| STONEWALLED |

STONEWALLED

My Fight for Truth Against the Forces of
Obstruction, Intimidation, and Harassment in
Obama's Washington

Sharyl Attkisson

HARPER

NEW YORK · LONDON · TORONTO · SYDNEY

HARPER

A hardcover edition of this book was published in 2014 by Harper, an imprint of HarperCollins Publishers.

HarperCollins books may be purchased for educational, business, or sales promotional use. For information, please e-mail the Special Markets Department at SPsales@harpercollins.com.

FIRST HARPER PAPERBACKS EDITION PUBLISHED IN 2015.

Designed by William Ruoto

Library of Congress Cataloging-in-Publication Data has been applied for.

ISBN 978-0-06-232285-2

17 18 19 OV/RRD 10 9 8 7 6 5 4 3 2

The truth eventually finds a way to be told.

ACKNOWLEDGMENTS

With much appreciation to: the journalists who shared their experiences; to Tab Turner, Nick Poser, Jonathan Sternberg, and Rick Altabef for keeping me legal all these years; Richard Leibner; my computer forensics team and helpers; Les; Don; Owen; Mark; Bill; Sen. Coburn and Keith; Keith and Matt at Javelin; Adam and the entire Harper team; Brian; Jim and Sarah; and my whole supportive family.

AUTHOR'S NOTE

The content of this book is based on my own opinions, experiences, and observations. Some quotes contained within are based on my best recollections of the events and, in each instance, accurately reflect the spirit and my sense of the conversations.

Some proceeds from this book are being donated to the Brechner Center for Freedom of Information at the University of Florida.

CONTENTS

| Big Brother |

My Computer's Intruders

Reeeeeeeeeee."

The noise is coming from my personal Apple desktop computer in the small office adjacent to my bedroom. It's starting up.

On its own.

"Reeeeeee . . . chik chik chik chik," says the computer as it shakes itself awake.

The electronic sounds stir me from sleep. I squint my eyes at the clock radio on the table next to the bed. The numbers blink back: "3:14 a.m."

Only a day earlier, my CBS-issued Toshiba laptop, perched at the foot of my bed, had whirred to life on its own. That too had been untouched by human hands. *What time was that?* I think it was 4 a.m.

Some nights, both computers spark to life, one after the other. A cacophony of microprocessors interrupting the normal sounds of the night. After thirty seconds, maybe a minute, they go back to sleep. I know this is not normal computer behavior.

My husband, a sound sleeper, snores through it all. Half asleep, I try to remember how long ago my computers first started going rogue. A year? Two? It no longer startles me. But it's definitely piquing my curiosity.

It's October 2012, and I've been digging into the September 11 terrorist attacks on Americans at the U.S. mission in Benghazi, Libya. It's the most interesting puzzle I've come across since the *Fast and Furious* gunwalking story, which led to international headlines and questions that remain unanswered.

Solving these kinds of puzzles is probably the challenge that drives me most. There's nothing like an unsolved mystery to keep me at the computer or on the phone until one or two in the morning. Most mysteries can be solved, you just have to find the information. But too often, the keepers of the information don't want to give it up . . . even when the information belongs to the public.

Now my computers offer a new mystery to unravel. I already had begun mentioning these unusual happenings to acquaintances who work in secretive corners of government and understand such things. Connections I'd met through friends and contacts in the northwest Virginia enclaves. Here, so many work for—or recently retired from—one of the "alphabet agencies." CIA. FBI. NSA. DIA. They're concerned about what I'm experiencing. They think something's going on. Somebody, they tell me, is making my computers behave that way.

They're also worried about my home phone. It's practically unusable now. Often, when I call home, it only rings once on the receiving end. But on my end, it keeps ringing and then connects somewhere else. Nobody's there. Other times, it disconnects in the middle of calls. There are clicks and buzzes. My friends who call hear the strange noises and ask about them. I get used to the routine of callers suggesting, half-jokingly, "Is your phone tapped?" My whole family's tired of it. Verizon has been to the house over and over again but can't fix whatever's wrong.

On top of that, my home alarm system has begun chirping a nightly warning that my phone line is having "trouble" of an unidentified nature. It chirps until I get out of bed and reset it. Every night. Different times.

I'm losing sleep.

I'm the one who tries to get information from the keepers and I can be relentless. That kind of tenacity doesn't always make friends, not even at CBS News, which has built an impressive record for dogged reporting in the tradition of Edward R. Murrow, Eric Sevareid, and Mike Wallace. But that's okay. I'm not in journalism to make friends.

My job is to remind politicians and government officials as to who they work for. Some of them have forgotten. They think they personally own your tax dollars. They think they own the information their agencies gather on the public's behalf. They think they're entitled to keep that information from the rest of us and—make no mistake—they're bloody incensed that we want it.

The Benghazi mystery is proving especially difficult. The feds are keeping a suspiciously tight clamp on details. They won't even say how long the attacks went on or when they ended. What they do reveal sometimes contradicts information provided by their sister agencies. And some of the most basic, important questions? They won't address at all.

For months, the Obama administration has dismissed all questions as partisan witch-hunting. And why not? That approach has proven successful, at least among some colleagues in the news media. They're apparently satisfied with the limited answers. They aren't curious about the gaping holes. The contradictions. They're part of the club that's decided only agenda-driven Republicans would be curious about all of that. These journalists don't need to ask questions about Benghazi at the White House press briefings, at Attorney General Eric Holder's public appearances, or during President Obama's limited media availabilities. It might make the administration mad. It might even prompt them to threaten the "access" of uncooperative journalists. Other journalists simply think it would be rude—maybe even silly—to waste time pursuing a topic of such little consequence.

There are so many more *important* things going on in the world.

But still, *I'm* curious.

What did the president of the United States do all that night during the attacks? With Americans under siege and a U.S. ambassador missing—later confirmed dead—what actions did the commander in chief take? What decisions did he make?

I'm making slow but steady progress in finding answers to some of the mysteries. Some of my sources are in extremely sensitive positions. They say lies are being told. They're angry. They want to set the record straight. But they can't reveal themselves on television. It would end their careers and make them pariahs among their peers. Little by little, with their help, I'm piecing together bits of the puzzle.

Those involved in the U.S. response to the attacks tell me that the U.S. government was in sheer chaos that night. Those with knowledge of military assets and Special Forces tell me that resources weren't fully utilized to try to mount a rescue while the attacks were under way. Those with firsthand knowledge say that the government's interagency Counterterrorism Security Group (CSG) wasn't convened, even though presidential directive requires it. Others whisper of the State Department rejecting security requests and overlooking warning signs in the weeks leading up to the attacks.

There are those in government who don't like it that the sources are talking to me. "Why are they speaking to reporters," they grumble to each other, "revealing our dirty laundry, telling our secrets?" These are powerful people with important connections.

I start to think that may be why my computers are losing so much sleep at night.

| FIRST WARNINGS

Months before the rest of the world becomes aware of the government's so-called snooping scandal I already know it's happening to me.

Snooping scandal.

As serious as the implications are, the media manages to give it a catchy little name. Not so much intruding, trespassing, invading, or spying. Snooping. You know, like a boyfriend snoops around on his girlfriend's Facebook account. Or kids snoop through the closets for Christmas packages. It's like dubbing HealthCare.gov's disastrous launch a "glitch."

In the fall of 2012, Jeff,* a well-informed acquaintance, is the first to put me on alert. He's connected to a three-letter agency. He waves me down when he sees me on a public street.

"I've been reading your reports online about Benghazi," he tells me. "It's pretty incredible. Keep at it. But you'd better watch out."

I take that as the sort of general remark people often make in jest based on the kind of reporting I do. As in: *You'd better watch out for Enron, they have powerful connections. You'd better watch out for the pharmaceutical companies, they have billions of dollars at stake. You'd better watch out for Obama's Chicago mafia.* I hear it all the time.

But Jeff means something more specific.

"You know, the administration is likely monitoring you—based on your reporting. I'm sure you realize that." He makes deep eye contact for emphasis before adding, "The average American would be shocked at the extent to which this administration is conducting surveillance on private citizens. Spying on them." In these pre–NSA snooping scandal, pre–Edward Snowden days, it sounds far-fetched. In just a few months, it will sound uncannily prescient.

"Monitoring me—in what way?" I ask.

"Your phones. Your computers. Have you noticed any unusual happenings?"

Yeah, I have. Jeff's warning sheds new light on all the trouble I've been having with my phones and computers. It's gotten markedly worse over the past year. In fact, by November 2012, there are so

---

* Not his real name.

many disruptions on my home phone line, I often can't use it. I call home from my mobile phone and it rings on my end, but not at the house. Or it rings at home once but when my husband or daughter answers, they just hear a dial tone. At the same time, on my end, it keeps ringing and then connects somewhere, just not at my house. Sometimes, when my call connects to that mystery-place-that's-not-my-house, I hear an electronic sounding buzz. Verizon can't explain the sounds or the behavior. These strange things happen whether I call from my mobile phones or use my office landlines. It happens to other people who try to call my house, too. When a call does manage to get through, it may disconnect in mid-conversation. Sometimes we hear other voices bleed through in short bursts like an AM radio being tuned.

One night, I'm on my home phone, reviewing a story with a CBS lawyer in New York and he hears the strange noises.

"Is (click) your phone tapped (clickity-click-bzzt)?" he asks.

"People (clickity-bzzt) seem to think so (click-click)," I say.

"Should we speak (click-click) on another line?"

"I don't think a mobile phone is any better (bzzzzzt) for privacy," I tell him.

Our computers and televisions use the same Verizon fiber optics FiOS service as does our home phone and they're acting up, too. And the house alarm going off at night gets me out of bed to scroll through the reason code on the panel to reset it. It makes the same complaint night after night: trouble with the phone line. Two a.m. one night. Three forty-seven a.m. the next. No rhyme or reason.

The television is misbehaving. It spontaneously jitters, mutes, and freeze-frames. My neighbors aren't experiencing similar interruptions. I try switching out the TV, the FiOS box, and all the cables. Verizon has done troubleshooting ad nauseam during the past year and a half. To no avail.

Then, there are the computers. They've taken to turning themselves on and off at night. Not for software updates or the typical, automatic handshakes that devices like to do periodically to let each other know "I'm here." This is a relatively recent development and it's grown more frequent. It started with my personal Apple desktop. Later, my CBS News Toshiba laptop joined the party. Knowing little about computer technology, I figure it's some sort of automated phishing program that's getting in my computers at night, trolling for passwords and financial information. I feel my information is sufficiently secure due to protections on my system, so I don't spend too much time worrying about it. But the technical interruptions get to the point where we can't expect to use the phones, Internet, or television normally.

Around Thanksgiving, a friend tries to make a social call to my home phone line. I see his number on the caller ID but when I pick up, I hear only the familiar clicks and buzzes. He calls back several times but unable to get a clear connection, he jumps in his car and drives over.

"What's wrong with your phone?" he asks. "It sounds like it's tapped or something."

"I don't know," I answer. "Verizon can't fix it. It's a nuisance."

"Well, if it's a tap, it's a lousy one. If it were any good, you'd never know it was there."

Numerous sources would tell me the same thing in the coming months. When experts tap your line, you don't hear a thing. Unless they *want* you to hear, for example, to intimidate you or scare off your sources.

Well, it's silly to think that my phones could really be tapped. Or my computers, for that matter. Nonetheless, I tell the friend who'd tried to call my house about the computer anomalies, too.

"If you want to get your computer looked at, I might know

someone who can help you out," he offers. Like so many people in Northern Virginia, he has a trusted connection who has connections to Washington's spook agencies. I say I'll think about it.

On one particular night, the computer is closed and on the floor next to my bed. I hear it start up and, as usual, I shake myself awake. I lift my head and see that the screen has lit up even though the top is shut. It does its thing and I roll over and try to go back to sleep. But after a few seconds, I hear the "castle lock" sound. That's what I call the sound that's triggered, for example, when I accidentally type in the wrong password while attempting to connect to the secure CBS system.

They're trying to get into CBS, I think to myself. Hearing the castle lock, I figure they've failed. Gotten locked out. *Nice try.* Only later do I learn that they had no trouble accessing the CBS system. Over and over.

When I describe the computer behavior, my contacts and sources ask me when I first noticed it. I don't know. I didn't pay much attention at the time. On the Apple, I figure it was at least 2011. Maybe 2010. My husband would sleep through it. Later, I'd remark to him that the computer woke me up last night.

"Do you think people can use our Internet connection to get into our computers at night and turn them on to look through them?" I'd ask him, thinking only of amateur hackers and spammers.

"Of course they can," he'd say matter-of-factly.

The second week of December 2012, my Apple desktop has just had a nighttime session. A night or two later, it's my CBS News laptop. I look at the clock next to the bed. The green glow of 5:02 a.m. blinks back at me. Later than usual. Considering the discussions I'm now having with my contacts who think I may be tapped, I decide it might be useful to start logging these episodes. But no sooner do I begin this task than the computers simply . . . stop. It's as if they know

I've begun tracking them and the jig's up. The first time I attempt to formally log the activity would be the very last time I'd notice them turning on at night. This time frame, when I noticed the activity halts, December 10 through December 12, 2012, later becomes an important touchstone in the investigation.

| DISAPPEARING ACT

In late December 2012, I take up my friend's offer to have my computer examined by an inside professional. Arrangements are made for a meeting.

In the meantime, Jeff wants to check out the exterior of my home. To examine the outside connections for the Verizon FiOS line and see if anything looks out of order.

"If you're being tapped, it's probably not originating at your house, but I'd like to take a look anyway," he says.

"Sure, why not." I don't think he'll find anything but there's no harm in having him look. Maybe I should be more concerned. What if the government *is* watching me? What if they're trying to find out who my sources are and what I may be about to report next?

"I did find some irregularities," Jeff tells me on the phone after inspecting the outside of my home. "It could be nothing, but I'd rather discuss it in person." We meet at my house and he walks me to a spot in the backyard just outside my garage. His primary concern is a stray cable dangling from the FiOS box attached to the brick wall on the outside of my house. It doesn't belong.

"What is it?" I ask.

He picks up the loose end and untwists a cap exposing a tiny glass dome underneath. "It's an extra fiber optics line," he tells me. "In addition to your regular line."

"What's it for?"

"I'm not an expert, but someone could remove the cap and attach a receiver and download data. Or they could put a tiny transmitter here," he points to a place under the cap, "and send information to a receiver off site once a day, once a week, or whenever. You need to have this checked out."

I photograph the cable and decide to begin by asking Verizon reps if they installed the extra line for some unknown reason. For the moment, I'm operating under the assumption that the company will be able to explain everything. So on New Year's Eve 2012, I place the call to Verizon and describe the mystery cable.

"Can you tell me if this is something you installed?" I ask. I tell the representative that Verizon has made repeated troubleshooting visits to my house in the past year. Maybe a spare line got left behind.

The Verizon rep puts me on hold for long periods as she contacts one department, then another in hopes of answering my question. Finally, she tells me authoritatively: "That's nothing that we would have installed or left there. You need to contact law enforcement."

"Can I email you a photograph and have your technicians look to be sure?" I ask.

I'm not convinced it's time to call the cops. What would they do, anyway, other than tell me that they don't know why the cable is there and recommend that I call Verizon? My husband, a former law enforcement official, agrees. Besides, in the unlikely event that there's a legal tap on my phone, neither Verizon nor the police would tell me.

But the Verizon rep won't let me send the photo for technicians to review. She insists they have no process that allows a customer to email a picture. For the moment, I give up. We'll wait until the holidays are over and get some advice on what we should do.

An hour later, my phone rings. A woman identifying herself as a Verizon supervisor says she's following up on my call and wants to dispatch a technician to my house the next day to take a look. That's New Year's Day. I find that unnecessary and somewhat surprising. It's not always easy to get a service call scheduled quickly, let alone on a holiday when I didn't even ask for one.

"You don't have to send anybody out on New Year's Day," I tell the supervisor. "Why don't you let me just email this photograph and you might be able to save yourself the trouble. Maybe it's just a piece of equipment your technicians installed or left here. Can't someone look at the picture and see if they can tell?"

"No," she insists. "We'll just send a technician out tomorrow."

I report this to Jeff, who also finds it curious that Verizon would rush out a technician, unsolicited, on New Year's Day.

"Mind if I come by when he arrives?" he asks.

"That would be great."

So I begin the first day of 2013 by answering a knock on the door. The Verizon technician introduces himself and hands me a business card with his first name and phone number handwritten on it.

"Be sure and call me anytime if you need anything or have any questions," he says.

I begin by asking him if he has a record of the work that Verizon has done at our house in the past year. That might help tell us whether a previous technician left the cable. He says he has no access to such records and that the main office wouldn't have any, either. He'll just need to take a look at the box himself. As I lead him to the back of the house, I text Jeff to come over.

The technician takes one look at the cable and says it doesn't belong.

"Yeah, that shouldn't be there."

"Why's it here, then?" I ask.

"Well, we deal with a lot of third-party contractors. It probably got left here when some work was done and a contractor was supposed to pick it up but didn't. Something like that," he says. "I'll just remove it."

He goes out to his truck to get some tools and Jeff arrives. We watch together as he removes the cable, coils it up, and prepares to take it with him.

"Just leave that here," I say.

"Why?"

"I just want to keep it," I tell him. I figure when I drop off my computer for analysis in a few days, I'll send along the mystery cable, too. The Verizon technician seems hesitant but puts down the cable on top of the air-conditioning fan next to us. We continue to chat and I make a mental note: *Don't leave the cable there. If you do, it might disappear.* The Verizon man really seems to want to take it. Am I imagining that?

Jeff and I walk the technician back to his truck. Jeff has a few more questions for him but it's chilly outside and I leave the two of them to finish their conversation.

A couple of days later, I'm driving to work when I remember the cable. I call my husband at home.

"Go get that cable off the air-conditioning fan," I tell him.

I listen as he walks outside with the phone to look. "It's gone."

"Gone? Are you sure?"

"Yeah, it's nowhere around here," he says. Also gone are several other pieces of wire that Jeff had pulled up from the ground in front of the Verizon man.

"Well what happened to it?"

"The Verizon guy must've come back and taken it," my husband speculates.

Later, at the office, I decide to call the Verizon technician and ask him myself. I want to know if he took the cable after I'd said to leave it, and why. More important, I hope he still has it so that I can have it examined. I have that handwritten business card he gave me. I call the phone number on it, it rolls me to his voice mail, and I leave a message. But he doesn't call back. That day or any other. I call almost every day, sometimes twice a day, for the next month. But the once-helpful Verizon man never responds.

At least I still have my photographs.

And an expert source who's willing to peer inside my laptop and see what secrets it might reveal about covert attempts to monitor my work.

| Media Mojo Lost |

Investigative Reporting's Recession

The first time you catch the government in a lie, it changes you.

I was twenty-one years old and working as a reporter at WTVX, the local CBS News television station in Vero Beach, Florida. ("*X-34 Newwwwwws,*" sang our theme song over video of our smiling news anchors, Michelle and Jim, wearing matching bright orange blazers with big *X-34* patches on the breast pockets and the geographically incorrect globe spinning behind them.) It's such a small station and I'm so enthusiastic that I happily perform additional duties as videotape editor and producer.

I'm covering one of my first big, original stories there when I make contact with a whistleblower who tells me there are places in the county where raw sewage is being secretly, illegally dumped into local waters. The worst part, he says, is that the county water and sewer department knows about it.

It's a simple enough story to check out: I figure all I need to do is to call the county and ask. This was at a time when I believed the government *had* to tell the truth. It's silly in retrospect, but I nonetheless thought there was some sort of unofficial code of ethics, if not something more formal, that required government officials to be honest in their dealings with the public and press. That they'd be kicked out of the government club if they weren't.

When I ask the county about the raw sewage allegations, the officials tell me the information I've received is absolutely, unequivocally false. And I believe them, at first. Why wouldn't I? So I go back to my whistleblower but he remains insistent. With his information and assistance, I eventually locate and videotape multiple incidences of raw sewage pouring into public tributaries and find evidence that the county had been well aware.

This is my first big lesson on the subject that the government—our government—can lie. And as I continue my career, I come to understand that this type of deception is not an anomaly.

A few years later, I'm working at WTVT, "Big 13," then the local CBS station in Tampa, Florida, where again I pull multiple duties as a reporter, producer, editor, and anchor. (*"Pulse News,"* says our baritone-voiced announcer in promos, *"Where News Comes First."*) It's one of the best local news markets in the country and I'm sharpening my reporting skills. I make contact with an insider from the Florida agriculture department. He wants to blow the whistle on the fact that there's been an outbreak of a terrible agricultural disease called citrus canker, and the state is covering it up. If true, this would be a major story: a confirmed outbreak would subject Florida's powerful citrus industry to a restrictive quarantine to prevent the disease from spreading. It could devastate citrus growers in the Sunshine State, and roil international markets in citrus futures.

Here again, the path forward seems simple enough: all I need to do is call the state agriculture department and ask for comment. When I do, they tell me it's all hogwash. Confidently, assuredly. But this time I'm a little wiser. I press them; give them a chance to hedge their answer. They don't. The allegation is absolutely, unequivocally false, they say: there's been no citrus canker in Florida since 1933. Period.

But once again, my source remains insistent and he has specific information to back up his claims. He gives me a geographic area in

Manatee County south of Tampa where the outbreak has supposedly been discovered. I get the plat records and identify the farmer who owns the grove in question in the town of Bradenton. I look up his phone number and call him cold.

"Hi there. I'm Sharyl Attkisson, a reporter with Channel 13. I hear you have some citrus canker in your groves."

"Yup," the farmer readily admits.

I'm shocked it's that easy. I ask a few more questions and then, "Can I come over and take some pictures for a story?"

"Sure," says the farmer. "In fact the state fellas are here right now getting ready to burn a bunch of the bad trees."

The state fellas are there . . . *right now*? *My luck can't be this good.*

I arrive with my cameraman. We park our news truck and walk down a dusty pathway between the rows of orange trees until we come upon several state agriculture officials. They're carrying clipboards and overseeing a large pile of trees that have been cut down and stacked together. There are men wearing gloves and boot covers and they set the trees on fire. As plumes of gray smoke billow into the afternoon sky, the officials whisper to one another and look over at me. They won't speak to me but the farmer tells the whole story: how the state confirmed the presence of canker through lab tests a while back, how the state has been working with him what steps to take. As he talks, I'm thinking about how blatantly the state lied. We wrap up our shooting and one of the state officials stops us. He directs me and my cameraman to a shallow pan of liquid and tells us to step in it before we exit the grove. It's a bleach mixture, he explains, to kill any canker we may have picked up on the bottom of our shoes so that we don't spread it outside the grove. The man sprays our hands and camera equipment with the mixture, too.

Within hours of Big 13 breaking the news of the citrus canker outbreak on the local evening news, the Florida agriculture department issues a brief press release confirming what they'd known for quite some time but denied: citrus canker had been discovered in Manatee County. The result is a statewide quarantine by the U.S. Department of Agriculture. No citrus can be shipped outside Florida without a special permit.

I wonder whether we would have ever known about the outbreak if it hadn't been for that insider. I also wonder whether, in the supposed fifty-three years between canker outbreaks in Florida, there were ones that we just never found out about because the state covered them up.

Since that time, government and corporate authorities at the heart of many of my stories have proven time and again to be less than forthright—even dishonest—in their portrayal of facts. The following are just a few examples of assertions by the powers that be that were all later proven false:

Until the 1990s, tobacco companies claimed cigarettes didn't cause cancer.

The FBI said that Wen Ho Lee, accused of spying for China in 1999, had failed his FBI lie detector test.

Government officials claimed all links between autism and vaccines were debunked in the early 2000s.

During the rash of Firestone tire–Ford Explorer rollovers in 2000, the government claimed there was no inordinate danger. Firestone and Ford said their products were safe and that any problems were due to driver error.

The Red Cross claimed it did not mishandle donations intended for September 11, 2001, terror attack victims.

Also in 2001, the behemoth energy company Enron said it wasn't cheating employees or the public. Auditor Arthur Andersen said Enron's books were solid.

In 2002, the Los Alamos National Laboratory denied that employees were purposefully abusing their government credit cards.

The makers of the dietary supplement Ephedra said it was safe in 2004.

The Bush administration claimed the 2008 Troubled Asset Relief Program would help homeowners facing foreclosure by helping banks purchase their troubled assets.

In 2010, oil company BP and the government said a relatively small amount of oil was leaking from the Deepwater Horizon wreckage.

In 2011, the Obama administration insisted to Congress that no guns were "walked" in *Fast and Furious* or any other government case.

The State Department said it did not refuse security requests prior to the September 11, 2012, attacks on Americans in Benghazi, Libya.

The government defended the safety of prescription drugs such as Rezulin, fen-phen, Duract, Vioxx, Trovan, Baycol, Bextra, and Propulsid, as well as the first rotavirus vaccine and the oral polio vaccine: all later withdrawn from the market for safety reasons.

The State Department said Secretary of State John Kerry was not out on his boat the day the coup in Egypt was unfolding in 2013.

Also in 2013, James Clapper, the director of national intelligence, told Congress that the National Security Agency doesn't collect data on hundreds of millions of Americans.

You can see how things begin to look from where I sit.

| PUZZLE SOLVING

I'm politically agnostic . . . motivated by the desire to solve puzzles and uncover public information that the government, corporations, and others in positions of authority are trying to keep from you. I'm not here to tell you how to think. I just want to give you information. What you do with it is your business. Do your own research. Consult those you trust. Make up your own mind.

Think for yourself.

There's nothing more intriguing than a good puzzle or an un-solved mystery. The building blocks of a story are there, but pieces are missing. Things don't make sense, documents are withheld, nobody wants to talk. My goal is to chip away at the secrets little by little and put the bits of information together to ultimately reveal a larger truth. It takes time, persistence, and a tin ear for criticism from the targets of a story and the peanut gallery.

In the quest to reveal information, the logician in me is troubled when I see the media treat stories differently depending upon who we think did the bad deed, what ideologies we personally hold, or how we secretly wish a story would turn out. Everyone has opinions and biases; our job is to keep them out of our journalism.

It's not always easy. It's an intellectual challenge. A matter of train-ing our brains to think differently. As students in the Journalism Col-lege at the University of Florida, we were taught to think outside our own belief systems when reporting. The ultimate accomplishment is to report stories on issues about which we have strong opinions based on personal convictions, yet produce results that are so cleanly absent our biases that nobody really knows which side we're on (or they may incorrectly guess that we're on the opposite side). To do this success-fully, we must be able to disconnect ourselves from our personal opin-ions for the sake of our reporting. And we have to remain unmoved by the inevitable criticism and attacks that come from the interests who feel criticized.

Believe it or not, journalists are still capable of doing this. One such example comes from the 2008 presidential campaign.

I prefer not to cover political campaigns. They're no-win assign-ments. You follow a candidate around the country: if you expose their flaws, you're viewed as being politically biased against them and it jeopardizes your access. If they have a good day and you report it as such, you risk critics accusing you of being their cheerleader. And if your observations from the front lines aren't in synch with what the news managers back in New York see on cable news or read on the wire services or hear on the competition, you may find yourself eternally second-guessing and getting second-guessed. Nonetheless, a campaign story occasionally falls into my lap and draws me into the fray. That happened in 2008 when I returned from a trip overseas to be greeted with a strange question from my husband.

"When you went to Bosnia with Hillary Clinton in 1996, were you guys shot at?" he asks.

"No," I reply. "Why?"

"Are you sure?" he presses.

"Of course. I'd know if we'd been shot at," I say.

It seems that Democratic presidential candidate Hillary Clinton has been publicly saying that we took sniper fire on that trip to Bosnia twelve years before when she was first lady. Some observers theorize that Clinton is saying this now because she believes that getting shot at in a war zone would help voters view her as being qualified to serve as commander in chief. More so than a young senator from Illinois named Barack Obama with no such experience.

"She must be speaking of a different trip," I postulate. Nothing else makes sense.

I do a little research and discover Clinton *is* referring to the trip on which I accompanied her. She's claiming that, as our military plane landed in Bosnia, we took sniper fire. She even says she had to duck and run for cover to escape the flying bullets.

The idea is ludicrous. Yes, we flew into a recent war zone and were told it could be dangerous. We were prepared for the possibility of hostile fire. But it never materialized. And the fact is, had hostile forces fired upon our aircraft, our military pilot wouldn't have just flown right into them and landed. Especially considering that accompanying us on the trip were the president's daughter, Chelsea, and two entertainers who came along to perform for the troops: comedian Sinbad, and singer Sheryl Crow. If there had been any threat of our plane being shot at, we simply would've flown to an alternate, safe destination.

I rarely hang on to story materials for very long, but in this case, I go to my office in Washington, dig through some boxes of records, and discover I still have notes, photographs, and videotape from that trip in 1996. The video clearly disproves candidate Clinton's story. It shows Clinton and Chelsea disembarking from the plane on the tarmac in Bosnia, leisurely smiling for photographs and greeting a local schoolgirl on the runway.

No sniper fire. No ducking and running.

I tell *CBS Evening News* executive producer Rick Kaplan what I have. He orders up a story for that night's newscast. I'm aware that he and the Clintons are acquaintances. An hour before the broadcast, he looks over my script.

"It's kind of awkward," I comment to Kaplan. "I know you're friends with the Clintons."

"We're not that good of friends," Kaplan replies, not missing a beat. "A great story's a great story."

I'm comforted by his sentiments. This manager isn't trying to steer or influence reporting on the basis of his own personal beliefs or relationships. His successor, in my view, would be the polar opposite.

Kaplan approves the Clinton Bosnia script and makes it that night's lead story. The result is devastating to Clinton's campaign. Some political observers say her sniper fire claim, in stark contrast to the video evidence, is the final blow that knocks her out of serious contention in the Democratic primaries. This paves the way for her opponent, Obama, to win the nomination.

In this instance, the executive producer was able to disconnect his personal feelings from a legitimate news story. Today, the public rightly has come to assume that many of the news media just don't do that. The public believes we report the news through the lens of our own biases. Or amid influence by political or corporate interests. And so they try to take that into account when they view and read our stories. But they're sick and tired of hedging the news based on the reporter or channel they're watching.

This *news outlet did the story?* they subconsciously think. *They're probably trying to make Republicans look good. So I'll only believe about forty percent of that report.*

That *reporter did the story? He's probably doing the bidding of Democrats. I'll bet only half the truth is being told.*

All these people really want is the News. They're thirsty for news that they don't have to place odds on or discount. They want reporters to follow a story wherever it leads, no matter how unpleasant, no matter whom it touches or implicates. They just want the truth, to the extent it can be known.

The perception that opinions are intertwined with news may have grown sharper in recent years, but the reality is long-standing.

As a high school student, I observed that my hometown newspaper's sportswriters often seemed to be rooting for the opposing high school in town.

"Sir," I wrote in an indignant letter to the editor of the *Sarasota Herald-Tribune*, "Sarasota High has always gotten top billing in your paper—especially in sports. I, being a student of Riverview High School, consider this unfair. When Sarasota wins a football game, it's 'Sarasota Rips Apart . . .'—but when Riverview wins, it's more likely to be 'Riverview Barely Escapes . . .'" I went on to use the example of a specific article that I felt demonstrated blatant favoritism.

I concluded: "Sir, I challenge you to reread that article and many others similar to it and declare it unbiased."

I don't think my letter led to any big changes at the local paper. But the process really got me thinking and, in a way, it helped shape me.

Not long after, in college, I found myself confronting opinions presented under the guise of news. I was researching an issue for a speech class debate when I noted instances of journalists at news magazines and newspapers clearly expressing their opinions in their reporting without attribution, as if fact. For example, one might write: "advocates who want bean balls in professional baseball to be punished more severely are only hurting the sport and doing a disservice to fans."

That's an opinion, I'd think to myself, as I'd reread the passage to make sure. *There's no evidence cited. And it's not attributed to anybody. Yet it's stated as if it's an established fact.*

I brought this complaint to the attention of one of my journalism professors.

"They're allowed to do that," the professor explained professorially. "Especially in the print press, they often take editorial positions on controversial subjects."

"But this isn't an editorial," I argued, pointing to the offending news article. "Shouldn't they have to label their opinions as *opinions*? How is the rest of the article to be trusted when the reporter is advancing his own personal viewpoint?" The question was rhetorical.

Thereafter, I remained on the lookout for news stories in which reporters appeared to be presenting their own disguised opinions rather than information or viewpoints based on reporting.

| THE "SUBSTITUTION GAME"

It's not too difficult to root out cases of unattributed opinions in news. But there are other, less obvious ways we may skew coverage, sometimes unintentionally. As a test to see whether our stories are leading us, or our biases are leading our stories, one can employ a simple logic exercise. I call it the Substitution Game. It takes a given news scenario and posits how we might treat a similar event if key players were substituted.

For example, on May 9, 2008, Democratic presidential candidate Obama said he had visited fifty-seven states in America. Everyone knew that Obama probably meant that he'd visited forty-seven states, not fifty-seven. He knows there are only fifty states. The remark, nothing more than a verbal gaffe, didn't make big headlines. Substitution Game: What if Republican vice presidential candidate Sarah Palin had uttered the same misstatement? Do you think the news media would've been so quick to overlook it?

They weren't quick to forgive Palin when she made a comparable geographical gaffe in July 2010. She referred to Kodiak Island in Alaska as "America's largest island." Everyone knew she probably meant that Kodiak is the largest island on the continent; Hawaii is the largest island in the United States. But unlike the overlooked Obama incident, some treated Palin's error as major national news. Then, when President Obama accidentally referred to Hawaii as being part of Asia on November 15, 2011, most of the news media didn't find it noteworthy.

National news outlets also prominently featured Palin's November 24, 2010, remark about hostilities between North and South Korea. She told conservative radio host Glenn Beck "we've got to stand with our North Korean allies." She meant South Korean.

But nobody made much of President Obama mistakenly saying on August 6, 2013, on *The Tonight Show* that Charleston, South Carolina; Jacksonville, Florida; and Savannah, Georgia, are on the Gulf of Mexico. (They're on the Atlantic side, not the Gulf.)

The press also pretty much looked the other way when President

Obama invented a language called "Austrian" in April 2009. Austrians actually speak German. Substitution Game: Would the major press have ignored the same, understandable error had it been made by President Bush?

Poor Republican vice president Dan Quayle got more bad press for a gaffe he never even committed. Maybe you've heard the story: Quayle remarked that he wished he'd studied Latin harder in school so that he could converse with the people of Latin America. It turns out the quote is no more than a joke about Quayle told in 1989 by Republican congresswoman Claudine Schneider. But several national publications were apparently so eager to believe it, they printed the anecdote as a fact and it took on a life of its own.

The point here isn't which politicians are smarter or which gaffes are substantive versus meaningless. It's that similar faux pas should elicit relatively similar treatment.

Too often they don't.

And that's just one way in which we're losing our mojo. There are others.

By "we," I mean the news media. And by "mojo," I mean our ability to serve vigorously and effectively as the Fourth Estate. Watchdog to government and other powers that may otherwise overstep their bounds.

And we're losing it without so much as a whimper. We're voluntarily relinquishing it.

| THE COMPLIANT NEWS MEDIA

There are exceptions, of course, but it's difficult to deny that the news media as a whole seems largely disinterested in some of the most important and controversial happenings on a given day. It must mystify those in the public who notice such things.

Often, our journalistic skepticism is misplaced. We're more skeptical of those who blow the whistle than we are of those being exposed. When someone steps forward with information and accusations against powerful people or corporate interests, we're too eager to buy the label that their enemies place on them, such as "disgruntled," "publicity-seeking," or "nutty" without carefully examining the facts at hand. *After all*, we think, *why would somebody step out of line, even risk their job for the public's good—for the truth?* Perhaps it's because we, ourselves, would never do such a thing that we're suspicious of the mentality.

When a government entity or corporation calls a press conference or issues a news release, we're often too quick to rush to report their "news," accepting the information uncritically as if it's an established fact just because they said so. We allow them to set the agenda for the day's news without regard to the notion that they may be steering us in one direction to keep us from looking in another.

In fact, they're so used to dictating the terms, they sometimes become enraged when we veer off script.

In January 2014, after President Obama's State of the Union address, New York congressman Michael Grimm, a Republican, appears before an NY1 television camera in the U.S. Capitol in Washington for commentary. But when the questioning by reporter Michael Scotto pivots from Grimm's chosen topic and into a federal investigation into his campaign finances, Grimm storms off. He returns a moment later, seemingly unaware that the camera is recording, and angrily whisper-yells to Scotto, "If you ever do that to me again, I'll throw you off this fucking balcony. . . . I'll break you in half."

Scotto protests, "Why? It's a valid question."

The exchange, captured on video, goes viral. The public and other news reporters are understandably outraged at the physical threats and Grimm later apologizes. But we should ask, why does a news environment exist whereby Grimm comes to believe that he should be exempt from questions of public interest when they aren't of his own design? (Three months later, Grimm was indicted on federal charges of tax evasion and perjury; charges he denied.)

The fact is, many of us in the media are more comfortable when we're on the right side of the government and corporations that guide us. When we are, there's less stress. Life is simpler. We can go home at night without work nagging at us. Nobody threatens to sue us. No one writes nasty emails or calls our bosses to complain.

In fact, the powers that be, prominent government leaders or corporate entities that we cover, may even pat us on the head.

They might as well be remarking "Good boy!" when they toss us a compliment as if we're obedient lapdogs after we dismiss a story that could have damaged them. "Glad you didn't fall for that old trick. *You're* smarter than that," they tell us with a figurative pat-pat. Sometimes, they even hint that one day, we might be offered a job working with *them*. That is, if we keep doing our jobs so well. Maybe we can become the press flack for the federal department of so-and-so. Or the pharmaceutical division of this-and-thus. We're flattered by the offers, but we don't *really* want to work for them. (Well, at least not now. Maybe later. Maybe down the road when we're tired of the news business or it tires of us. We have families to feed, college educations to pay for, after all . . .)

All the while, they're gaining more control over how we think and what we report. In reality, for those who bother to look, history and experience teach that the biggest dose of skepticism should be reserved for the authorities that seek to influence us and the information they want us to receive.

But the biggest way in which the Fourth Estate is losing our mojo has less to do with disguised opinions or inconsistent treatment and more to do with a trend toward favoring the establishment, whoever it may be. We're falling down on the job of being vigilant watchdogs of government and corporations. Today, they're not to be bothered by persistent reporter questions about their behavior and motives. That's viewed as harassment rather than watchdogging. A distraction if not an outright nuisance.

NBC investigative correspondent Lisa Myers departed NBC in 2014 not long after I parted ways with CBS, and she expressed a similar observation.

"I think journalism at its best is a matter of holding powerful people and institutions accountable and exposing injustice," Myers told C-SPAN host Brian Lamb during a June 2014 edition of *Q-and-A*. "I fear today that we are not doing that enough."

Are investigative and watchdog reporting dying a slow and painful death? Or has the pendulum just temporarily swung too far in the wrong direction? Can we coax it back?

None of this is to say that investigative journalism is entirely gone. There are strongly committed local television news stations, newspapers, and online organizations such as the Center for Public Integrity. On a national level, the networks employ many talented journalists, and programs such as *60 Minutes* still produce strong work such as the 2011 report by correspondent Steve Kroft and producer Ira Rosen that exposed how members of Congress, the executive branch, and their staff use inside information gained through their jobs to profit financially. PBS produces excellent investigations such as its 2013 *Frontline* documentary examining why Wall Street executives escaped fraud prosecution in the mortgage crisis.

But overall, listen to the community of investigative reporters and there's little doubt that it's getting tougher to get investigative stories approved and published. I and my colleagues from other networks, local news outlets, and major newspapers compare notes and commiserate over drinks at investigative reporting conferences.

We're running into resistance from supervisors and meeting with increasing interference from commercial concerns.

"Right now, we're not allowed to do stories about hospitals or pharmaceutical companies," says one local news reporter in our group as another nods.

"For us it's hospitals and car dealerships," adds a third.

Sometimes, when an investigative story is accepted, it's begrudgingly. After one of my hard-nosed story ideas got the green light from a broadcast executive in September of 2013, a subordinate manager sent me a message through a back channel.

"That story's really a *downer*," he complained, ordering me to leave out critical facts that he found depressing. "Isn't there any way you can make it *inspiring*?"

Pushing original and investigative reporting has become like trying to feed the managers spinach. They don't like the taste, but they occasionally hold their nose and indulge because it's good for them—or because it looks good. They much prefer it to be sugarcoated, deep-fried, or otherwise disguised so that it goes down easier.

Many good reporters have learned not to bother. Why come to work and fight every day for original and investigative reports when your superiors want to repeat stories that have already appeared in the *New York Times*, on the Internet, or on the competition? What's the point of breaking new ground on an important story only to be told there's no room for it because the news hole is filled up with the same dozen or so popular topics du jour? While many of those topics are perfectly legitimate, they're often skin-deep summaries that don't shed any new light. They're not tough and challenging. They're definitely not holding the powers that be accountable.

And more and more, those we're supposed to hold accountable are calling the shots and naming the terms of our coverage. They've changed the way we do business and we've allowed it largely without objection.

In my experience covering Capitol Hill, public servants rarely agreed to conduct interviews on topics raised in the course of naturally occurring news. Instead, they schedule appearances and press conferences on the topics they wish to publicize. They email press releases announcing when and where we and our cameras should be, and wait for us to show up to be spoon-fed. But try doing an original story that demands an interview with them. Even public officials who sit on important committees over key issues beg off when it's not a topic of their own choosing.

In the summer of 2013, CBS News decides to do a story on the controversial decision by the Transportation Security Administration to allow small knives back on planes. The knives were banned after the September 11, 2001, terrorist attacks. We request an interview with the head of TSA: John Pistole. TSA denies the request. The government doesn't feel a responsibility to be accountable. And the media accepts the denial without pressing.

As the days pass, criticism mounts over the TSA's proposed policy change. The issue has captured the public's attention. A week after denying our interview request, the TSA calls us and the other television news networks. TSA says Pistole will be available to us today. He wants to make TSA's case. His press officers dictate the terms: the boss will do brief one-on-one interviews at the agency's Virginia offices. The problem is, we did our story a week ago—*that's* when we needed the interview. We weren't planning another story today and the Pistole interview, a week later, wasn't exactly promising to be newsy.

But instead of telling the TSA no, we dutifully rush our cameras to their offices as directed, and do the interviews in the order they determine in the time slots they assign, for the length of time that they determine, during which Pistole offers carefully prepared, well-vetted answers—and no new information. Then we clear a spot in the evening newscast for the resulting story and call it "news."

What's just happened here? The TSA has dictated the terms of our coverage. When the media initiates a story worth covering, the government balks—but when *they* need *us,* we're compliant. It's important for us to resist this dynamic because we risk becoming little more than tools in their propaganda efforts: serving their interests rather than holding them accountable and serving the public's interests.

As an aside, for the same news report, I sought comment on the knife policy from members of Congress who lead the House Transportation Committee, but they declined. A spokesman for one of them said his boss had "no interest" in doing an interview. I was asking an elected official to fulfill his duty as the public's representative on a key committee, but the request was treated as if I were asking for a favor.

| SPINNING YOU—WITH YOUR OWN TAX DOLLARS

That attitude in Congress is the rule rather than the exception. Many elected officials don't seem to recognize that they work for the public and have an obligation to answer public controversies and speak to how they make their decisions and spend your tax dollars. Tax dollars even supply members of Congress with money to hire press officials who are supposed to be responsive to the media but often behave instead as if they're privately paid public relations officers whose job is to spin the news media and run interference for their bosses.

This is never more apparent than during my "Follow the Money" reports, circa 2007–2009, which question Congress's awards of coveted, no-bid earmarks of tax dollars to corporate and special interests in their home districts. In some cases, there are questions of fraud. In other cases, it's about waste, patronage, and conflicts of interest.

With ample earmarks to examine and plenty of offenders, I split the targets of my inquiries between Democrats and Republicans. For Republicans: North Carolina's Virginia Foxx gave generously of tax dollars for a new teapot museum building that never came to pass; California's Jerry Lewis earmarked to improve neighborhoods suspiciously close to property that he owned, possibly increasing his own property values; and Alaska's Don Young handed out $10 million that stood to benefit one of his supporters.

Among Democrats it's Congressman Rahm Emanuel of Illinois in 2008 (later to become President Obama's chief of staff and then Chicago mayor). He agrees to an interview with me about one of his earmarks but he's clearly annoyed about it. I'm asking about his part in a $1.8 million grant of federal tax dollars to subsidize the Shedd Aquarium in Chicago, which has just cleared $8 million after expenses, has several hundred million dollars in net assets, boasts 159 corporate donors, and pays its chief executive $600,000 in salary and benefits. Emanuel explains to me that he nonetheless supports the Shedd Aquarium with your tax dollars because it raises awareness about the Great Lakes. He goes on to suggest during the interview that the reason America is growing suspicious and wary of earmarks is that I've been doing a series of reports about them. He becomes so hostile toward me during the interview, I finally ask, "Is something wrong? Are you angry with me?"

"You don't really want to know what I think," Emanuel barks back as we continue rolling the camera for editing shots. "*I'm fully medicated!*"

As I make my way further down the list of equally resentful congressmen responsible for a seemingly endless list of earmarks, nobody owes taxpayers more answers than Senator Ted Stevens, a prickly, powerful Republican leader from Alaska. Nicknamed by some critics as the "emperor of earmarks," he personally directed at least $3.4

billion in tax dollars to projects in his home state of Alaska. Yes, I said 3.4 *billion* as in: $3,400,000,000.00. A single billion is a pretty big number, let alone three. One billion minutes ago the Roman Empire was dominating the earth. One billion hours ago, we were in the Stone Age.

Stevens's controversial earmarks include major ones that appear to benefit his friends, donors, and family members. But he doesn't think he has to justify how he's spending your billions. Even when he's the subject of several investigations. When I ask for interviews, Stevens's press officer employs the nonrefusal-refusal that's become so familiar. Here's how it works: instead of declining the interview request outright, which would give rise to a phrase in the news story that says something like "Senator Stevens refused to do an interview," the press officer never calls back with a final answer or he stonewalls with a list of excuses.

> *Senator Stevens is just too busy.*
> *It's not that he doesn't want to do an interview. It's just that he has to go straight from a meeting to a vote.*
> *He has to rush to the airport. There's just no time. Not one spare second.*

On one occasion, I press the matter. I offer to come to Stevens anytime, anywhere, at his convenience.

"I wish that were possible," says the press aide, most sincerely. "But as soon as he votes, he has to rush to the airport for a flight back to Alaska.

I call *Evening News* executive producer Kaplan.

"If I can get an interview with Senator Stevens, will you give me the time to fly to Alaska to do it?"

"Hell, yes," says Rick, no questions asked.

I call Stevens's press assistant.

"Since the senator is rushing back to Alaska, to make it convenient for him, I can come to Alaska and do the interview with him anytime this weekend," I say.

He's at a loss. Then, I finally get a direct answer.

"Sharyl, he's not going to do an interview with you," says Stevens's spokesman.

Sometimes, when members of Congress avoid me, I have to stake them out with a photographer and try to hunt them down on their own turf so that they will be answerable to public questions.

They don't like that.

For one report, I need Democratic congresswoman Stephanie Tubbs Jones to explain why she earmarked $2 million in tax money to a well-to-do paint company in her Ohio home district: Sherwin-Williams. The earmark is to help Sherwin-Williams develop a biological repellent paint for the Defense Department. It sounds promising on its face—all earmarks do. Their descriptions are often creatively written to make it seem as though there's a great deal of public benefit when there may not be. Experts tell me the paint idea actually has almost zero viability and that the earmark is just a $2 million favor from a member of Congress to a business at home.

Tubbs Jones's press representatives give me the runaround and eventually deny the interview request. So I stake her out near her office on Capitol Hill. When I see her approach from a distance, I walk down the hall toward her and offer a handshake.

"I'm Sharyl Attkisson from CBS."

"Hi, Sharyl, how are you?" She takes my hand.

"I've been trying to talk to you about the Sherwin-Williams earmark—" I begin.

"Excuse me," interrupts Tubbs Jones, her manner suddenly turning dark. She continues through gritted teeth. "Don't you ever walk up like this . . ."

I explain that I've requested interviews through her office but to no avail.

"Ma'am, turn the camera off," she commands, as if royalty to her obedient subjects.

"You can't order us to turn our cameras off," I reply.

"Well then, I can't be forced to talk to you," she says in an exasperated voice, waving an arm. Then, she flashes in anger and grabs me tightly around my right wrist. And squeezes.

"Don't play me like that. Don't play me like that!" she says threateningly.

It looks like we're going to rumble. As a former judge and prosecutor, Tubbs Jones knows better. She's just committed battery. On a news reporter. With a camera rolling. I instinctively consider a defensive martial arts move. But instead, I touch the top of her grasp with my free hand and say, "Please take your hands off me."

This seems to jolt her back into reality. She releases her grip. "I didn't mean any offense, okay?"

With that, she says that if I'll turn my camera off and give her a few minutes, she'll do the interview. (For the record, she explained that she gave Sherwin-Williams the $2 million because they—the company—told her they're the most qualified for the project. "They came with a proposal that looked good to me," Tubbs Jones said. "They showed me testing, they showed me a video and I said 'let's go for it!'")

But perhaps the member of Congress who goes the furthest to avoid speaking to public questions on camera is legendary earmarker John Murtha, a Democrat from Pennsylvania. An unindicted co-conspirator in the ABSCAM public corruption scandal in the early 1980s, Murtha is notoriously camera-shy. But almost thirty years later, he's said to be under FBI investigation again for his relationships with lobbyists, corporations, and donors. A firsthand, trusted source has described to me how Murtha's staff shakes down defense contractors for campaign contributions as a quid pro quo in exchange for getting them government contracts. But Murtha doesn't want to answer any such allegations or explain his earmarks on camera. So CBS News Capitol Hill producer Jill Jackson and various camera crews help stake him out on the Hill.

He knows we're looking.

One morning, Jackson and our photographer spot Murtha boarding the small escalator leading from the underground electric train that shuttles members between the Capitol and the adjacent House office buildings. Murtha spots our camera. In an instant, he vaults over the divider from the "up" escalator to the "down" side, and quickly disappears into the Capitol bowels before the photographer can get his camera on his shoulder and hit the ON button. "I've never seen a seventy-five-year-old move so fast," the cameraman would later marvel in relaying the account.

As powerful people in positions of authority work to avoid us and dictate the terms of our coverage, we too easily buy into their spin without question.

| THE POLITICAL-INDUSTRIAL COMPLEX

Big corporations rule the world. You may choose not to believe it. That's exactly what they're counting on. They influence vast amounts of information we receive. They control some facets of government so effectively that the government has all but given up trying to resist it. And it's the same whether we're talking about Democrats or Republicans.

That's not to say that big corporations are evil. Of course many do positive things for their employees, shareholders, and the public. They're engines that can power a healthy American economy. But when left unchallenged to control information so secretly and cleverly that we don't even realize they're doing it, they can get away with bad things. They can partner with the government and avoid meaningful government oversight. They can fool a complacent news media. They can hurt the economy. They can convince us that propaganda is the truth. They can prompt us to make decisions that are wrong, unhealthy, or dangerous.

What's even more dangerous is the fact that, today, government, politicians, and big corporations might as well be one and the same. Their self-interests are inextricably intertwined. Members of Congress serving on pivotal committees solicit contributions—legal payoffs—from the very special interests they're supposed to oversee. It results in a perverse dynamic where Congress ends up protecting and defending those it should be watchdogging. Likewise, federal agencies view the companies and industries they're supposed to regulate as "clients" or "stakeholders." These agencies are largely bought and paid for. They act as partners working in tandem for a common purpose. They exchange information between themselves that they keep secret from the public, which actually owns the information. Big corporations write and approve press releases that the government issues. As allies, they hold closed meetings and make decisions about matters of public interest without the public's input.

And because they make the rules: it's all legal.

In the early 2000s the government is debating how to regulate the mortgage industry. Countrywide Financial—among the biggest offenders in the brewing subprime mortgage crisis—gets caught attempting to curry favor by offering politicians and regulators red-carpet treatment and sweetheart loans through a VIP program called "Friends of Angelo," as in customers-referred-personally-by-

CEO-Angelo-Mozilo. VIPs include Democratic senators Kent Conrad of North Dakota and Chris Dodd of Connecticut. Both helped oversee the mortgage industry; each got at least two VIP loans.

VIP mortgages also went to President Clinton's former housing secretary Henry Cisneros, President Bush's housing secretary Alphonso Jackson, and Jackson's daughter Annette Watkins. (An internal Countrywide email noted Annette Watkins's father was expected to be confirmed by the Senate as secretary of housing and urban development.)

Another example is the case of Dr. Julie Gerberding, who was head of the U.S. Centers for Disease Control and Prevention (CDC). She's at the helm when the government secretly agrees to pay damages to the family of Hannah Poling, a child who developed autism after multiple vaccinations. The landmark case—which ultimately amounts to $1.5 million for Hannah the first year and $500,000 each year after—is ordered sealed, protecting the pharmaceutical vaccine industry and keeping the crucial information hidden from other families who have autistic children and also believe vaccines to be the culprit.

After she finishes as head of the government's CDC, Gerberding becomes president of vaccines for Merck.

Think about it. The very government that we pay to serve us and protect our interests ends up marginalizing us, working against us, or even leaving us out of the equation entirely.

Months before health-care industry lobbyists wrote the fine points of Obamacare to their own advantage, there was the Bush administration's $700 billion Troubled Asset Relief Program, or "TARP" for short—brought to you by the Wall Street banking industry.

It's September 24, 2008, and Secretary of the Treasury Hank Paulson is fervently lobbying members of Congress to pass TARP into law. It's a tough sell. I'm at a Washington, D.C., restaurant, meeting with Republican senator Lindsey Graham of South Carolina over iced tea. Our talks are interrupted by the important business of TARP. I get to be a fly on the wall for some important legislative discussions as they unfold.

Graham is acting as the intermediary between Secretary Paulson and Republican presidential nominee John McCain, who's on the campaign trail. Paulson calls Graham's cell phone making the pitch for TARP. Graham calls McCain's cell phone to relay information. McCain responds to Graham. Graham calls back Paulson. And so on.

In between calls, Graham relays to me the justification Paulson is giving for TARP. How tax dollars will be used to buy up so-called toxic assets in the subprime mortgage crisis. How, if this exact thing isn't done *now*, the U.S. economy—perhaps the world economy—will fall apart. Nothing short of the American way of life is at stake. Eventually, for the good of the nation, McCain is sold and so is the Democratic presidential nominee, Barack Obama. They set aside politics and issue a joint statement supporting TARP. Congress passes the TARP legislation on October 3, 2008.

It's not long before I break the news that Treasury secretary Paulson has quietly redefined TARP's mission out of the public eye. *It's now a cash program for banks, not consumers.* Instead of buying up so-called toxic mortgage-related assets, the TARP tax dollars will purchase massive amounts of the banks' preferred shares, giving them wide freedom to spend the money how they choose. Including acquiring other banks. I spend the next few days doing more research and then share the findings with Senator Graham, double-checking to confirm my understanding of how Paulson had originally sold the TARP concept to him and to Congress.

"Paulson fucking lied to us," Graham responds flatly, in his opinion.

I don't know if Paulson sold Congress a bill of goods because he figured they'd never approve a big bank bailout. Or if he did a genuine about-face as soon as TARP became law. I only know that the banks were clued in well before the American public was.

And what America got was fooled.

But there's no better exemplar of the political-industrial complex at work and the damage that it can do than the aftermath of the Deepwater Horizon oil rig explosion in the Gulf of Mexico on April 20, 2010. Eleven workers are killed instantly. The explosion itself is thoroughly covered in the media. But in the early days, the massive oil spill that follows doesn't generate commensurate interest among the news media.

Three weeks into the disaster, *CBS Evening News* executive producer Kaplan asks me to turn my attention to the story. I get up to speed and am surprised at the lack of enthusiasm over this environmental disaster from many in the traditionally environmentalism-friendly news media.

My first question is an obvious one: *Where's the video?*

Logic and experience tell me that BP would have undersea cameras watching and recording everything. Unbelievably, three weeks into the spill, there's no record of any other reporters yet seeking the video. When I raise the question with BP, the company refers me to the Coast Guard, as if the Coast Guard is acting as BP's press agent. (The government-corporate partnership—starting to sound familiar?)

I come to learn that after previous environmental accidents, government initiatives were put in place to hold oil companies more responsible for cleaning up their own messes. But with the Deepwater Horizon disaster, a perverted implementation of these rules leads to a bizarre relationship in which BP calls the shots, and the Coast Guard and U.S. Department of the Interior act, in some respects, as the oil company's agents, defending it rather than holding it accountable.

When I call the Coast Guard, media officials there confirm that video of the undersea disaster exists but they tell me that I can't have it because it belongs to BP. I argue that the video qualifies as public information and quickly file a demand for it under the federal Freedom of Information Act.

I might still be waiting today if it weren't for three Democrats in Congress who were on the same trail: Congressman Ed Markey of Massachusetts, Senator Bill Nelson of Florida, and Senator Barbara Boxer of California. I discover that they, too, are seeking the video. With combined efforts, I hope the cumulative pressure will force the video's release.

It works.

Fewer than two days after I start covering the story, three weeks into the spill, the *CBS Evening News* airs the world's first underwater glimpse of BP's catastrophe (May 18, 2010). Shocking black plumes of oil gushing from the uncapped well at a rate that surpasses all estimates. The video engages and galvanizes viewers around the world. Even more outrageous, as far as I'm concerned, is that we learn the Coast Guard—the very agency paid by the public to protect our interests—has been watching video of this disaster in real time but keeping it secret from the public and Congress from the start. It's not surprising that the company might seek to keep the video hidden, but the government shouldn't be helping the cause. In subsequent days, the *CBS Evening News* and *Face the Nation with Bob Schieffer* continue airing my reports exposing BP's and the government's wildly lowball estimates of how much oil is leaking. (It's three million gallons a day rather than the 42,000 gallons initially claimed, or the 210,000-gallon figure later provided to Congress.) I also catch the U.S. Interior Department giving interviews and issuing press releases that misrepresent its own experts' opinions for the purpose of understating the scope of the disaster.

This is the first time I witness what will become a recurring observation under the Obama administration. Normal political and news media relationships seem to be turned on their head.

Substitution Game: If a corporate environmental disaster had occurred under a Republican administration, the lines would be clear. Democrats and most in the media would fault Republicans and their hostility toward the environment, aversion to regulation, and cozy relationship with industry. But under a new, popular, African-American, Democratic president, few are as eager to point fingers.

Some Democrats in Congress privately confess to me that they can't risk criticizing the government's response to the oil spill for fear that it would look like a criticism of the Obama administration. Some in the press seem to have similar concerns. Their heart just isn't in it—which is evidenced by the fact that three weeks into the spill they hadn't even bothered to ask: *where's the video*?

In November 2012, BP pays a record $4.5 billion fine for, among other crimes, lying about how much oil was spilling from the Deepwater Horizon wreckage. The government officials who marched in lockstep with BP the whole way are not held similarly accountable.

| THE POLITICAL-INDUSTRIAL PR MACHINE

As they've melded into one, the government has adopted and perfected many of the public relations and crisis management strategies employed by big corporations. It's a natural outgrowth of their incestuous relationship. The big difference is the government is using your tax dollars to promote itself and advance its propaganda.

One way they do this is by self-producing videos and building their very own television production facilities where the upper echelon give interviews and speeches, controlling everything from content to lighting. While the nation has descended into unprecedented debt, Congress and federal agencies ranging from the Department of

Health and Human Services to the National Institutes of Health have been using millions of your tax dollars to build or expand their television studios. The Food and Drug Administration's facility boasts "a number of mobile and fixed sets, as well as various configurations, to allow for a studio audience of over 100." The Transportation Security Administration sports a studio with "Hitachi high-definition cameras, Fujinon lenses and LCD based teleprompters mounted on Vinten Vision studio pedestals and Vision 20 fluid heads." And when top officials with those federal agencies appear on camera, naturally, they have to look good. So your tax dollars may kick in for the cost of their hairstylists, makeup artists, and wardrobe consultants. One insider told me the head of a federal agency even had her fashion "colors" analyzed at taxpayer expense (are you a winter, spring, summer, or fall?).

In addition, the Pentagon has its own twenty-four-hour channel, which features military news, interviews with top defense officials, and programs such as *The Grill Sergeants*. While the Pentagon frets over sequestration cuts, and the troops listen to talk of cutting their pensions, your tax dollars pay to produce programs such as a cooking show competition that features mess hall cooks and aides to generals battling it out over dishes such as seared ahi tuna and lamb with blueberry wine sauce.

Both the Defense Department and the Centers for Disease Control provide taxpayer-funded advisors to television and Hollywood entertainment producers to promote accuracy—or propaganda— depending on your view.

Some of the public interest justifications for these assets are dubious.

In 2013, Congress catches the IRS making *Star Trek* and *Gilligan's Island* parody videos to "educate" federal employees at a conference. When Secretary of Energy Steven Chu resigns from the Obama administration, the federal agency that he led produces a slick photo tribute to him—using your money. It touts Chu's incredible "successes," but forgets to mention any of his scandals, such as his failed efforts at playing venture capitalist with tax dollars in green energy initiatives like Solyndra. And by its own admission, the Pentagon's Film Liaison Office gives for-profit filmmakers free use of taxpayer assets, from tanks to jets, but only if the film portrays the positive images the Pentagon wants. If not, the assets are withheld. According to the documentary *Hollywood and the Pentagon: A Dangerous Liaison*: "Scripts are cut and sometimes watered down. Characters are changed and historical truth, sometimes fudged. One director might be loaned combat ships and jets. . . . Another director, whose script displeases the army, may be refused any kind of support. . . . Few great war films have escaped the influence, or even the censure, of the U.S. Army."

It's "pure propaganda," according to the documentary. And you're paying for it.

Like big corporations, each federal agency and all 535 members of Congress have teams of taxpayer-funded media and communications specialists to advance their messages. A few years ago, a well-placed insider at the U.S. Department of Agriculture confessed to me that even he was surprised to learn that his own agency supposedly had more than 1,200 employees working in some sort of media relations capacity nationwide. (And on a given day, exactly zero of them may provide information requested by the media on a timely basis.) Your tax dollars pay their salaries, but many times they're little more than private publicity agents for their bosses: spinning, avoiding, and obfuscating as expertly as any of their corporate counterparts.

Too often, we let them get away with it.

If the news media were to collectively hold public officials accountable, the officials wouldn't be able to run and hide. At least we could make it more difficult. But it seems that there are a relative few journalists doing all the chasing and more who see all that as—well, unnecessary and perhaps a bit rude. They don't seem to share the view that public officials are answerable to the public. They make it easy for politicians to believe that the public serves them rather than the other way around.

Combine complacency in the news media with the incredible publicity forces behind the political-industrial complex and you begin to understand how little of the truth you sometimes get. They often have unlimited time and money to figure out new ways to spin us while cloaking their role in doing so.

| BLURRED LINES

If you're confused about all the influences behind what you see on the news and how they affect the product, there's good reason. At times, there's a liberal political bias in the mainstream media that tilts toward stories favoring liberal social issues and philosophies. But there's also a competing conservative, corporate bias that favors specific companies, industries, and paid interests. Unfortunately, the result isn't an ideal balance of complete information about the world; it's often a distorted and perplexing mix. This trend has become more predominant in the last couple of years as powerful interests have mastered their methods of influencing us, and some of our managers have embraced the influence believing that they'll keep their lucrative jobs by going along, rather than resisting.

The capitulation to special interests may preserve these news managers' jobs in the short term, but in the big picture they're ensuring a quicker demise of the entire platform by alienating and eroding the audience that we supposedly serve. While the network evening newscasts brag that increasing numbers of people are watching, the total television broadcast network news audience compared to that which is available remains minuscule. Many in the public believe that we're feeding them a lot of pabulum. I've never before heard so many people say so—liberals, conservatives, and people who define themselves as neither.

In February 2014 I'm at 524 West Fifty-Seventh Street, the main CBS News offices in New York, when a couple of colleagues happen to strike up a conversation that veers into the issue of corporate conflicts of interest. One CBS News producer who predates me at the network by at least a decade discusses how corporate interference has long been a hard reality in the news business. Several of us share our various war stories on the subject. All agree it's worse now.

So what is the mysterious process behind the decisions as to which stories make the news on a given night? Some stories are carefully chosen and edited by a small group of broadcast news managers because they serve a specific set of agendas.

In *Manufacturing Consent: The Political Economy of the Mass Media*, Edward Herman and Noam Chomsky state that commercial news organizations disseminate propaganda on behalf of dominant private interests and the government.

"The U.S. media do not function in the manner of the propaganda system of a totalitarian state," write the authors. "Rather, they permit—indeed encourage—spirited debate, criticism, and dissent, as long as these remain faithfully within the system of presuppositions and principles that constitute an elite consensus, a system so powerful as to be internalized largely without awareness."

I agree with the observations. We routinely convince ourselves that we're questioning authorities and approaching news stories with open minds. In fact, our discussions usually take place within the confines of the narrowest parameters preset by our own—or our supervisors'—"system of presuppositions and principles that constitute an elite consensus."

There are also other factors at play. Many story topics are selected by managers who are producing out of fear and trying to play it safe.

Playing it safe means airing stories that certain other trusted media have reported first, so there's no perceived "risk" to us if we report them, too. We're not going out on a limb; we're not reporting anything that hasn't already been reported elsewhere. But it also means we're not giving viewers any reason to watch us.

Playing it safe can mean shying away from stories that include allegations against certain corporations, charities, and other chosen powerful entities and people. The image of the news media as fearless watchdogs poised, if not eager, to pursue stories that authorities wish to block is often a false image. Decisions are routinely made in fear of the response that the story might provoke. The propagandists' heavy-handed tactics have worked: they don't even have to pick up the phone and complain— news managers demonstrate a Pavlovian-style avoidance response when presented with a story they fear will bring about negative reaction. We're weak and diffident when we needn't be.

Many investigative reporters around the nation are experiencing the same thing. It's a trend. Longtime Emmy Award–winning reporter Al Sunshine retired from the CBS owned and operated station in Miami, WFOR-TV, the summer before I left the CBS News network. Afterward, he made similar observations.

"Because of the recent lack of support and commitment for my investigations, I faced an almost daily battle to get the time to work my stories and had to fight harder than ever for airtime," Sunshine told me. Though his brand of investigative and consumer stories was wildly popular with viewers, sometimes resulting in new laws being passed and criminals getting prosecuted, he says he was told his stories were "too negative." Instead, he was often reassigned to day-of-air news coverage.

"Advertisers are dominating news judgment in news organizations all over the country. The public interest is being diminished in the interest of corporate advertisers and lobbyists. What's almost universally accepted as 'business as usual' in Washington, corruption between lobbyists' dollars and political favoritism, is slowly but surely becoming the norm for many news organizations as well," Sunshine contends.

It may be growing worse, but historical narrative implies there's always been an element of this conditioned avoidance response in the corporate news world. In his 1967 memoir, *Due to Circumstances Beyond Our Control*, CBS News president Fred Friendly expressed the discomfort that top management felt over its star reporter Edward R. Murrow: "During the 1954–55 season we did a two-part report on cigarettes and lung cancer, and both CBS and [CBS sponsor] Alcoa aluminum company felt the pressures of the tobacco industry, which buys both air time and aluminum foil. The attitude at CBS was: 'Why does Murrow have to save the world every week?'"

In another instance, Friendly quoted CBS founder Bill Paley as telling Murrow, "I don't want this constant stomach ache every time you do a controversial subject."

These tendencies to censor topics that generate objections from their powerful targets aren't necessarily spoken or even consciously addressed. Those of us who report on these sorts of subjects aren't *told* that our original stories are undesirable because they're not "safe" or because they challenge powers.

"News management manipulation is subtle," observes Sunshine. He says it comes in many forms, like the withholding of resources such as cameramen and producers, and conveniently dropping investigative reports from the newscast when the timing of the show happens to run too long to fit it in.

We've figured it out.

Ironically, management's avoidance response can result in absurd machinations that inadvertently generate the very liabilities that they're trying to avoid.

Some of us have boiled it down to a saying: "They're often worried about the wrong things; not worried about the right things."

In one instance, I reported a story on a credit card scam that showed surveillance video of a suspect caught on camera allegedly using one stolen card after another at Target, Wal-Mart, and Macy's. Neither the story, nor our use of the surveillance video, was precarious in any sense. The police had publicly released the video, it had already appeared on the local news, the suspect had been identified, and I had run my story through the CBS legal department for clearance. Even under the standards of the current skittish *Evening News* management, this story was "safe."

But just prior to air, executive producer Pat Shevlin views the finished piece in New York, and rings the hotline phone to the Washington newsroom.

"We can't show the suspect's *face*," she protests.

"Why not?" I ask.

"He hasn't been *convicted* of anything," Shevlin sputters back.

I take a breath. The idea that a criminal suspect's face can't be shown on television comes from someone who lacks the most basic knowledge of law. I'm having way too many of these conversations lately and I already know it means that she won't listen to me: she's scared of the story. What I tell her from here on out won't matter.

Nonetheless, I patiently explain that somebody doesn't have to be convicted of a crime for us to identify him or show his face. Under Shevlin's mistaken idea of the law, arrest mug shots would never be shown on the news. We wouldn't have shown O. J. Simpson's face when he was accused—but never convicted—of murder. We wouldn't have identified any criminal suspects prior to conviction: Timothy

McVeigh. John Gotti. Jack Kevorkian. Lorena Bobbitt. Tom Delay. Martha Stewart. Michael Jackson. Bernard Madoff. The Unabomber. Osama bin Laden. None of those stories would have been done if we were to consistently apply Shevlin's warped view of the law.

Still, she balks. "Call his lawyer and ask for permission to show his client's face."

Another breath. I look at the clock. It's nearly 6 p.m. The story is set to air at 6:30 p.m. The odds that I'll reach the suspect's public defender and get a yes from him in the next half hour are remote. But more important, the idea that we would set a precedent by asking the suspect for permission to use his image has to rank as one of the more preposterous suggestions I've ever heard. Even in a newsroom.

"Well, we don't *need* his permission," I reiterate. "And I doubt he'd give it. I wouldn't if I were him."

"Okay," she says, still sounding unconvinced. We hang up the hotline phone. Within seconds, she sends a message telling me to blur the suspect's face, anyway.

"Just wuzz it a little," she says.

With time ticking, I rush back to the editing room and break the news to my producer, Kim Skeen, and our editor.

"You're not going to believe this, but she wants us to get permission from the defendant's lawyer to use his face or else wuzz it out."

"What?!?" says Kim, dumbfounded. "That's outrageous."

Kim makes another attempt to reach the attorney, whom we'd tried earlier. It's futile at this hour. And we know that, if asked, he'll say no anyway. So we go ahead and blur the suspect's face and refeed the story to New York.

In some ways, this may not sound like a big deal. What's the harm in masking a criminal suspect's identity? I know the answer and it nags away at me. The executive producer's misguided and capricious decision hasn't avoided risk; it's actually created a potential liability.

We've now set a precedent that sets us up for accusations of bias and inconsistent treatment.

For example, Substitution Game: Following the February 2012 fatal shooting of the black youth Trayvon Martin in Florida, which ignited allegations of racism, we rightfully identified the gunman, George Zimmerman, though he hadn't been arrested, let alone convicted of anything. But under the executive producer's current reasoning, we shouldn't have identified Zimmerman or shown his face—unless we had his permission. That's absurd, of course, but it's the sort of comparison invited by her order to blur the face of the alleged credit card thief. I imagine the lawyer for other suspects whom we've previously identified asking CBS:

"Why did you blur out the face of this credit card suspect?"

"Well, because he hadn't been convicted of anything," we would answer.

"*My* client hadn't been convicted of anything either—why did you show *his* face? Do you have something against *my* client?"

Worried about the wrong things and not worried about the right things.

The tendency to stick to mostly "safe" stories means you'll see a lot of so-called day-of-air reports on topics that won't generate pushback from the special interests we care about. Think: weather, polls, surveys, studies, positive medical news, the pope, celebrities, obituaries, press conferences, government announcements, animals, the British royals, and heartwarming features. They fill airtime much like innocuous white noise.

Crafting the special news concoction of safe stories and ones that push certain agendas requires finding reasons to avoid—I would say censor—stories and topics that don't fit the bill. That includes much of the original and investigative reporting that we supposedly covet. Yes, strong, original reporting still exists. But the behind-the-scenes struggles to get it on the air have grown more pitched and fruitless. And much more of that sort of reporting is cast aside than ever sees a national audience.

In short: people assume a great deal of effort goes into putting terrific stories on the news. They'd be shocked to learn how much effort goes into keeping some of them off.

On more than one occasion, I've been encouraged to stop reporting on an original topic that's generating strong pushback from powerful entities or people.

"Just wait and report if there's a day-of-air story about it, you know, a congressional hearing or something," I'm told by various managers.

Translation: You're pissing off important people. Stop breaking news on this topic. If something happens that everybody is reporting, we can join in. That's . . . *safe*.

It's unconscionable that a news organization would actually forgo breaking important news in favor of staying safely back with the pack, but that's exactly what happens, day in and day out. Instead, we spend our efforts chasing down an interview with the local news reporter who fainted during a live shot, resulting in a viral video.

Often replacing what used to count as true and independent news is a new brand of reporting that assists paid interests who are pushing a business agenda.

The lines have become blurred as corporations that own news divisions have come to view them as potential profit centers. This is understandable: corporations have a fiduciary duty to make financial decisions that benefit the business and any shareholders. If a network's pharmaceutical client were to threaten to cancel millions of dollars in advertising if the network's news division investigates and reports on its controversial product, the corporation may believe its fiduciary responsibility is to block the news division from doing the report. But therein lies the inherent conflict: the news division is supposed to shun the influence of financial interests. It's sort of like saying that politicians are supposed to be above the influence of money while knowing that, in reality, they rely on cash from influential powers to get elected.

Some broadcast managers' idea of what constitutes "news" has shifted to fit the cold, hard reality. They instinctively shy away from stories that may offend advertisers or other powerful corporate interests. They don't necessarily have to be told to do so. They've learned to self-censor. At the same time they insist there's no room in the broadcast—or interest among viewers—for many investigative stories, they clear even more generous blocks of time for segments that promote commercial interests and have little genuine news value.

One example is *The Mysterious Case of the Incredibly Unwarranted National News Coverage of Taco Bell Dorito Shells*. On March 21, 2012, *CBS This Morning* features a four-and-a-half-minute interview with Taco Bell CEO Greg Creed.

"Listen to this! A taco shell made of nacho cheese Doritos!" reads one of the anchors, enthusiastically introducing Creed. That's followed by such hard-hitting questions as "I'm curious about where the idea came from?" and "Are you handing out the breath mints?"

Creed is pushing Taco Bell's "reinvention of the taco" through the cross-promotional partnership with Doritos. As Creed puts it, "these two great products coming together . . . [are an] amazing combination . . . we have great quality, we have great taste, we have great value." He points out that Taco Bell has "one hundred percent all-white all breast meat chicken" and concludes, "There's so much happening at Taco Bell . . . You can customize anything at Taco Bell."

Viewers have just witnessed what amounts to little more than a product promotion presented under the guise of news. A few of us in the news division wonder aloud how Taco Bell managed to get *CBS This Morning* to do that.

Ten months later, on January 29, 2013, Taco Bell's Creed is back on *CBS This Morning*. This time, the news segment begins with the broadcast showing Taco Bell's upcoming Super Bowl ad, after which the anchors bestow compliments on Creed as if they're at an ad agency screening.

"Nicely done, Taco Bell!"

"I love it, I love it!"

Then: probing questions.

"How many times will this run during the Super Bowl?"

"Let's just talk about the Doritos Locos Taco—I mean that is *quite* a concept, essentially putting taco in a Dorito!" And—wait for it—the big reveal, provided exclusively to *CBS This Morning*: "Cool Ranch" flavor Dorito tacos are on the horizon!

Whatever the motivation, these appearances are a marketing coup for Taco Bell. A national news organization has been convinced to treat a product promotion as if it's a big breaking news story. Once the "news" is codified on the network news, other media outlets pick it up. The New York *Daily News*, *Time Newsfeed*, *Buzzfeed*, *Business Insider*, *Gawker*, *Daily Finance*, and *Huffington Post* advance the promotion, crediting *CBS This Morning* for being first to "break" the story.

Note to self: there's no time for an exclusive story exposing wrongdoing inside a corporation or government agency. They're too busy chasing that Taco Bell Doritos exclusive.

If we're to believe that this is legitimate news coverage with no financial consideration provided by Taco Bell and Doritos, then why do the stories fail to address any of the obvious news controversies? Doritos, while an incredibly successful and yummy product, is nonetheless junk food in its purest form. But none of these news segments mentions the debate over scientific research linking some of the artificial food coloring used in Doritos to ADHD and other health problems in children. There's not a whiff of the news that European lawmakers require health warning labels on foods that contain some of the same artificial dyes. Critics could reasonably argue that these news segments uncritically push a potentially harmful product without making the public aware of the significant debate. Well, they *could* argue that if they were offered a voice in any of these segments, but they aren't.

A colleague in television network news tells me such "silliness" takes time away from a meaningful story we might have told. "I'm disappointed because of what is taken off the table. . . . We always believed we served the public interest and that doesn't exist anymore. Our public interest is incidental to success."

Now that I've pointed it out, you'll recognize how widespread this syndrome is and how much "news time" appears to be influenced by paid, commercial interests.

On June 9, 2014, the *Today* show on NBC features a segment that's little more than an ad for Dove products. Like the Taco Bell segment on *CBS This Morning*, the *Today* show begins by actually showing a commercial from the company. After that, there's four more minutes promoting Dove, including interviews with a Dove ad campaign's vice president of marketing and "an advisor on Dove Men research" (what is that, exactly?). The broadcast then promotes a Dove-created social media hashtag and encourages viewers to contribute by tweeting or Facebooking "real dad moments."

What stories weren't told on this day because news time was filled with this promotion for Dove? What stories might not get covered in the future because of the news' financial relationships with advertisers?

Even though it's a given that the *Today* show isn't meant to be a hard news broadcast, the Dove episode caused quite an uproar among some inside the NBC News division. They were outraged over what they viewed as a number of steps taken within the news division to please the Dove corporate officials in the reported attempt to convince the company to provide a paid sponsorship for the news. They say internal news division emails refer to a Dove executive as "the client," and indicate that news officials were letting him call the shots on "news coverage" of his product.

Then, in July 2014, *CBS This Morning* spends two minutes and forty-five seconds of broadcast time on what amounts to a commercial for TGI Friday's. It promotes the restaurant's latest promotion: all-you-can-eat-appetizers on Fridays.

"We're at TGI Friday's to take a look at their new recipe for profits and—*here it is*!" says the correspondent on the scene.

The camera zooms out, similar in fashion to a TV ad, to show a display of all the tempting appetizer offerings on the menu.

"This deal is only good for the summer," adds the reporter, as if to say *hurry, hurry!*

The anchors comment, "Smart idea! Everybody wins with all-you-can-eat" and "I think it's a good idea!"

It's a telling glimpse into a TV news environment that has less appetite and less time than ever for serious, original, and investigative stories, but all the time in the world to promote commercial interests.

When corporations approach news organizations with a press release on a product or concept they want to promote, we're supposed to say, *No thanks, we don't usually do stories on press releases. That's advertising, not news.* If an advertiser tries to get a "news story" produced with the agenda of promoting its product, we should say, *That wouldn't be proper.*

But clever marketers may have learned that it's easy to trade on their financial relationship with the parent corporation or manipulate us into treating promotional material as if it's news. They may contact us and tell us that we can have an exclusive! *How would you like to have the first interview with our CEO?* They play one news organization against the other implying that our competitor might get the interview first if we don't commit. Or, the opposite approach: they tell us that everyone else is interested in doing it and we'll be left out if we don't do it, too. They offer "round robins," as we call them, in which compliant news organizations take turns, one right after the other, conducting the same interview with the same executive who's promoting the same idea so that we can all publish roughly the same story and call it news. They play off our desire to be part of the pack. They exploit our fear that our competitors might have something that we don't. They institute ground rules and embargoes on the information until a certain date and time that make it feel as though we're brokering a very coveted deal! Pretty soon, we're wrapped around the corporate finger: all competing to be first to do the company's bidding, and touting it as a coup when we do. I can't help but think that there must be marketing experts patting each other on the back as they watch, laughing all the way to the bank. But the public isn't laughing.

Maybe the airlines have figured this out. Several of us at CBS notice a rash of oddly uncritical airtime offered to various airline CEOs.

On February 14, 2013, *CBS This Morning* interviews US Airways CEO Doug Parker and American Airlines CEO Tom Horton about their proposed, controversial merger. They need to put a good public face on the pending union to win crucial federal approval and this media outreach is part of their PR campaign. And we're apparently delighted to be of service. For nearly four minutes in a joint interview, they promote their business deal, unchallenged, and dispel the notion that it could mean higher ticket prices for consumers. The anchors ask questions like:

"You've been pushing for the merger for a long time. Why and why now?"

"What's the benefit for American with this merger?"

"Sounds like a good deal . . . can't wait to fly!"

There's no voice provided to consumer groups or antitrust experts who argue the merger is anticompetitive. In fact, you'd never know it from the interview, but there's so much opposition to the merger that the Justice Department and a half dozen states would eventually sue to try to stop it.

On May 22, 2013, Spirit Airlines CEO Ben Baldanza is provided three minutes and forty-eight seconds on *CBS This Morning* to counterspin a consumer survey that faulted Spirit for poor customer service. Of course, there's nobody to present the consumer viewpoint. In the interview, Baldanza repeatedly touts his company's cheap ticket prices and other advantages, adding: "We *do* have great customer service."

On August 1, 2013, United CEO Jeff Smisek is given more than seven minutes on *CBS This Morning* to insist that mergers in the industry are good and that there's no major issue with Boeing's beleaguered Dreamliner, which United flies. (It's significant to note that CBS producers and management killed one of my in-depth stories on the Dreamliner's battery problems six months earlier, despite strong verbal and written objections from me and several producers. More on that later.)

On December 10, 2013, American CEO Parker is back on *CBS This Morning*. The US Airways–American merger is nearly complete and now he's getting another unchallenged opportunity to push back against experts who still insist the consolidation will be bad for consumers. Except none of those experts are interviewed in the segment. "Nothing about this merger should affect prices," says Parker, earnestly.

Maybe Southwest Airlines felt left out. Three days later, on December 13, 2013, it's Southwest's chance to get four minutes and thirty seconds on *CBS This Morning*. CEO Gary Kelly reassures viewers that the controversial consolidation within the industry won't result in higher fares. As usual, there's nobody in the segment to challenge that contention, though there are plenty of formidable voices in the business world saying so. Instead, the time is taken up with Kelly making promotional points like "Southwest has the best Wi-Fi," "You can count on companies like Southwest," and "We have, we believe, the best people . . . the best service."

Many in the public recognize they're not hearing about the news that's important to them. They're getting the news that other interests want them to have.

With so many important topics left unexplored, the topics are ceded to the interpretations and whims of social media, special interests, and bloggers whose mission is very different than that of a news journalist. The public is left with the choice of big media outlets that pretend certain topics of interest don't exist, or conflicting, off-brand sources that publish opinion and rumor. That's our fault.

A network colleague observes, "In England they call us presenters. They don't call us reporters. And in many ways, that's what we've become."

| THE ASTROTURF EFFECT

As the money trail leading from big corporations to government and nonprofits has become subject to more exposure, they increasingly use more surreptitious methods such as astroturf. As in fake grass roots.

If you're not familiar with the term, astroturf is when special interests disguise themselves and write blogs, publish letters to the editor, produce ads, establish Facebook and Twitter accounts, start nonprofits, or just post comments to online material with the intent of fooling you into believing an independent or grassroots movement is speaking. There's an entire industry built around it in Washington,

D.C., and some lobbyists now say that astroturf is more important and effective than traditional forms of influence, such as directly lobbying members of Congress.

The whole point of astroturf is to give the impression there's widespread support for an agenda when there's not. Businesses may fund fake, astroturf "consumer campaigns" against competitors. Government may call upon its corporate partners to use astroturf methods to discredit reporters who threaten their mutual interests. You will no doubt see astroturf techniques used to attack the opinions and themes in this book, for obvious reasons.

Once you begin to know what to look for, you can detect astroturf everywhere. Hallmarks include the use of inflammatory language such as "crank," "paranoid," "quack," "nutty," "lies," "truther," "conspiracy theorists," "shoddy," "witch hunt," and "pseudo" in targeting the political-industrial complex's enemies. Astroturfers often claim to "debunk myths" that aren't myths at all. Another astroturf technique is to simply shove so much confusing and conflicting information into the mix, the public is left to throw up its hands and disregard all of it—including the truth.

Astroturfers also disguise a special interests' role by forming or co-opting a benevolent-sounding nonprofit or other third party. The nonprofit peddles a "story" that serves its corporate masters, and unwitting journalists report it as news. Or the nonprofit secretly defends the propagandists' interests without offering to disclose the financial ties.

One example is the cosmetic industry's use of the American Cancer Society. I discovered this tie several years ago when reporting on an FDA source's tip about the suspected link between antiperspirants and breast cancer. The FDA official told me that the agency was contemplating requiring a breast cancer warning on antiperspirants based on several studies suggesting a possible link. But some inside the FDA felt that industry opposition would be insurmountable. It was an inside debate that would interest many in the public.

As I pursued the story, the cosmetics industry wouldn't do an interview but referred me to the American Cancer Society, which, they assured me, would defend their interests.

Indeed, the American Cancer Society was all too happy to agree to appear on camera debunking any idea of a link between antiperspirants and breast cancer. But in my pre-interview with the Cancer Society's chief doctor, I discovered he hadn't read—and apparently didn't know about—the latest peer-reviewed, published studies suggesting a link.

That's when I thought to ask the Cancer Society if it got funding from the cosmetics industry. The answer was a very defensive "Yes." But the charity wouldn't disclose how much and said they wouldn't go through with the on-camera interview unless I agreed not to ask about the antiperspirant industry funding.

I forwarded the studies to the American Cancer Society's doctor. When he did the on-camera interview with me, he reversed his earlier position that had claimed the antiperspirant–breast cancer link was a "myth." Instead, he answered my questions by deflecting—repeatedly stating, when asked about the latest antiperspirant studies, that women have more important things to focus on, such as getting regular mammograms.

I strike even more sensitive spots when I dig into conflicts of interest among the supposed independent forces that promote and defend vaccines. When I ask, the not-for-profit American Academy of Pediatrics won't disclose how much money it receives from vaccine makers, but I find plenty of examples in the public domain, including a $342,000 payment from vaccine maker Wyeth; a $433,000 contribution from Merck the same year the Academy of Pediatrics endorsed Merck's controversial HPV vaccine Gardasil; and donations from Sanofi-Aventis, maker of seventeen vaccines, including a five-in-one combo shot added to the childhood vaccine schedule.

Beyond the exploitation of nonprofits, there's Wikipedia: astro-turf's dream come true.

Billed as "the free encyclopedia that anyone can edit," the reality can't be more different. Anonymous Wikipedia editors acting on behalf of corporate interests co-opt and control pages to forbid or reverse edits that threaten their agenda. Two steps ahead of everyone else, these agenda editors wield the most powerful editing authority, having joined Wikipedia years ago and worked their way to the top of the editing power structure. They skew and delete information, blatantly violating Wikipedia's own established policies with impunity, always superior to the poor schlubs who believe "anyone can edit" Wikipedia—only to discover they're blocked from correcting even the simplest factual inaccuracies.

Some of Wikipedia's conflicts of interest are exposed by a group called Wikipediocracy.com, which states that it exists to "inoculate the unsuspecting public against the torrent of misinformation, defamation, and general nonsense that issues forth from one of the world's most frequently visited websites."

In September 2012, famed author Philip Roth tried to correct a major fact error in his Wikipedia biography. But Wikipedia's editors wouldn't allow it, telling him that he simply was not a credible source. On *himself.*

A week later, a far more embarrassing conflict-of-interest scandal came to light. Wikipedia's dark side was publicly revealed as Wikipedia officials got caught offering a "PR service" that skews and edits pages on behalf of paid, publicity-seeking clients. An ad for one of the Wikipedia officials who allegedly put up his PR editing services for hire states, in part: "A positive Wikipedia article is invaluable [Search Engine Optimization]: it's almost guaranteed to be a top three Google hit. . . . WE HAVE THE EXPERTISE NEEDED to navigate the complex maze surrounding 'conflict of interest' editing on Wikipedia."

And then there are the powerful pharmaceutical interests that deftly use Wikipedia to distribute their propaganda and control the message. They maniacally troll specific Wikipedia pages to promulgate positive but sometimes-false information about medicines, vaccines, and their manufacturers; and delete negative but often-true information about the same topics. They unabatedly violate Wikipedia's own rules and disparage scientists, advocates, and reporters who research medical and vaccine controversies by controlling their Wikipedia biographical pages. Conversely, they scrub all of the controversial information from the biographical pages of those pharmaceutical and research officials whom they are paid to defend. This phenomenon is surely one factor contributing to shameful study results that compared several Wikipedia articles about medical conditions to peer-reviewed research papers, and found that Wikipedia contradicted medical research 90 percent of the time.

You may never fully trust what you read on Wikipedia again. Nor should you.

| SPIN CYCLE

Besides astroturf, both government and corporations use many other tried-and-true PR strategies to spin the news media and public opinion. Once you learn to recognize them, you'll come to see that they are utilized far and wide.

"Know Your Enemy"

PR officials get to know the reporters on the story and their supervisors. Research them. Lobby them. Look for their weak spots. If they don't adopt the preferred PR viewpoint, the PR officials launch a campaign to controversialize and discredit them.

"Mine and Pump Strategy"

When asked to provide interviews and information for a story, the

PR officials stall, claim ignorance of the known facts, and mine and pump the reporter for what information he has.

"Controversialize"

The PR officials wait until the story is published to see how much the reporter really knows. Then they launch a propaganda campaign with surrogates and sympathizers in the media to divert from the damaging facts. The officials controversialize the reporter and any whistleblowers or critics to try to turn focus on personalities instead of the evidence. They start a whisper campaign saying that the critics are paranoid and agenda driven.

"The Inversion Diversion"

This strategy that works quite well when practiced on the unsuspecting in the media: clever PR officials label damaging information as "propaganda." They do this by buddying up to reporters and convincing them to dismiss the truth—the damaging information—as spin that's being advanced by political opponents. Less experienced journalists are easily manipulated and react as scripted, now viewing the damaging information as tainted and not to be trusted.

I won't be used as a propaganda tool! the exploited reporters proudly think as they congratulate themselves for being so savvy.

They've effectively been swayed from reporting the reality, having no idea that they've succumbed to propaganda, even as they were led to believe they were resisting it.

"Old News"

The PR officials delay providing the true facts and information for as long as possible. Then, when the facts finally are revealed, they claim it's all "old news" and not worthy of a story.

There are as many variations of these common techniques as there are stories to be spun.

Here's an approach often employed by authorities who are defending themselves in a controversy: blanket-deny everything and hope the news media doesn't come up with proof to refute the denials. If they do, modify your position. Say they misunderstood you earlier. Parse wording. Tell them you never meant to deny *that* particular thing.

Rinse. Repeat.

The evolving denials in the Bureau of Alcohol, Tobacco, Firearms and Explosives (ATF) *Fast and Furious* gunwalking scandal are a prime example of this strategy in practice.

It's pretty clear to see that the government can't always be trusted to tell the entire truth. Yet each step of the way in covering *Fast and Furious*, I was faced with naysayers and colleagues who pointed to the government's spin—one disproven story after another—as if the latest version were to be believed. As if it put the matter to rest. Obviously, I wouldn't be doing my job if I were to accept—uncritically, without skepticism, at face value—proclamations from government and others in power as absolute truth.

| THE DREADED "PUSHBACK"

Fast and Furious isn't the only case that some journalists or their managers wrote off simply because the government said the allegations weren't true.

"We're getting some serious pushback [from the government]," concerned-sounding managers might say to one another or to the reporters on the story. The managers think, *Oh no! We'd better back off. The story's wrong because the government says so.* Pushback makes them uncomfortable. It makes them nervous.

I think it should have the opposite effect. If it's my story generating the pushback, I think, *That usually means there's more to uncover.* It makes me want to keep digging.

"Serious pushback" is mediaspeak for the-accused-parties-are-mounting-a-full-force-campaign-to-stop-or-discredit-a-story. And they often get a big assist from others in the media club. Because there are few things news outlets enjoy more than undermining each other's big stories.

In 2000, there's pushback on the story about Firestone tires and Ford Explorer rollovers. Our CBS affiliates in Houston and Miami were first on the case and had great leads investigating the rash of people injured or killed in Ford Explorer rollovers after their Firestone tires blew out, sometimes at low speeds. Some consumer groups and reporters feel that the government safety agency, the National Highway Traffic Safety Administration, is in the business of protecting Ford and Firestone rather than being on top of their safety issues. But the agency is ultimately pushed and prodded by consumer complaints and media coverage to investigate the claims.

My producer, Allyson Ross-Taylor, and I are assigned to look into the allegations and I'm lucky to get some help from *60 Minutes* staffers who have already been gathering research. The story is moving too fast to wait for a big *60 Minutes* piece so they share their list of contacts. I get up to speed and we begin breaking news.

It's 6:28 p.m. one night, just two minutes before the opening of the *CBS Evening News with Dan Rather.* I'm sitting at the tiny newsroom set in the Washington, D.C., bureau waiting to lead the broadcast when I hear the voice of Executive Producer Jim Murphy in my earpiece. He's in the control room in New York.

"I just got a fucking fax from Firestone threatening to sue us," Murphy tells me.

"For what?" I ask.

"They say your story's wrong and unfair," he replies.

"Shouldn't they wait and see the report before they sue?" I ask rhetorically.

"Just tell me, is your story solid?"

"Of course," I tell him confidently. "Definitely."

"I thought so," says Murphy. "Fuck 'em." The open of the broadcast rolls live and the newscast begins.

It takes a certain kind of manager to stand up to pushback. I think there are fewer and fewer of them around these days.

Murphy asks me to continue aggressively reporting the Ford-Firestone story. Although pushback continues, we do a report almost every night for more than thirteen weeks. CBS becomes the go-to source for the latest developments in a story that millions of people are following. Eventually, after all of our coverage and the tally reaching at least 271 people dead in Explorer rollovers involving Firestone tires, the tires are recalled. Had we and the rest of the news media succumbed to the pushback back then, the story would have died and the tires would never have been pulled from the market. Had we taken the government's word at the outset, as some managers would have us do today, we would never have pursued the story.

Some of the hardest pushback I ever receive comes after Murphy assigns me to look into the reported cover-up of adverse effects of various prescription drugs and military vaccinations. That series of reports leads to me to investigate related stories about childhood vaccinations and their links to harmful side effects, including brain damage and autism. At the time, the Bush administration is marching in lockstep with the pharmaceutical industry in denying problems with the prescription drugs at issue as well as both military and childhood vaccines. It's one thing for them to want their side of the story told: that's understandable. But it's quite another for them to want the stories censored entirely. They're trying to keep them from airing altogether. They don't want Americans to know about the many controversies or hear from the scientists doing peer-reviewed, published research that contradicts the official party line.

Minutes before one of my first stories about childhood vaccinations and autism is to air, a spokesman for a nonprofit group called "Every Child by Two" calls the network in New York. The spokesman evokes the name of former first lady Rosalynn Carter, who cofounded the group.

The call reaches Murphy, who then calls me on the hotline that rings directly into the Washington bureau newsroom. I'm preparing for my live shot.

"Why is some group called 'Every Child by Two' supposedly fronted by Rosalynn Carter calling me about your story?" Murphy asks.

"I have no idea," I reply. I'd never heard of Every Child by Two, which promotes children getting fully vaccinated by age two and rejects the idea of investigating harmful vaccine side effects that could injure the very youngsters they purported to protect. (The dynamic was later explained when I discovered a major vaccine manufacturer, Wyeth, funded the nonprofit and a Wyeth spokesman was listed as the group's treasurer.) I wondered how they knew we planned to air a story on the news that night.

"Your story's solid, right?" Murphy asks.

"Yes," I assure him. There's not a sliver of doubt.

Resisting the pushback, we air the story as planned and Murphy asks for more. We continue digging into FDA-approved prescription drugs that are allegedly proving problematic from a safety standpoint.

When we do, hired guns for pharmaceutical interests flood me and CBS News with emails, phone calls, and requests for meetings. They write letters to CBS attorneys. The spokesman for Secretary of Health and Human Services Tommy Thompson calls the CBS News

Washington bureau chief to exert pressure to discredit our stories. Pharmaceutical company lawyers set up secretive meetings with CBS officials in New York. Pharmaceutical interests contact CBS executives to complain.

At one point, when I'm covering safety concerns about the highly profitable cholesterol drugs known as "statins," whose makers buy advertising on CBS, Murphy receives what he views as a harsh threat from one of the CBS sales bosses. The manager leaves Murphy a loud, angry voice mail saying that the stories could "really harm business."

My producer and I are also receiving direct pressure from news executives in New York who begin unnaturally inserting themselves into the newsgathering and approval process for the pharmaceutical-related stories as they had never done with me before. Even after our scripts go through the normal editorial process and receive approval from the legal department, the executives enter to dissect and question each fact and sentence. We vigorously defend our work and, in one story after another, they end up finding no fault. No legitimate reason to kill the reports. But the process is uncomfortable and grueling; their actions convey a clear, underlying message that's intended to discourage us.

After one particularly thorough examination of one of my scripts, an executive confesses to me in frustration that she's been given a mission of trying to stop my stories but that they're so thorough and well reported, she can't find any reason to.

Fortunately, Murphy brushes off the heat and we successfully cover news on the pharmaceutical front for several years. He understands that the stories are alienating some in the Bush administration, including officials at the Department of Health and Human Services and the Centers for Disease Control, as well as the pharmaceutical industry and its many connected special interests. But he doesn't care.

"I know what I'm doing," he tells me in keeping me focused on reporting the controversies at hand. "You're the bad cop. [Our regular medical beat reporter] can be the good cop and stay on the government's good side." He doesn't mind the pushback. And I don't care if I piss off the entire government-pharmaceutical complex. So it works out.

Eventually, our own effectiveness catches up with us. The pushback comes from within.

One memorable incident happens after I've written a script that had received approval from my Washington senior producer, the *Evening News* executive producer in New York, and our CBS lawyers. It's a story about a documented danger involving an automaker's cars. I'm called into the office of the Washington bureau chief, who had never before been involved in my script approval or story reporting process.

"Why are we doing this story?" she demands.

"Well, *Evening News* assigned it to me, and it turned out to be a good story. It's also an important story," I answer. "A lot of cars are catching fire and being recalled due to this safety issue."

"But [the car company] says there's not a problem," she retorts. "*So why are we doing this story???!?!*"

I'm puzzled. Why would she take the PR claim of the automaker that's accused of the wrongdoing as gospel? Why would she imply that's justification to keep us from doing the story?

I reply with an analogy.

"Well, Ford and Firestone said their tires on Explorers weren't dangerous," I point out. "It doesn't mean they're telling the truth."

There's a succession of similar meetings over a period of months and the message is clear. My producer and I should steer clear of stories that accuse corporations of doing anything wrong. At least that's the message we infer.

Regardless, as long as Murphy wants the stories, and he does, we continue onward.

Then one day, my bureau chief calls my office and tells me she "wants to see my notes" on a story I'm preparing that raises questions about an American Red Cross disaster response. I'd never been asked such a thing in all my years as a reporter and hardly knew how to respond. Especially since, as I mentioned, the bureau chief traditionally had played no role in my reporting chain of command. I gather what I've scribbled on various notepads and papers and take the stairs from my third-floor office to the second floor, where the bureau chief resides.

"You can look at my notes on this or any story," I tell her. "But there's no way that will give you a total picture of what we've done during weeks of research. Frankly, I think it's wholly inappropriate."

She exhales and looks deflated.

"I know," she tells me, sounding exasperated. "I don't know what else to do." Then she says something unexpected: the directive to discourage my stories had come from high up in the news division.

"We must do nothing to upset our corporate partners," she confesses she's been told.

I'm temporarily dumbfounded. *Who are our "corporate partners"? Advertisers? Somebody else?*

"For how long?" I ask.

"Until the stock splits," she answers.

"Well, when is that supposed to be?"

She names a date a few months down as the time period when the stock is expected to split. In the end, it didn't. But the episode leaves no doubt in my mind that there are corporate pressures behind the effort to discourage my hard-hitting reporting.

When it comes to our coverage of the terrorist attacks on Americans in Benghazi, Libya, on September 11, 2012, I don't know about all the pushback CBS News received. But I do know I'm the target of some of it.

For example, on April 30, 2013, I write an article for CBSNews.com about Benghazi whistleblowers who are still working in the government. They want to speak to Congress but feel that the Obama administration is blocking them from doing so.

Shortly after my story is published, my mobile phone rings. It's CBS News Washington bureau chief Chris Isham. He says White House spokesman Jay Carney is trying to reach him.

"I haven't called him back yet," Isham says. "Any idea why he's upset?"

"I'm sure he doesn't like the Benghazi story," I answer. I'm used to the routine.

"It's fair and accurate," I tell Isham. "It also quoted a State Department spokesman and the president directly from his press briefing today."

"Yeah, that's what I thought. It looks pretty straightforward. I just wanted to know the story before I call him back."

The next day, Isham reports to me that he had followed up with Carney, who was, indeed, "very upset."

"What did he say was wrong with the article?" I ask.

"He didn't really have anything specific," Isham says with a chuckle. "He just didn't like the whole thing."

Even absent a legitimate complaint, those who spin the media know that pushback tends to aggravate news managers. It forces them to deal with uncomfortable phone calls and nagging emails. It's time consuming. It follows them home. They'd rather avoid it. That's the whole point—and it's one reason why pushback often works. There's nothing better than news managers who stand strong and resist pushback. They listen to the complaint, consider it, and if it lacks merit, politely tell the complainer to fuck off. As a result, frivolous complaints lessen over time.

I've heard more stories than I can possibly recount about the Obama administration's unique brand of pushback and retaliation against any pesky media that prove uncooperative. There's no better example—all wrapped up in one—of what's wrong with this government misbehavior than what happened when the White House press gang became angered by a national television outlet in 2010. An outlet that refused to go along with the Obama agenda like others had.

What outlet? you ask. FOX? CBS? The *New York Times*?

No. It's C-SPAN. The cable television network that has to be considered by more Americans to be fairest of them all.

It's summer of 2010. C-SPAN wants to add footage of President Obama to a White House documentary it produced in the final years of the George W. Bush administration.

President Obama agrees to tape a brief interview in the Oval Office on August 12 with Brian Lamb, founder and executive chairman of C-SPAN's board of directors. The nine-minute interview, conducted with both men standing, is innocuous.

"What have you changed in this room?" Lamb asks.

"We have not redecorated yet," answers the president. "Given that we are in the midst of some very difficult economic times, we decided to hold off last year in terms of making some changes."

All is well until about two weeks later when a C-SPAN official gets a call from Obama's director of broadcast media, Dag Vega. Vega tells C-SPAN that in two days, the *Washington Post* will be breaking the story of the president's reported multimillion-dollar renovation of the Oval Office. Vega is calling to make sure C-SPAN won't follow up the news by running its interview with the president. The one taped just days before in which President Obama had implied that, in the spirit of austerity, there would be no Oval Office redecoration.

"You're going to save the interview for the documentary [set to air a few weeks later], right?" Vega reportedly asks the C-SPAN official. If the public sees the president's interview now, they might wonder whether he'd been clueless or intentionally misleading about the impending makeover.

From C-SPAN's viewpoint, this is a problem. There was never any agreement as to when the president's interview would air. And it would be foolish to hold the relevant material only to air the inaccurate interview later in the documentary.

Discussions go back and forth with the White House saying that the agreement was for the president's interview to air in the future, around the release of the updated documentary. But with the turn of events, C-SPAN decides it has no choice but to air the interview sooner, when the story breaks about the Oval Office redecorations. The White House follows by pressuring C-SPAN to change its mind, and suggests the cable television network will be punished with lack of access if they do air it.

On August 31, as Vega had foretold, the *Washington Post* breaks news of the president's Oval Office facelift. C-SPAN airs the president's interview the same day.

That night, Josh Earnest, then-White House deputy press secretary (now White House press secretary) reportedly fires off an angry email to C-SPAN. The biggest surprise is that he sends it in the middle of the president's live address to the nation about the drawdown of U.S. troops from Iraq. You'd think he'd have bigger fish to fry.

In the email, Earnest accuses C-SPAN of being egregiously unethical and of violating terms of the interview. Though there's no evidence of the existence of any prior agreement, he continues to insist the White House would not and did not agree to an interview with the president without specifying the terms under which it would air. Earnest says no other news organization has done such a thing to the Obama White House. And he threatens to withhold future access.

For its part, frustrated C-SPAN officials feel they're the ones who have been wronged. After all, the president gave an interview containing incorrect information, in which the content was almost immediately invalidated.

Like a bad-tempered child stomping his foot against the exercise of logic and reason, Earnest accuses C-SPAN of a violation of trust and says they'll be unlikely to see any further cooperation from the president as long as he remains in office.

One can only guess whether the Obama White House has made good on that threat to withhold cooperation. But C-SPAN's programming since that date reflects no interview with either the president or the first lady.

The message? Don't cross the White House even if it involves the simple act of airing an on-the-record, on-camera, unedited interview with the president of the United States—the consummate public official. This White House gets to direct its coverage and the terms. Good behavior will be rewarded with access. Dissenters will be punished.

I hate to say it, but I think many news organizations would have agreed to the White House demand to hold the president's interview, no questions asked.

There's nothing more heartening than confident news managers unintimidated by pushback. Conversely, there are few things more disheartening than weak news managers who succumb to pushback. You can tell when it's happening. No matter how solid the sources, no matter how fact-based and proven the reporting is, no matter that it's been cleared by the network law department: you can pretty much kiss it good-bye.

News managers who hate pushback the most tend to be most affected by it. The irony is that it ensures they'll be the target of even more. The complainers smell blood. They have a sixth sense for the weak, for those seeking the path of least resistance. Word gets around. Succumbing to pushback begets more pushback.

And if you, the reporter, push back against the pushback? You just might be labeled a troublemaker. Bosses who don't like you pushing them to defend a story might turn on you. They might whisper that you hang on to unanswered questions too long. They might accuse you of having an agenda. Otherwise, they mutter, you'd just move on to something else and make things easier on everyone. You'd believe your government when it says a story isn't true. You'd relinquish your mojo. Voluntarily.

Without so much as a whimper.

| "IT'S TOUGH ALL OVER"

Not long ago at a reporting conference, a colleague from another news division discussed among a small group the disturbing trend away from investigative reporting.

"Do they want your investigative stories at your network?"

"Nope," I answered. "Yours?"

"Nope. Nobody wants them anymore. We just end up posting most of them on the Web."

"That's what *I* do!"

Later, a network news colleague remarked about how weather stories had never been so popular as they were in the 2013–2014 winter season. You don't tick off powerful people by reporting on the weather. It fills the broadcast. And the ratings go up. (Of course, I could argue that the ratings would go up if we had topless female anchors presenting the news. Or I could argue that the ratings might go up more if we devoted ourselves to putting on an original, fearless newscast.) In any event, resorting to weather stories so often became such a shameless fallback position, some in the CBS New York fishbowl took to calling it "weather porn."

It happens in local news, too. In some cases, reporters are outright told to stay away from certain topics or industries. Sunshine, the longtime Miami reporter, recounts a meeting he attended years ago where he says he overheard a top station manager tell the head of an auto dealers' association that his newsroom wouldn't be doing any "negative car stories."

"I sat at the table stunned," Sunshine says.

And years earlier, when Miami was seriously plagued by drug-related violence, Sunshine says local news management told him his continued reporting on drug seizures and murders was "bad for local tourism."

"Suddenly, those stories got a lot less airtime. I was branded a troublemaker" for pushing the stories, Sunshine told me.

It's tough all over. In 2012, I was in a New York hotel room getting ready to attend the Emmy Awards, where I didn't yet know it but I was about to receive the year's investigative reporting award for *Fast and Furious*. It had been a year and a half of me pushing an important story that few at my network wanted pursued. Some of them put a great deal of effort into marginalizing and ridiculing the reporting to try to discourage it. But I didn't allow the resistance to interfere with what I saw as my job as a journalist. I was a troublemaker. Now, to have the series of stories recognized by esteemed, independent peers in the industry validated my instincts rather than the misguided efforts of some of my CBS managers. Anyway, I'm preparing for the award ceremony when I get a call on my cell phone from a number I don't recognize. It's from a colleague who works at a national publication. I don't know this person terribly well. The colleague sounds extremely distraught.

"I didn't know who else to call . . . I hope you don't mind."

"What's wrong?" I ask.

"I just spent months investigating a huge story—and they're blocking it. Keeping it out of the paper. It's *criminal*."

I stop getting ready and sit down on the bed in the hotel room to listen. Someone I am only acquainted with is calling me to share; to unload. The colleague goes on to explain—tearfully—the story and the obfuscation. It sounds familiar. I've been there, too. This person had done nothing more than to bring a terrific, well-researched story to the table. Something that should draw accolades. But as the story worked its way up the editing chain, somebody in the organization had deemed it to be untouchable material. The reporter began to be treated like an outcast for arguing that it was an important and valid story that the public should be told. That censoring it would be improper. The reporter came to be excluded from meetings about the story. Supervisors implied the reporter was uncooperative. Controversial. Colleagues began avoiding the reporter. The whisper campaign began. This is how whistleblowers in the government and at corporations often get treated. But it happens in the news business, too. Groupthink is a powerful thing.

In February 2014, a colleague at a competing news outlet emailed one of my coworkers. He was discouraged because he said that his organization was increasingly turning away from investigative reporting. My coworker showed me the email, remarking, "I hate to tell him—it's the same way here."

And in March 2014, another competing-network colleague shares with me a tale of frustration regarding a truly meaningful story that took weeks of research and prodding to get the original information. A story that I would have been proud to have dug up myself. But once completed, the story's airing was postponed from one day to the next and ultimately died on the vine.

"I eventually just posted it on the Web," says the colleague.

He continues by telling me that a short time later, the government released official statistics mirroring the information that he'd gathered weeks earlier. Only now was it considered *real* news— *safe* news—since the government was pushing it and other news outlets picked it up. Now it was widely reported. The colleague's news organization could've had the story, exclusively, long before everyone else. But they'd taken a pass.

It's tough all over.

And most network correspondents who do original reporting and have been around awhile will tell you this is the case. We're supposed to be the ground-level newsgatherers who have the contacts, sources, and editorial judgment to bring unique ideas to the broadcasts. But more often than not, that's not what the broadcasts want anymore.

| COPYCAT COMFORT

What they *do* want infuriates producers and correspondents far and wide. The broadcasts want what they see on the competition.

It's counterintuitive to the whole idea of journalism. When I attended the University of Florida College of Journalism and Communications, there were two ways to ensure an automatic F on an assignment. One was by making a fact error. The other was by copying a story idea from the newspaper. That was strictly verboten for two reasons. First, it was considered ethically akin to plagiarism. Second, we were taught that the foundation of our mission as journalists is to find and develop stories that the audience isn't getting on an alternate source. We learned to shun basic news conferences and press releases except as a starting point: they're what somebody *wants* you to report. Now dig in: what is it you *should* report?

But today, too many of the broadcast producers lack a solid foundation themselves and don't trust the judgment or skills of their own people. If it hasn't been reported elsewhere, how can they be sure it's news? In fact, it's *only* news after somebody else reports it. Or after one of our relied-upon special interests, such as the government, says it's news. These managers don't trust that their own experts in the field can produce ideas as good as, and often better than, the competition. They desire what the others have. This means they manically monitor sources like the *New York Times*, the *Washington Post*, the *Daily Beast*, the *Huffington Post*, and *Buzzfeed*. They follow the Twitter accounts of their favorite bloggers and sources. They watch the cable news channels all day long and dispatch a relentless stream of notes and phone calls to the bureaus in the field.

> *Here's a story from the* New York Times. *Can you do this for us tonight?*
> Buzzfeed *is reporting (fill in the blank). . . . Can someone confirm?*
> Politico *just tweeted out (fill in the blank). . . . Have we confirmed?*

A colleague from a competing network told me, "Once it's in the *Huffington Post*, you'll get a call from a senior producer saying 'we need you to do this story.' . . . To them, it's a fact because it's in the *Huffington Post*. But if you provide the fact [from your original sources], it's not a fact to them because they need to see it in the *New York Times* or the *Huffington Post* or whatever is the website of the moment. It's just disappointing."

To them, newsgathering is defined as, quite literally, gathering *other* outlets' news. Far more emphasis is put on watching the competition than digging up our own unique stories. We've become expert confirmers. Experienced field reporters and producers who seek to advance a story are relegated to copying or matching what other news outlets' reporters have already reported, often tasked with finding the people others already interviewed to repeat the things they've already said. I liken it to assigning a talented artist to do a paint-by-numbers project. *Use the colors we instruct you to use. Fill in the preselected image. Stay in the lines.*

A colleague at another news outlet recently got a tip from one of his sources about a developing story and told a young broadcast producer about it.

He says the producer responded by saying, "I haven't seen this on the wires, how do you know it? Where can I find it?"

"It never occurred to this producer," says my colleague, "that news that's original to us doesn't come from the wires, it's not on the Web. So then, the young producer says, 'Can we confirm this? How do we confirm this?' and I'm saying, '*I'm* confirming it to you. I'm telling you I just spoke to the source who was there.' That's what we're dealing with."

This syndrome is so endemic that good reporters are always trying to figure out ways to beat the flawed system. One shared a successful strategy with me a few years back. Too often he'd get a great interview or exclusive piece of information on a big breaking story in the field only to have supervisors in New York tell him to find, instead, the witness interviewed by the Associated Press or shown on CNN. So now, if he's out on a big breaking story and lands a fantastic interview, he might let someone from a wire service listen to an excerpt of the interview recording. The wire service then publishes its own account of the story, using the witness's quote. Sure enough, often within minutes, the New York supervisors call and say, *We need you to find that guy interviewed by the wire service. . . .*

"No problem," answers the reporter in the field, who already has the interview in hand. He had it first but knows that New York wouldn't have valued it unless they'd seen it elsewhere first. They covet what they see on other outlets, not what their own expert reporters can bring them.

In some cases, we're little more than casting agents. Entire stories are conceived of by New York managers who not only assign a given topic but also tell us whom we should interview, what they should say, and how the story should be written. We're asked to create a reality that fits their New York image of what they believe, what they've read, what they've been told by their contacts, or what they've heard at parties. For these types of managers, you gather the information in the field and if the truth doesn't reflect their preconceived notion, they'll either change the story so that it does, or it won't air. They use heavy-handed editing to alter the script so that it's written in *their* style, using *their* thoughts and vernacular. One network producer told me, "When I wrote stories about workers protesting to gain a hike in the minimum wage, I was not allowed to write that the majority of the people protesting were not minimum wage workers, but were paid by outside groups to protest. . . . [W]e conducted 10 separate interviews of actual workers who make minimum wage. In these interviews, all 10 revealed to us that they had several times been offered raises, but turned them down because of the added responsibility that came with the pay hike. I was told directly by my supervisor, 'you can't put that into the story because it will skew the viewer's impression of the demonstration.'" More accurately, it would have skewed the supervisor's preconceived notions of the story that he wished to be told, or the agenda that he sought to advance, regardless of the facts encountered in the field.

Another colleague observes, "You have these executive producers and senior producers in New York who attend the same social gatherings, they all read the same newspapers, they all listen to the same radio, they all go to the same birthday parties with their kids. And they're all trapped in their socioeconomic groups. The stories are happening in New Mexico, Arizona, Georgia, Alabama, Iowa. But if they've ever been to those places, they've made fun of the people while they were there."

I got a call on February 28, 2014, from a CBS colleague who, like many of us, had been put in the position of defending the *CBS Evening News's* content and, at times, its perceived political tilt.

"You know, people ask me and I tell them it's not as if everyone at CBS News is a raving liberal. In fact, there's a pretty diverse spread among the correspondents and a lot of the producers. It's this small group of managers in New York that's affecting *everything* right now."

It's as if they're ordering up their own little novelettes instead of allowing us to seek out and portray the reality.

If you resist, you're considered a troublemaker. Or controversial. Because first and foremost, they know best and they're always correct.

A network field producer I know recently boiled it down to this metaphor: "New York tells us to write in our script that the car is red. We tell them it's blue. They insist it's red because the wire service says it's red. We tell them we're here on the scene, looking at the car right now, and it's blue. 'Okay,' they say 'but make it red.'"

A typical conversation about assigning a story often begins with "We need to find someone who will say . . ." what we want them to say. Or "We need to find a sympathetic character to show . . ." that a policy we like is good or one that we don't like is bad. In other words, we've decided what the story is before we've researched it fairly and thoroughly ourselves. All we need is the right actor to portray our managers' viewpoints.

Almost every journalist with a few years in network television knows exactly what I'm talking about and none of them likes it. Correspondents and producers have had countless *fuck you* battles over this very issue, and more that I know of in the last three years than in the past two decades. They've lost their tempers, walked out of the building, threatened to quit, had screaming matches, or complained about it almost every day. Sometimes, they're considered troublemakers, too.

Many who are starting out in journalism know no other way. They take the lead from their elders or non-journalist managers who have worked their way up the ranks and help codify the syndrome. They eagerly scan the Web for celebrity news and political scandals, they monitor social media of selected bloggers and opinionmakers, they subscribe to the edgiest Twitter accounts. They report their findings to their superiors so that the best pickings can be passed along for us to confirm or repeat. Nothing frustrates a good reporter more than having to use his time chasing other reporters' efforts when he, in fact, has a better story that he can't get the broadcasts to take seriously.

| HOMOGENIZED, MILQUETOAST NEWS

The result of all this is a homogenization of the mainstream news. It helps explain why, on a given night, the three evening news broadcasts are often more alike than they are different. It's not that there are only ten stories in the world that matter. It's that we all employ similar decision-making processes that result in the selection of the same ten stories.

On February 21, 2014, all three networks lead with three minutes on the troubles in Ukraine. Everyone has two to three minutes on the weather: a new popular favorite dominating the news almost every night. Everyone has stories on the Olympics. Everyone does the *exact same feature* in the middle of their broadcasts about a woman who saved her baby nephew's life (a story widely circulated on the Web the day before). Everyone reports President Obama's decision to award the Medal of Honor. Two of the three networks devote more than two minutes of their precious, limited news time to tributes to their own network's employees: one who passed away and another who is retiring. Are we producing a newscast more for ourselves and each other rather than the public? What did we really tell America on this night that they didn't already know?

My own network is passing up stories on the crumbling Affordable Care Act; an exclusive investigation I offered about a significant military controversy; an investigation uncovering a history of troubles surrounding Boeing's beleaguered Dreamliner; and massive government waste, fraud, and abuse. Largely untouched are countless stories about pharmaceutical dangers affecting millions of Americans, privacy infringement, the debate over President Obama's use of executive orders, the FDA monitoring of employee email, the steady expansion of terrorism, the student loan crisis, the confounding explosion in entitlements, the heartbreaking fallout from the Haiti earthquake, continuing disaster for government-subsidized green energy initiatives, the terrorist influences behind "Arab spring," various congressional ethics investigations and violations, the government's infringement of and restrictions on the press, escalating violence on the Mexican border, the debt crisis, the Fed's role and its secrecy, to name just a few.

We do stories on food stamps but only to the extent that we prove the case that they're needed, without also examining well-established fraud and abuse. We look at unemployment but only to the extent that we present sympathetic characters showing that benefits should be extended rather than examining, also, the escalating cost and instances of fraud. We cover minimum wage but only to the extent that we help make the case for raising it, without giving much due to the other side, which argues it will have the opposite effect than intended. We cover sequestration but only to the extent that we try to show how much the cutbacks hurt Americans, rather than also cover the abuses by those who attempted to make the cutbacks more visible and hurtful to build a political case against sequestration.

| ACCOUNTABILITY INTERRUPTED

It's June 20, 2013, and I'm at the annual Investigative Reporters and Editors conference at the Marriott Rivercenter in San Antonio, Texas. Five weeks ago, the Associated Press exposed the Obama administration's shockingly broad seizure of AP reporters' phone records as part of a government leak probe. Four weeks ago came news that the Obama Justice Department targeted a FOX News reporter and his source in a different criminal leak investigation. Two weeks ago, former NSA contractor Edward Snowden began revealing massive, secretive surveillance methods the government is using on American citizens. And one week ago, CBS News officially announced that an unauthorized intruder remotely accessed my work computer on repeated occasions using sophisticated methods to search and remove data.

But I've known that, and more, since January.

At the Marriott with hundreds of investigative journalists in attendance, there are several conference sessions examining the new surveillance revelations and the chilling effect it has on our work. My own situation is part of the official discussion as well as the conference gossip. My producer Kim, who arrived before me, alerted me in an email ahead of time.

"So many people have asked about you and voiced support over the computer issue," she tells me. Later, in person, she says that one conference attendee told her they heard that I'm "radioactive." I imagine a cartoon of myself surrounded by green waves of a radioactive glow, as other cartoon journalists hover just outside the aura to avoid me.

As I meander through the crowd on the third floor, some of my peers stop me to ask questions.

Do you know who did it? How did you find out?

They express a mix of support and outrage. "It was the government, wasn't it?" they ask. "You don't have to tell me. But you *know*, don't you?"

A few of them think the government is surveilling their work, too. A high-ranking executive from another network sends me a text message. He wants to set up a meeting. He's curious about the symptoms my computer displayed that led me to suspect it was being hacked. His computer has been acting strangely of late and his techs can't seem to fix it.

I duck into an investigative reporting session underway on the topic of How Not to Get Sued. It includes broadcast network lawyers and, prior to my arrival, the conversation has somehow deviated from

Topic A. They're now discussing how the Obama administration has crossed the line in withholding public information from the public.

"In all my experience, this is, by far, the worst, least transparent administration," says one of the network lawyers on the speaker's panel.

He goes on to describe what he sees as the Obama administration's outrageous pattern of rejecting Freedom of Information Act requests—and he pulls no punches. He tells the audience of investigative reporters that he's worried about what's happening to journalism under this administration. About the liberties that the government is taking. He says it's unprecedented. "We'd better start doing something about it or it's just going to get worse."

Looks like the bloom is beginning to fall off the Obama rose. Albeit, belatedly.

In 2009, President Barack Obama pledged to make history with the high level of transparency his administration would bring to government.

The directive he issued to federal executives reads in part:

My Administration is committed to creating an unprecedented level of openness in Government. We will work together to ensure the public trust and establish a system of transparency, public participation, and collaboration. Openness will strengthen our democracy and promote efficiency and effectiveness in Government.

It looks so good on paper. The Clinton years had proven difficult for the cause of transparency. Any hopes that George W. Bush would usher in a new era of openness were quickly dashed. But Barack Obama—here he was placing a value and emphasis on openness that really set him apart. It could only mean positive things to come for journalists. Especially for investigative journalists, whose effectiveness as watchdogs of government is directly proportional to our ability to access public information and inside sources.

But barely into his second term, the Obama administration finds itself making history instead for its secrecy and assaults on the press. I, and other investigative reporters who are fully experienced in the indelicate art of prying public information from the tight grip of the government's hands, have now begun comparing notes about the daunting challenges this administration poses. There's delay, denial, obstruction, intimidation, retaliation, bullying, surveillance, and the possible threat of criminal prosecution. In my view, and that of other national reporters, this is proving to be the least transparent administration we've covered.

It's so bad that practically every major national news outlet, including *CBS News*, the *Washington Post*, and the *New York Times*, signs a scathing letter to the White House on November 21, 2013, objecting to unprecedented restrictions on the press. "As surely as if they were placing a hand over a journalist's camera lens, officials in this administration are blocking the public from having an independent view of important functions of the Executive Branch of government," reads the letter addressed to White House spokesman Carney. It calls some Obama administration press policies "arbitrary restraint and unwarranted interference on legitimate newsgathering activities. You are, in effect, replacing independent photojournalism with visual press releases." The letter also states that the White House behavior raises constitutional concerns.

It's so bad, the free press advocacy group Reporters Without Borders gives a serious downgrade to America's standing in the 2013 global free press rankings, rating the Obama administration as worse than Bush's. "The whistleblower is the [government's] enemy," writes the group in explaining its findings under the Obama administration. "Amid an all-out hunt for leaks and sources, 2013 will also be the year of the Associated Press scandal, which came to light when the Department of Justice acknowledged that it had seized the news agency's phone records."

In March 2014, *New York Times* reporter James Risen speaks at a journalism conference and calls the Obama administration "the greatest enemy of press freedom" in at least a generation.

President Obama seems to be either oblivious or in denial. Or maybe he just thinks that repeating the same thing often enough will make people believe it to be true. During an Internet question-and-answer session hosted by Google on February 14, 2013, he proudly declares to the online audience: "This is the most transparent administration in history." Then he presents his evidence in support of the bold assertion. "Every visitor that comes into the White House is now part of the public record. Every law we pass and every rule we implement we put online for everyone to see."

The Obama administration measures its supposed transparency accomplishments by the sheer number of documents published online and the amount of paper turned over to Congress. On Benghazi, the president says, "We've had more testimony and more paper than ever before." Never mind all the paper they're withholding, the ignored and denied Freedom of Information Act requests or the fact that they refuse to answer many basic questions.

The job of getting at the truth has never been harder. In part, it's because the Obama administration has figured out how to avoid questions and accountability by cutting out the news media middleman. White House officials have perfected exploitation of the non-news media to spoon-feed unfiltered messaging—at times, pure propaganda—directly into the public's mouth. That Google-sponsored chat? It came with a preselected audience and questions submitted in advance via the White House's own YouTube channel. That's the way they like it. They generate their own content. Rely on surrogates to help spread it on partisan blogs, Twitter, and Facebook. Give lots of interviews to entertainment programs, digital media, and feature press. And when they feel the situation demands an appearance of newsiness, such as a presidential apology for HealthCare.gov's disastrous launch, they look for a soft landing with a handpicked outlet and reporter.

All of this impacts not only how well-informed we can keep the interested public, but also the very survival of investigative journalism. In three decades of polling by the Pew Research Center for the People and the Press, news organizations are near all-time lows when it comes to the public's view of our accuracy, fairness, and independence. But there's one thing the public still values most, and it makes no difference whether they're Democrat, Republican, or independent: they overwhelmingly support our role as government watchdogs. That support rose a full 10 percentage points from 2011 to 2013 amid revelations about government-conducted surveillance of the public and the press.

The 2013 Pew poll also reflects the public's rising concern about loss of civil liberties. If the press doesn't challenge and expose government secrecy and overreach, then who can?

I'm attending the luncheon on the last big day of the Investigative Reporters and Editors conference. They're presenting the very first "Golden Padlock" award. The idea is to call out an entity deemed to have made the most egregious violation of public information laws. The Centers for Disease Control is nominated for withholding public data on Lyme disease. The U.S. Border Patrol wins for its secrecy on deaths of illegal immigrants. And this year, special recognition is given to Attorney General Eric Holder's Justice Department for its improper monitoring of journalists. For that, the Obama Justice Department is awarded a prominent place in the Investigative Reporters and Editors inaugural "Hall of Shame."

It's a start, but we need to go far beyond naming government violators to the Hall of Shame. We must challenge any administration both publicly and legally if they violate ethics or the law, or betray the public they're supposed to serve.

| *Fast and Furious* Redux |

Inside America's Deadly Gunwalking Disgrace

It's Sunday night. I'm sitting on my bed with my laptop computer open, papers strewn about, and my phones next to me. Personal BlackBerry. CBS smartphone. Home phone. The television's on but it's just white noise. I'm not listening. I'm trying to solve a puzzle. For the fifth time tonight, I look at the phone number I've scratched on the back of an envelope. I'm deciding whether to call it.

I've spent nearly every night for weeks, often until the early hours of the morning, trying to piece together what would become the biggest investigative news story of the year: the *Fast and Furious* gunwalking story. I've already aired my first report, but it only scratched the surface.

That story revealed a scheme that sounded nothing short of crazy. The federal Bureau of Alcohol, Tobacco, Firearms and Explosives (ATF) had, in essence, helped supply Mexico's killer drug cartels with fearsome weapons. Why would an agency that's supposed to do the opposite—stop the flow of weapons—engage in this kind of dangerous behavior for any reason? I've been able to speak to many sources, including six veteran ATF agents and executives who don't want to be quoted by name for fear of retaliation. They told me that ATF secretly enlisted the help of licensed gun dealers in Arizona and encouraged them to do the unthinkable: sell AK-47–type semiautomatic assault rifles, .50-caliber guns capable of taking down an elephant, and other firearms to suspected traffickers for the cartels. Instead of intercepting the weapons or the suspects, ATF intentionally allowed the criminal operations to proceed unimpeded. ATF knew the guns would hit the streets and be used in crimes both north and south of the border. That was part of the plan. It's called letting guns "walk," and as an unintended consequence, people were dying.

Supposedly, the idea was that all this would lead ATF to dangerous cartel leaders in Mexico . . . the "Big Fish." The Big Fish could then somehow be arrested and brought to swift justice, though nobody could ever say how that would have really worked since the bad guys are on foreign soil and, under international law, the United States can't exactly march into Mexico and just take them. In the end, it didn't matter because they never caught any Big Fish anyway.

But innocent people were killed. Once U.S. law enforcement agents did the unthinkable and let guns onto the streets and into the hands of criminals, the weapons were used by cartel members in shoot-outs with Mexican police. They were used by cartel gangs who shot at a Mexican federal police helicopter. They were used by cartel thugs in fights with the Mexican military. And they were used by criminals on the U.S. side of the border. A single gun can be used to kill over and over again. The *Fast and Furious* weapons will be turning up in crimes on both sides of the border for decades to come. That's why in law enforcement one of the cardinal rules is: never, *ever* let guns walk.

As part of my initial contact with insider sources in January 2010, I learned that some ATF agents questioned the wisdom of letting guns walk, only to be rebuffed and marginalized by their supervisors. The "time to crime" was both astonishing and frightening. Sometimes, it was just a few days after being sold in Arizona that *Fast and Furious* weapons surfaced at crime scenes in Mexico. One ATF agent told me the strategy was "insane." I asked where the name *Fast and Furious* came from but nobody seems to know. The title was apparently pulled from a street racing action movie by the same name that hit theaters in 2009 because some of the initial suspects raced cars and worked at an auto repair shop, like the film's star. I know just how significant the story is when several inside sources say they think it's the biggest scandal ever to hit the beleaguered federal agency. Bigger, they say, than ATF's deadly assault on the Weaver family at Ruby Ridge, Idaho, in 1992. Bigger than ATF's controversial siege of a religious cult's compound in Waco, Texas, in 1993, which almost caused Congress to decimate and dissolve the agency.

Things might still be going along just that way today, with guns surfacing at Mexican crimes and the U.S. government publicly tsk-tsking over the evil U.S. gun shops selling all those weapons to drug cartels, if it hadn't been for what happened on December 14, 2010. On that date, U.S. Border Patrol agent Brian Terry was gunned down in the dark Arizona desert night by Mexican "rip crew" bandits who'd crossed into the United States illegally.

Rip crews are considered more dangerous than your average, everyday smugglers. They prey upon the drug mules and others who cross the border illegally. It's one of the little-discussed ironies about Brian Terry's demise: he didn't die protecting Americans. He died on a mission to protect illegal, foreign smugglers from worse illegal, foreign smugglers.

The rip crew that shot Terry used at least two AK-47–type rifles trafficked by *Fast and Furious* suspects. With Terry's tragic murder, all hell broke loose inside ATF. The agency had been on the verge of arresting a group of gun-trafficking suspects in the *Fast and Furious* case and making a big publicity deal out of it. Attorney General Eric Holder himself was considering making the trip to Phoenix to appear in front of the television news cameras for the case announcement.

But with Terry's murder, the Phoenix ATF group, as well as their superiors at headquarters in Washington, knew that they could be in deep trouble. That is, if the connection between Terry's murder and their gunwalking scheme got out. Could they count on agents who disagreed with the strategy to keep their mouths shut? Some agents were so distraught over Terry's death and the truth behind it that they risked their careers to talk outside the protection of their government walls.

I first heard about the story when someone anonymously sent my producer a copy of a letter that Senator Charles Grassley had written to the Justice Department outlining the alleged facts and asking about the controversy. ATF insiders were confidentially giving Grassley information. We called Grassley's office several times but nobody would speak with us about the case. How could I find out more? If the facts in Grassley's letter were true, then we were looking at a story with incredible impact on both sides of the border.

Grassley is a grandfatherly, plain-talking Republican from Iowa. His claim to fame came in the 1980s when he exposed the ridiculous waste of tax dollars by the Defense Department, such as the Pentagon buying a toilet seat for $750 and paying $695 for an ashtray for air force planes. There's no better clearinghouse than Grassley's office for whistleblowers on most any topic and—an added bonus—he and his investigators aren't afraid to upset members of their own party.

We found that a lot of the background regarding this emerging controversy was anonymously posted by ATF insiders on the blogs of gun rights activists Mike Vanderboegh of Sipsey Street Irregulars and David Codrea of Examiner.com. So my producer and I contacted Vanderboegh and Codrea, who were in direct contact with some of the principal players. We asked the bloggers to pass along my name and number in hopes that their sources would be willing to talk to me. After a few days passed with no luck, I registered with the forums of the blogs and posted a public notice. It said that I was interested in pursuing a possible story for CBS News and needed insiders to contact me.

It worked.

Meanwhile, the Justice Department, which oversees ATF, responded to Grassley's inquiry, in writing, and insisted that no one in the government would ever let guns walk. This is a wildly false claim they would later recant once the evidence became irrefutable.

When I first propose the *Fast and Furious* story to *CBS Evening News* executive producer Rick Kaplan, he's fascinated.

"Who approved the strategy? What were they thinking?" he asks. It's his job to prompt reporters with the questions any viewer would want answered.

"I don't know," I tell him. "We don't have the answers. But this first story will shake the tree and we'll get closer to some answers."

Kaplan is sold. I'm lucky he's from the school of *follow-the-story-where-it-lead*s rather than the school of *you-must-know-in-advance-where-it's-going-and-how-it-ends-and-then-we'll-decide-if-the-public-should-know*. This is how real news is committed.

Instead of giving me the typical length of about two minutes' time to tell my story, Kaplan does something bold and unusual. He tells me to write it the way it needs to be written. When I'm finished, it's five minutes long. Almost unheard-of on an evening news broadcast. But Kaplan airs it as is. Without this kind of time and commitment, the story would be over before it ever got started. The complexities and nuances of *Fast and Furious* would be lost in a story if it were half the length. It would have very little lasting impact.

The five-minute-long report airs on the February 22, 2011, edition of the *CBS Evening News* and makes an instant splash. Viewers are intrigued, colleagues pepper me with questions about what else I know, and I receive calls of interest from congressional staffers, both Democrats and Republicans.

One colleague approaches me and says he has a close contact inside ATF.

"He says your reporting is right on target," he tells me. "And they're rooting for you inside ATF. He says keep going."

But as outrageous and remarkable as the allegations are, most of the media don't pick up on the story. They're steering clear. I know from my sources within the Justice Department and on Capitol Hill that other reporters are calling them, wanting to know about *Fast and Furious*. But these reporters say that they can't get their own stories published. The bosses don't want them. And with a few exceptions, the beat reporters who have regular access to Attorney General Holder choose not to press for answers, much to the delight of the government.

Fast and Furious provides a prime example of the syndrome I've described in which federal agencies use public information officials—paid by your tax dollars—as private PR agents advancing the agendas of their bosses rather than serving the public. Exhibit One is an internal memo written by ATF's chief of public affairs, Scot Thomasson, in response to my initial *Fast and Furious* report. Thomasson dispatches the memo to other public affairs officers inside ATF and a source supplies it to me. The purpose of the memo, Thomasson explains to his public affairs staff, is to "lessen the coverage of such stories in the news cycle by replacing them with good stories about ATF."

When potentially damaging news stories loom, the federal government seems to magically produce positive news stories calculated to counteract or even replace the negative ones. Often, it works. Our federal contacts call us and breathlessly announce a hastily called news conference. They tantalize us with a few details and advise in hushed tones, *"You'll want to have a camera there,"* as if they're imparting secretive, valuable information. We alert our managers. News is about to happen! And thanks to our well-placed sources, *we've* got the heads-up! We divert our cameras from whatever they're doing and rush to the "news" conference, grateful and puffed up with pride that we have such important contacts in the federal government.

For example, in October 2011 Holder was revealed to have given inaccurate testimony about his knowledge of *Fast and Furious* and Congress hit him with a subpoena: suddenly Holder announces a major, dangerous international terror plot is busted. Good news! ABC, NBC, CBS, FOX News, *USA Today*, the *Washington Post*, the *Wall Street Journal* . . . just about everyone runs with the headlines.

A week later, amid furor over FBI evidence discrepancies in the Brian Terry murder—more good news!—ATF invites reporters along on a giant illegal cigarette bust!

In June 2012, just as an historic House contempt vote against Holder was scheduled and widely reported by news organizations, the attorney general announces $111 million in tax-dollar funding for law enforcement agencies to hire military veterans. The *Huffington Post*, Reuters, the *Chicago Tribune*, and many local news outlets in markets receiving the funding write up the good news, helping counteract the negative publicity surrounding the scheduled contempt vote.

More recently, amid questions about the Justice Department's controversial decision to seize telephone records of journalists with the Associated Press, Holder announced a giant Medicare fraud strike force crackdown.

I'm not saying the aforementioned cases aren't worthy of coverage. But what if federal officials wait to reveal them until they're needed to bump negative news out of the headlines? The timing may be purely coincidental, but in light of Thomasson's ATF memo, we have every reason to be cynical.

The Thomasson memo directs ATF's public information officers to "[p]lease make every effort in the next two weeks to maximize coverage of ATF operations/enforcement actions/arrests at the local and regional level" to try to drown out the "negative coverage by CBS News. . . . The bureau should look for every opportunity to push coverage of good stories."

The memo goes on to note: "Fortunately, the CBS story has not sparked any follow up coverage by mainstream media and seems to have fizzled." The subjects of negative news are always relieved when a story remains confined to one or two outlets. And if one of them is FOX News, all the better. The administration knows that some in the media reject, out of hand, stories that FOX News follows closely, regardless of merit. So if it's a FOX story, half the battle is already won.

But the Obama administration is particularly worried when the story appears on CBS News. They can attempt to pin a right-wing label on me, but CBS itself can hardly be portrayed as a bastion of conservatism. And my record of reporting on mischief within both parties makes my stories credible, and therefore dangerous.

Thomasson's memo reiterates, "ATF needs to proactively push positive stories this week, in an effort to preempt some negative reporting. . . . If you have any significant operations that should get national media coverage, please reach out to the Public Affairs Division for support, coordination and clearance."

Think about it. Your tax dollars are paying the salary of an ATF manager who's using taxpayer time and resources to direct his teams of taxpayer-supported public affairs officials to "push" propaganda in order to drown out an important, truthful story of public interest.

So here I am, sitting on my bed, laptop computer open, with the first *Fast and Furious* story under my belt, contemplating the next step. I need a good source to go on camera. The Justice Department is counting on the fact that I won't get that. They're telling other reporters that my unnamed sources are lying.

But I have a lead.

Just a few days before, I had received a call at my office.

The voice on the other end sounds hesitant. It's a woman.

"My boyfriend wants to talk to you," she tells me. "He has information about the story you've been working on."

She won't give his name. Or hers. I don't yet know whether this source will bear fruit or is just another in a long list of people who, in the end, have no real information that I can use. I instinctively look at the caller's telephone number displayed on my phone and scribble it on the back of an envelope.

The woman goes on to explain that her boyfriend isn't with her at home right now because he's attending a conference. She says he needs to get approval from congressional investigators to speak to me. But he wants to talk. The mention of Congress elevates his potential importance, as I know that several bona fide whistleblowers are in contact with Senator Grassley.

I thank the woman for calling and tell her I'm very interested in speaking to her boyfriend. I don't press too hard. As badly as I need the information, potential sources need to be handled gingerly and respectfully. They're easily scared off. Get too aggressive and they may never call back.

The importance of handling sources delicately should become clear when I tell you that, while I may have broken a lot of *Fast and Furious* news, I wasn't actually the first network news reporter following the trail. Early on, when my producer and I contacted the bloggers Vanderboegh and Codrea, they told us that an investigative reporter from NBC had already called them. But he ticked them off.

"He's an asshole," Vanderboegh told me more than once. "He demanded our contacts' names and phone numbers. Hell no, we're not handing over names and phone numbers to some asshole, pardon my French!"

I realize that the bloggers could well be saying the same thing about me pretty soon. The gun rights crowd is, by nature, mistrustful of reporters. So are the ATF agents whose confidence I need to gain. You can't lie to them. You can't mislead them. They can smell insincerity a mile off. And you most certainly can't cold-call them and demand names and numbers of their confidential contacts.

But if you do your research and show that you genuinely want to understand the facts, and if you're blessed with a little bit of luck, you might end up with the goods.

So I hang up from the call with the anonymous woman with the well-placed boyfriend who's talking to Congress, and I hope to hear from him later that day.

But he never calls.

Several days later, I decide it's time to try that phone number on the envelope. My hope is that the woman will answer the phone and tell me more or even let me speak to her boyfriend. On the other hand, it's entirely possible that she'll freak out over the fact that I even have her phone number and go dark on me entirely.

I punch the eleven digits into the phone and hold my breath. She answers.

"Hi, it's Sharyl Attkisson. You called me the other day and said your boyfriend might be willing to speak to me?"

She hesitates. I think she's trying to figure out how I got her number. But she doesn't hang up. She says her boyfriend still wants to talk to me but he doesn't want to mess up the investigation. And Senator Grassley's office hasn't given the okay.

But then she says her boyfriend is right there next to her!

"Can you give him the phone?" I ask her. "He doesn't have to say anything, he can just listen if he wants. I have a lot of information I haven't reported yet. I've confirmed some of it with people whose names I can't use. It always helps to run the information by additional sources. See if your boyfriend will get on the phone and just listen."

I hear a rustling noise and then a tentative but polite male voice on the other end.

"Hello, ma'am."

I do the talking, telling him pieces of what I know, and he provides additional bits of confirmation. He calls me "ma'am" at the end of almost every sentence. He must be from the South.

After a few minutes, I ask if he's a member of ATF's Group VII in the Phoenix, Arizona, office. That's the group assigned to *Fast and Furious.*

"Yes, ma'am," he tells me.

That narrows it down.

I've managed to piece together the names of the agents on the team with a good deal of confidence through insider sources who've contacted me as a result of my having posted my name and phone number on the gun rights blogs. I'm fitting together the puzzle pieces. You have to be patient and just gather a tiny bit of information at a time, if that's all you can get. Even if you don't know what the final picture is going to look like. When my sources initially contacted me, they often wanted to remain anonymous. But I'd ask, *Who's on the team? Who objected to the gunwalking?* I'd get a lead here, a name there . . . pretty soon I had a list.

There's ATF's Phoenix Special Agent in Charge Bill Newell.

Assistant Special Agents in Charge George Gillett and Jim Needles.

Group VII Supervisor David Voth.

Lead case agent Hope MacAllister.

Case agent Tonya English.

All of them are gung ho on *Fast and Furious.*

Then there are Group VII Special Agents Olindo "Lee" Casa, John Dodson, and Larry Alt.

Not gung ho.

Based on a bit of deduction, I believe it's Alt and Dodson who are talking to Senator Grassley.

"I think I know who you are," I tell the male voice on the phone. I'm taking a chance in trying to identify him. It might scare him off. But I don't have a lot of time to waste and if I don't make progress now, who knows if I'll ever speak with him again. My instincts tell me to try.

"Okay . . ." he says.

"You're either Larry Alt or John Dodson."

Sounding taken aback, he says: "I'm John Dodson, ma'am."

Special Agent Dodson seems relieved to be identified. He's lived with the secret of *Fast and Furious* for many tortured months. He's internally raised objections with his supervisors over what he views as the foolhardy strategy of gunwalking, only to feel retaliated against and marginalized. One of Dodson's bosses brushed off his concerns about innocent people getting hurt by saying, "If you're going to make an omelet, you've got to break some eggs."

"We just knew it wasn't going to end well." Dodson told me. "There's just no way it could."

One source had told me that, at one point, infighting over the gunwalking was so fierce, "it got ugly." Another said there was "screaming and yelling." A third said he warned: "This is crazy, somebody is gonna get killed."

But Dodson had asked the most chilling question of all when arguing with a superior: "Are you prepared to go to the funeral of a federal officer killed with one of these guns?" He says he got no reply.

In light of the gunwalking, every time there was a shooting near the border, the ATF agents would collectively hold their breath, "hoping it wasn't one of 'our' guns." When a madman shot Arizona congresswoman Gabrielle Giffords in January 2011, the tension at ATF could be cut with a knife. Nobody rested easy until the attack weapon was traced and found not to have been walked in *Fast and Furious*.

But for Dodson, the final straw came on that December night in 2010 when Border Patrol agent Brian Terry was shot. According to Dodson, a colleague approached him and said, " 'Did you hear about the border patrol agent?' And I said, 'Yeah.' And they said 'Well, it was one of the *Fast and Furious* guns.' There's really not much you can say after that," Dodson told me.

After Dodson and I talk on the phone for a few minutes, the door is opened for a possible interview. It may be unprecedented: an on-camera interview with a sitting federal agent, criticizing a major government law enforcement initiative.

When I hang up with Dodson, I finally get Grassley's office to engage with me and work out details so that I can quickly interview both the senator and Dodson. I make the arrangements to travel to Phoenix to meet up with Dodson. I don't need to clear it with my executive producer Kaplan. He'll want this story.

A few days later, my plane touches down in Arizona. My producer and I are early for our interview with Dodson, which we've scheduled to take place at a Phoenix area hotel, and we order food at the bar. I'm watching the door for Dodson. When he strides into the bar, I know who he is even though I've never seen him. Polite, law enforcement type. Short brown hair. Goatee. Dark pinstripe suit, blue shirt, blue tie, blue eyes.

"Hello, ma'am," he says and I stand up to shake hands. I ask if he needs to eat and he declines. He's nervous. We look around. We assume that either he's being followed or I'm being followed or we're both being followed. I don't ask a lot of questions before the interview. I want to hear his entire story for the first time as it's recorded on camera.

An hour later, we're wrapping the interview. The content of it and the passion with which it's delivered are nothing short of incredible.

Dodson is intelligent, sincere, and convincing. His interview wholly undercuts the Justice Department's attempts to claim *Fast and Furious* never happened.

A few days later, on March 4, 2011, the *CBS Evening News* airs our second report in the series. This one is longer than the first. Five and a half minutes. I'm watching from the Washington, D.C., control room when it airs. I glance around to find the other producers, correspondents, and technicians staring at the monitor with rapt attention. It's a tough crowd. If they're showing this much interest, I know Dodson and his story have captured our audience.

ATTKISSON "You were intentionally letting guns go to Mexico?"

AGENT DODSON "Yes, ma'am, the agency was. I'm boots on the ground in Phoenix telling you we've been doing it every day since I've been here. *Here I am.* Tell me I didn't do the things that I did. Tell me you didn't order me to do the things I did. Tell me it didn't happen. Now you have a name on it. You have a face to put with it. Here I am. Someone, now, tell me it didn't happen."

Fast and Furious has just become an undeniable reality.

If ever there's a story that transcends politics, I think, *surely this is the one.*

But on this point, I'm incredibly mistaken.

When a story makes major news, members of Congress often take an interest. Perhaps it's an issue of importance to their district. Maybe it affects their constituents. They might also see it as a way to raise their political profile.

Congressional interest can be a good thing. Congress has the power to hold hearings and issue subpoenas. I lack that authority but can use the information they obtain. Sometimes, though, congressional interest isn't such a good thing. Invariably, one party takes up the issue, the other adopts an opposing view, and matters of substance drown amid political posturing.

Congressional staffers and members from both parties privately tell me they agree that the ATF gunwalking is a travesty. But they're still trying to calculate how the story will play among their constituents.

For a time, it's Senator Grassley alone who's banging this drum. And there's only so much he can do. His Republican Party is in the minority in the Senate. They don't have subpoena power and can't call hearings. But on the other side of the Capitol, in the House, Republicans hold the majority. And the GOP chairman of the House Oversight and Government Reform Committee, Darrell Issa, has become interested in *Fast and Furious*.

Issa is a former CEO and a self-made millionaire from California. A dominant personality, quick study, and insanely confident, Issa is one of the most powerful members of Congress. He'll need that heft as his party leaders, Speaker John Boehner and Majority Leader Eric Cantor, are widely said to be slow-walking the *Fast and Furious* investigation behind closed doors.

Issa's interest becomes a double-edged sword. Oversight Committee chairmen are attack dogs on behalf of their parties and are thus polarizing and controversial. Issa's no different. And being a Republican, he's viewed even more harshly by some in the news media.

When Democrat Henry Waxman chaired this important committee from 2007 to 2009, and prior to that, as its top Democrat, he went after many Republican causes. I broke news on several stories that jibed with Waxman's interests, including the energy company Enron's fraudulent practices, and contract abuses in Iraq. Back then, there was no chorus from my colleagues or broadcast managers saying *that's all just politics.* They didn't accuse me of being a Democratic mouthpiece. They just liked the stories.

But, Substitution Game, Issa's involvement in *Fast and Furious* is treated much differently. Issa's name evokes obvious distaste among some of my colleagues. They imply that he's incapable of raising legitimate concerns on any issue: that he's purely political theater. These colleagues wish to view the story as nothing more than a political dispute between Issa and the Obama administration, which is exactly how the administration wishes to portray it. Issa's engagement becomes the excuse that opponents will use from that day forward to officially label *Fast and Furious* a phony, Republican scandal.

The fact that I don't think that way makes me Public Enemy No.1 among partisan Democrats and President Obama's most ardent supporters. And it gets me a special caseworker inside the White House.

Eric Schultz is a former spokesman for New York senator Charles Schumer. More recently, Schultz headed communications for the Democratic Senatorial Campaign Committee. He's no political ingénue and no stranger to scandal and controversy. He was deputy campaign manager for Al Franken's contentious 2008 Senate campaign in Minnesota, and before that, he headed the press shop for John Edwards's 2008 run for president, fielding the onslaught of questions about Edwards's extramarital affair and illegitimate child.

In May 2011, the Obama White House chooses Schultz, to be paid with your tax dollars, to handle press on *Fast and Furious.*

Our relationship is courteous enough. As far as I'm concerned, it largely consists of Schultz trying to discredit those who could harm the administration, and advancing story lines and ideas to help his boss. He seems to have a pretty well-organized network of support. For example, Schultz might suggest to his media contacts that they do a story dissecting controversies in Issa's background. It could be an editorial or blog written by party loyalists, an article penned by a like-minded reporter, or a favorable piece in the left-wing propaganda blog Media Matters. Schultz then circulates the resulting "story" to the rest of us in the media, sprinkled with his commentary. The strategy counts on the tendency of many bloggers and reporters to copy and codify each other's work. If things go according to plan, the story is regurgitated and excerpted by so many outlets that it appears, to the uninitiated, to be prevailing thought. It's self-fulfilling and self-legitimizing. Pretty soon, the theme bleeds into real news organizations and the cycle is complete. The message being delivered, of course, is that there's no real story behind *Fast and Furious*. Just a Republican vendetta.

It's not only liberals who operate this way. Conservatives do it, too. But their propaganda blogs are less likely to get treated as "news" by the regular media.

Along with Schultz, Media Matters is in touch with me about *Fast and Furious* and things start out friendly enough. They recently received a $1 million donation from George Soros, the multibillionaire funder of left-wing causes. On one occasion, they call to peddle the idea of a story that discredits *Fast and Furious* blogger Vanderboegh for his militia ties and other perceived transgressions. It's a propaganda campaign to divert from the damaging facts: *controversialize critics to try to turn the focus on personalities instead of the evidence.*

Media Matters emails me the summary of an extensive investigation their researchers have done on Vanderboegh's personal life. It's pretty impressive for the time and effort they've put into it. Propaganda groups know if they do all the work and make it easy, some writers will print a version of their story. With Media Matters' proposed Vanderboegh story, all a writer really needs is a few comments from relevant players and it's ready to go.

But it's not journalism and it's not how I operate.

It's not that I mind getting the idea. Good ideas can come from almost anywhere. Special interests can contribute valuable information for a story. But they shouldn't be researching and writing it for you. The *Huffington Post* and *Mother Jones* are among those that ultimately do publish stories about Vanderboegh. I wonder if it's because of a spark planted by Media Matters. Maybe it's just coincidence.

When I prove to be noncompliant, and continue covering stories considered potentially damaging to the Obama administration, Media Matters will strike me from their list of valuable media contacts—and make me a target of their aggressive campaign to smear and controversialize with false information. If one were to believe the liberal blog, in an overnight transformation, I went from being a trusted journalist whom they wanted on their side, to a shoddy reporter. Fortunately, few are swayed by the narrative.

As for me, I'm just focused on trying to solve the primary puzzles of *Fast and Furious*.

What was the real purpose?

Whose idea was it?

Who knew, how high up?

As the weeks progress, evidence mounts and the Justice Department's spin proves embarrassingly incorrect time and time again. As quickly as one of the administration's claims is contradicted, the Justice Department revises and reissues its position, only to be disproven once again. The missteps provide a textbook example of why journalists with any awareness of the track record simply cannot immediately accept the official government line as the truth. Too often, it proves not to be.

Perhaps the Justice Department's biggest blunder was its February 4, 2011, letter to Congress, which falsely stated that ATF doesn't let guns walk. Specifically, Holder's assistant attorney general Ronald

Weich wrote that the allegation that ATF "'sanctioned' or otherwise knowingly allowed the sale of assault weapons to a straw purchaser who then transported them into Mexico—is false," and ATF "makes every effort to interdict weapons that have been purchased illegally and prevent their transportation to Mexico."

Ten months later, when it's clear even to the Obama administration's fiercest supporters that guns *did* walk, the Justice Department formally retracts its earlier statement but implies there was no intent to deceive.

Blanket-deny everything and hope the news media doesn't come up with proof to refute the denials. If they do, modify your position.

In the coming months, Republicans ask for internal emails and other documentation to discover exactly how false information made it into the original letter to Congress, but the Justice Department refuses to turn over the material. Eventually, President Obama steps in and exerts executive privilege for the first time of his administration to keep the documents secret.

Once Justice Department officials are forced to acknowledge the gunwalking, the next story they tell is that rogue ATF agents in Phoenix are solely to blame, and that nobody higher up was aware that the strategy was being employed. But Congress manages to get its hands on internal documents that prove that's not true: officials at ATF headquarters in Washington were well aware of the gunwalking. So the Justice Department changes its story again and claims that all knowledge was isolated at the ATF level: the Justice Department was kept in the dark. But Congress receives documentation showing Justice Department officials very well knew about *Fast and Furious.* The department even approved wiretaps for the case, which involved criminal division officials reading detailed affidavits that explained exactly what was going on. For the first time, there's direct evidence leading to Holder's men.

It's about this time that the *CBS Evening News*'s interest goes from hot to cold.

It's the weekend and I see Katie Couric's name pop up on my BlackBerry as the sender of an email. She compliments my work so far on *Fast and Furious*. She wants to know if I've asked Holder for an on-camera interview. Yes, I reply, I've asked several times through the Justice Department press office, but it's a no-go. Couric knows Holder and his wife. She types back saying maybe she'll ask him for an interview. Is that okay with me? I tell her it's a good idea. Holder isn't going to talk to me. Maybe he'll talk to her. Couric is a good interviewer. We'll brainstorm on questions and she can do the job.

Holder never does the interview. But after that weekend email exchange, nothing is the same at work.

First, my next *Fast and Furious* report is inexplicably cut short. It's an exclusive interview with a second ATF official who has a very different piece of the story to tell. Special Agent Rene Jaquez was stationed in Juarez, Mexico, the most dangerous city in the world. He tells me, on camera, that he's outraged that, as he risked his life, facing daily brushes with death on assignment in Juarez, his own agency was helping arm the bad guys. Jaquez tells me he has family—uncles, aunts, a father, and a sister—living in Mexico and "any one of us could have been shot with one of those guns."

The idea that two active ATF agents are stepping forward to criticize the government initiative on camera is remarkable. But inside CBS, official interest has suddenly gone gray.

Then, my next story is killed from the *Evening News* entirely. It's a devastating, exclusive interview with ATF's lead official in Mexico City, attaché Darren Gil. I'd worked for weeks to convince Gil to go on camera.

As I continue to push for CBS to cover ongoing developments, one broadcast producer tells me, "The thing is, you've done such a great job covering this story, you were so far ahead of everybody else, you've reported everything. There's really nothing left to say."

In fact, we've barely begun to peek through the door.

I end up publishing many follow-ups online at CBSNews.com, where, unlike the broadcasts, there's the time and appetite for a diverse range of stories. Colleagues email me privately and ask why we're not airing these developments on television. Some view the story as more serious than Watergate because people have died. Others whisper, where my friends can hear, that I must have some sort of *agenda*.

It's pointless to explain that I'm just following the story where it leads. Deep down, they know it. They simply don't like where it's going.

Online, my *Fast and Furious* reports develop a following of tens of thousands who are thirsty for the news. Most are devoted conservatives. But I also hear from many liberals who think *Fast and Furious* is a horror story that crosses political lines. As for me: I don't view it as a gun control story. It's about corruption, cover-ups, and government misdeeds.

I've spent hundreds of hours researching leads. Internal ATF emails written in 2010 at the height of *Operation Fast and Furious* are leaked to me by sources or handed over to Congress. They portray the excitement among ATF managers, rather than the horror one might expect, as weapons turn up at crime scenes south of the border. In their view, it's Mission Accomplished.

But what, really, is the mission?

The whiteboard and poster I'm using to organize and cross-reference my leads become crowded with an ever-expanding network of cases with shades of gunwalking and unresolved questions. The cases have catchy titles. *White Gun. Operation Wide Receiver. Operation Castaway. Operation Head Shot. Too Hot to Handle.* Some are simply named after one of the defendants: *Ramos. Osorio. Hernandez.*

Medrano. Bazan. Kingery. There are still more cases connected to a gun shop in Houston: Carter's Country. So far, I've found evidence or allegations of gunwalking in Phoenix; Tucson; Dallas; Houston; Tampa; Evansville, Indiana; and Columbus and Albuquerque, New Mexico. I'm making a list of other federal agencies participating in or aware of the ATF cases, based on legal filings or press accounts. They include the Internal Revenue Service, Drug Enforcement Administration, FBI, Immigration and Customs Enforcement, the Border Patrol, the Department of Homeland Security, the U.S. Marshals Service, and the Justice Department's U.S. attorneys. Remembering that the Justice Department tried to portray the gunwalking as the brainchild of a few Phoenix ATF agents, I'm thinking that, on my whiteboard, it sure looks a lot more like a coordinated interagency strategy.

We know that cartel firearms traffickers do a lot of their shopping along the border in Texas, California, Arizona, and New Mexico. The feds commonly claim that up to 90 percent of the weapons used by the Mexican drug cartels are sold over the counter in the United States. But when that figure is cited before Congress to make the case for additional gun control, gun rights advocates ask: Where's the proof? They correctly argue that only a fraction of firearms seized from criminals in Mexico are submitted to ATF for tracing: the ones that the Mexicans conclude are most likely to have come from the United States. The rest are presumed untraceable for reasons such as missing serial numbers, or Mexican officials believe they came from other countries. Yes, of the traced guns, almost 90 percent come from the United States. But the fact that most of them *aren't* traced at all messes up that math and a fundamental gun control argument. It means that most of the weapons found in Mexico technically are *not* traced back to the United States.

But let's imagine a scenario in which a greater percentage of guns from Mexican crime scenes are traced in a fairly short, defined period of time, and hundreds—no, thousands of them—are discovered to have come from the United States.

Gun control advocates could have their checkmate.

But how to make that happen?

A simple three-step strategy could do the trick. ATF could:

1. Work with licensed gun dealers in a scheme to encourage and monitor sales to suspicious characters and known traffickers, entering the serial numbers into ATF's Suspect Gun Database on the front end so that tracings later are easy.
2. Let the guns sold to these suspicious characters and known traffickers "walk."
3. Wait, sometimes an incredibly short "time to crime," as the weapons are recovered at crime scenes in Mexico and their serial numbers easily trace back to their American origins.

There's just one big flaw with using such a strategy to argue that most guns used in Mexican crimes are from America: it's all a setup.

But maybe the public will never have to know that.

Whatever the true purpose of the gunwalking program, and whoever thought of it, it runs counter to the whole mission of U.S. law enforcement, which is to protect the public—and federal agents. The twisted logic for the indefensible strategy goes something like this: To protect the public, we need to prevent guns from flowing across the border. To prevent guns from flowing south, we need to stop gun traffickers. To stop gun traffickers, we need to prove that their guns are used in Mexican cartel crimes. To get proof, we need to let crooks freely traffic weapons so that they're used by the cartels to injure and kill. We then trace the weapons back to the U.S. source, arrest the traffickers and cartel kingpins, and stop the guns.

Wait a minute. The federal agents' ultimate duty is to protect the public—but to do so, they're feeding violence that hurts people?

ATF managers note, apparently with no intended irony, that as more guns from *Fast and Furious* flow into Mexico, the violence there escalates. An internal ATF email states, "Our [*Fast and Furious*] subjects purchased 359 firearms during March alone, including numerous Barrett .50 caliber rifles" and notes, "958 killed in March 2010 . . . most violent month since 2005."

In my February 2011 interview with Special Agent Dodson, I asked, "Did you feel that ATF was perhaps partly to blame for the escalating violence in Mexico and on the border?"

"Yes, ma'am," Dodson answered. "I even asked [my supervisors] if they could see the correlation between the two: the more our [*Fast and Furious* suspects] buy, the more violence we're having down there."

Setting aside the human consequences, letting weapons flow freely into Mexico could be viewed as beneficial to certain political motives. For example, it could nicely tee up a new gun control initiative being pushed by the Obama administration called "Demand Letter 3."

"Demand Letter 3" was a very controversial proposal that sought to require certain U.S. licensed gun dealers to report to the feds when someone buys multiple rifles or "long guns." It would be the third ATF program demanding that gun shops report tracing information.

The two sides in the gun debate have long clashed over whether gun dealers should have to report multiple rifle sales. The feds argue that a large number of semiautomatic, high-caliber rifles from the United States are being used by violent cartels in Mexico. They believe more reporting requirements would help ATF crack down. Gun rights advocates say the reporting mandates are unconstitutional, and would not make a dent in Mexican cartel crimes.

Two earlier demand letters were initiated in 2000 under the Clinton administration. They added reporting requirements for a relatively small number of targeted licensed gun dealers. Demand Letter 3 promised to be much more sweeping, specifically targeting rifles and shotguns, encompassing 8,500 firearms dealers in four Southwest border states: Arizona, California, New Mexico, and Texas. It sought to require additional reporting for gun dealers who sell two or more long guns to a single person within five business days, if the guns are semiautomatic, greater than .22 caliber, and can be fitted with a detachable magazine. But gun rights advocates saw it as a backdoor gun registration scheme. They say the government has no business tracking rifle purchases made by law-abiding citizens.

According to email evidence, some federal officials viewed *Fast and Furious* as an opportunity to help justify Demand Letter 3. On July 14, 2010, after ATF headquarters in Washington, D.C., received an update on the *Fast and Furious* case in progress, prior to its public exposure, Field Operations Assistant Director Mark Chait emailed ATF Phoenix Special Agent in Charge Newell.

"Bill, can you see if these guns were all purchased from the same [licensed gun dealer] and at one time. We are looking at anecdotal cases to support a demand letter on long gun multiple sales. Thanks."

As I research the federal government's push for Demand Letter 3, I begin to wonder about a yearlong investigation conducted by the *Washington Post* for a series of articles published in December 2010, just before *Fast and Furious* broke. The takeaway message from the article was: *Gun Shops Bad; More Gun Control Needed.* The *Post* named the U.S. licensed dealers that were doing the biggest business with Mexican cartel traffickers. I'll call the gun shops the "Dirty Dozen" because there are twelve of them and they sure don't look clean in the article.

The funny thing is, I now recognize two of the top three gun stores listed in the article—four in all—as names that were secretly cooperating with ATF in selling guns to the bad guys. Well before

Brian Terry's murder, months before the rest of the country learned of *Fast and Furious*, some of the cooperating gun dealers had privately raised objections about the gunwalking strategy that ATF wrapped them up in. They felt pressure to go along with the feds, who regulate them and inspect their shops. But they were reluctant.

For example, in April 2010, one dealer writes to Phoenix ATF officials, "We just want to make sure we are cooperating with ATF and that we are not viewed as selling to the bad guys." He's worried about potential liability. "[W]e were hoping to put together something like a letter of understanding to alleviate concerns of some type of recourse against us down the road for selling these items." But *Fast and Furious* group supervisor David Voth assures him there's nothing to be concerned about. Voth tells the dealer that ATF is "continually monitoring these suspects using a variety of investigative techniques which [*sic*] I cannot go into detail."

Two months later, the same dealer grows more agitated and his warnings become an eerie premonition: "I wanted to make sure that none of the firearms that were sold per our conversation with you and various ATF agents could or would ever end up south of the border or in the hands of the bad guys. I guess I am looking for a bit of reassurance that the guns are not getting south or in the wrong hands. . . . I want to help ATF with its investigation but not at the risk of agents [*sic*] safety because I have some very close friends that are US Border Patrol agents in southern AZ as well as my concern for all the agents [*sic*] safety that protect our country."

Apparently none of this was known by the *Post*, which gives no hint of this crucial backstory and seems to lay blame at the feet of the gun stores alone for selling to shady characters. No mention that the gun stores, in some cases, were doing exactly as ATF had instructed.

"All of the stores among the top 12 have had double-digit traces of 'crime guns' to their stores from Mexico," reads the article, "a statistic that can be a red flag for investigators." The owners of a Dirty Dozen gun shop in Texas called Carter's Country give an interview to the *Post* but don't reveal their confidential cooperation with ATF even as they're vilified. And, apparently, nobody in the government offers up this basic information. So in December 2010, the *Washington Post* report stands as a strong case for more gun regulation.

In a twist of fate, just two days after the *Post* series begins, Border Patrol agent Brian Terry is gunned down. Within hours of his tragic death, Holder's U.S. attorney in Arizona, Dennis Burke, notifies Holder's then deputy chief of staff Monty Wilkinson that the guns used to kill Terry are from *Fast and Furious.*

"The guns found in the desert near the murder [of the Border Patrol] officer connect back to the investigation we were going to talk about," Burke writes Wilkinson in an email.

"I'll call tomorrow," Wilkinson replies.

I reread the *Post* article several months later, in the context of what we now know about *Fast and Furious* gunwalking. I notice that the *Post*'s government sources used phrasing that's remarkably similar to what the Justice Department and others are now using to defend the gunwalking program. They say that laws backed by the gun lobby make it difficult to bring criminal cases against U.S. gun dealers who knowingly sell to criminals. The implication is that ATF agents have their hands tied and have to get creative with their strategies to do their job.

Around the same time the *Post* article is distributed to American readers, the Justice Department is preparing at last to round up the *Fast and Furious* suspects and do a victory lap for the media. In an internal email on January 4, 2011, ATF's Newell writes that the case will provide "another time to address Multiple Sale on Long Guns issue."

On January 25, 2011, ATF's Special Agent in Charge Newell

steps to the podium in Phoenix to lead the news conference. A cache of rifles is laid out on display for reporters to photograph. Newell announces the interagency effort called *Operation Fast and Furious*, which has resulted in the indictment of twenty suspects who bought scores of weapons from U.S. gun stores. There's talk of the escalating drug violence in Mexico as more American guns head south. New gun regulations are sorely needed, say the feds.

But the unspoken fly in the ointment is the inconvenient matter of Agent Brian Terry's murder forty-one days before. Apparently, there's been a decision within the Justice Department to keep its link to *Fast and Furious* guns quiet and hope that nobody is the wiser.

So the Newell press conference includes no talk of Terry. No disclosure that the rifles used by Terry's killers were trafficked by *Fast and Furious* suspects whom ATF had watched and allowed to operate week after week, month after month. Reporters aren't told that ATF had encouraged the sales then let the guns disappear, untracked, onto the mean streets of Nogales, Sonora; San Dimas, Durango; Tepic, Nayarit; San Miguel, Guerrero; Culiacan, Sinaloa; and Juarez.

Still, whispers of scandal are beginning to blow softly in the dry Arizona breeze. As the news conference wraps up, a local reporter asks Newell if his agents intentionally let guns walk. "Hell, no!" answers Newell, knowing full well that he'd led the effort. The reply isn't captured on videotape but it quickly makes the rounds of the media rumor mill and soon becomes legendary among the hardest-core followers of the scandal. (Two years later, in a private off-camera meeting, Newell would tell me, in his defense, that he didn't think *Fast and Furious* qualified as "gunwalking" under his own personal definition.)

Later, we learn that Attorney General Holder considered attending the news conference to thrust it further into the national spotlight. Just twelve hours before Brian Terry was murdered, on December

14, 2010, U.S. Attorney Burke emailed colleagues that Holder's office was "now expressing interest in the [attorney general] coming out" to speak to the press at the upcoming news conference.

But after Terry's murder came a change of heart. On December 21, 2010, Burke emailed Holder's deputy, Wilkinson. "I would not recommend the [attorney general] announce this case. I can explain in detail at your convenience."

Even with Holder a no-show at the press event, there's still hope among ATF managers that the indictment of *Fast and Furious* suspects will serve to advance gun control interests. A day after the press conference, Chait, at ATF headquarters, emailed Newell in Phoenix: "Bill—well done yesterday. . . . [I]n light of our request for Demand letter 3, this case could be a strong supporting factor if we can determine how many multiple sales of long guns occurred during the course of this case."

That optimism evaporates after Agent Dodson's March 4 interview with CBS News. After that, it's all about denial and damage control.

Later, many would refer to *Fast and Furious* as a "botched sting operation" in which agents "lost track" of weapons. The case may have been ill-advised, but it wasn't botched and it wasn't a sting. Nor did ATF agents lose track of the guns. They let them go on purpose.

On February 15, 2011, exactly two months after Terry is gunned down, I'm in the Washington, D.C., newsroom when one of my sources calls.

"Did you hear about the ICE shooting?" he asks.

"No," I answer.

"Two ICE agents ambushed in Mexico by drug cartels," he tells me. "One of them is dead. Headquarters is in a panic. They think that the guns the bad guys used might have been walked."

Before long, the news of the murder crosses the wire services. The two Immigration and Customs Enforcement agents, Jaime Zapata and Victor Avila, were traveling on assignment along a notorious Mexican highway controlled by drug bandits. Without warning, cartel bandits had cut off their vehicle and ambushed them. Zapata was killed, Avila seriously injured. Traveling without the usual escort, outnumbered and outgunned, they never had a chance.

At CBS, some of my superiors are paying so little attention to what I've reported, they're confused.

"Is this a separate shooting? Or is Zapata the same agent you've been reporting on?" one of them asks me. He's confusing Brian Terry's murder two months earlier with the Zapata murder that just happened. I'm taken aback. For the first time, I realize that certain managers have tuned out the whole story. Made up their mind without even knowing the broad-brush basics. They're making the editorial decision that developments in the *Fast and Furious* story don't qualify as "news," without bothering to learn the basic facts. They haven't thoroughly read the many notes I've circulated. They haven't read the stories I've published on our own website.

"They're two different shootings two months apart," I explain. "The first is a Border Patrol agent named Brian Terry in Arizona. This one is an ICE agent named Jaime Zapata in Mexico. But we need to find out if the firearms used against Zapata were also part of an ATF case."

As it turns out, they are.

It takes time and investigation to sort out the relationship, but through my sources, I'm able to obtain case files that show ATF had watched—and failed to arrest—suspects who trafficked two of the guns used in the ICE ambush. These ATF cases are not part of *Fast and Furious*. It further confirms that the federal government is using gunwalking strategies far and wide.

One of the traffickers had sent ten WASR-10 semiautomatic rifles to the Zeta drug cartel several months before Zapata was shot with one of them. Records show that ATF recorded a phone call in which the suspect "spoke about the final disposition of . . . firearms to Mexico and also about the obliterating of the serial numbers before they were trafficked." But even with that evidence in hand, the feds allowed him to continue operating his illegal trade for four more months. A warrant for his arrest was finally issued, coincidentally, the day before Zapata's murder.

New information is coming almost every day and it's hard to keep up with it. Insiders or, in some cases, the Justice Department under congressional demand are providing important internal emails and notes. The information unravels the story line that the Justice Department, attorney general, and White House knew nothing of *Fast and Furious*.

A huge blow to the administration comes at a congressional hearing on July 26, 2011. ATF Special Agent in Charge Newell testifies that he discussed the case with White House National Security Director for North America Kevin O'Reilly as early as September 2010. At that time, ATF managers were proud of their effort and saw it as something that headquarters in Washington, D.C., encouraged. O'Reilly emailed Newell asking if he could share information about ATF's efforts to combat cross-border gun trafficking, including the case that would become *Fast and Furious*, with other White House staffers. The two men also indicated they'd spoken on the phone about the subject.

It seems doubtful that Newell's discussion of *Fast and Furious* would fail to disclose the gunwalking strategy that was the heart of the case and, at the time, was perceived as vital to its success. Case briefings, complete with maps and charts, clearly delineated gun recoveries in Mexico and how federal officials tracked the weapons from the point of purchase to their endpoints. Wouldn't anyone with half a brain be able to deduce that this would only be possible if ATF were letting guns go?

Add the fact that American law enforcement officials were facilitating delivery of illegal weapons into a foreign, sovereign nation, where it's virtually illegal for private citizens to carry guns in public. Logic dictates that ground-level ATF officials would never be allowed to launch a major cross-border operation without knowledge and approval at high levels in the U.S. government. Such an operation, one would think, should pique high-level interest from a national security and international political standpoint. Federal law enforcement officials often won't do an interview with the media or put out simple facts on a case before navigating a mind-boggling bureaucracy to obtain upper-level approvals. Yet we're asked to believe that an international law enforcement initiative spanning over a year and reaching into almost every branch of federal law enforcement escaped all meaningful scrutiny. That nobody of any importance knew anything important.

Isn't the administration's story line, if true, a bona fide scandal of its own? That rogue ATF agents were able to spend millions of tax dollars on a secret, controversial, dangerous cross-border operation undetected, under their bosses' noses, without approval—and nobody had noticed?

After Newell's bombshell testimony that at least one White House national security staffer, O'Reilly, knew about *Fast and Furious*, a White House spokesman denies it. The spokesman claims that O'Reilly only spoke to Newell about other gun-trafficking efforts, not *Fast and Furious*. When asked why Newell would say otherwise, the White House spokesman says flatly, "I don't know."

By late summer of 2011, there's a full-scale meltdown inside the government. ATF's director Kenneth Melson resigns under pressure. Congressional investigators are demanding to know what information was shared with whom at the White House beyond O'Reilly and how far did it go. They're insisting that the White House turn over relevant documents and they want to interview O'Reilly. The White House responds that O'Reilly isn't around. It seems he's been tasked to the State Department, then sent out of the country to Iraq on assignment. He's "unavailable." I ask a congressional staffer who's trying to reach O'Reilly for an interview the obvious: *Don't they have telephones in Iraq?*

On Friday, September 2, 2011, I'm up at 4 a.m. to do a live shot for *The CBS Early Show*. My story covers newly obtained documents showing the U.S. attorney's office allegedly plotted to cover up the link between Brian Terry's death and *Fast and Furious*. Assistant U.S. Attorney Emory Hurley had sent an email the day after the murder indicating that the connection would be kept on the down low. "This way we do not disclose [*Fast and Furious*] or the Border Patrol shooting case," Hurley wrote.

After my live shot at 7 a.m., I head over to the White House. I have a special invitation.

During *Fast and Furious*, the Obama administration has improperly used its powers to ban me from the Justice Department building, where it was presumed I'd ask uncomfortable questions. On one occasion, a background briefing related to *Fast and Furious* was hastily scheduled for selected members of the media at the Justice Department. No sooner do I leave the office to attend than I get a call from Justice Department spokeswoman Tracy Schmaler.

"Don't bother to come," she says. "Only the regular Justice Department reporters are allowed." She tells me she won't clear me through security to come into the building.

My presence isn't a security issue. I'm a credentialed journalist who's gone through FBI background checks and had clearance to travel on jets with presidents and their families. Administration officials may not like me, but I'm pretty sure they know I'm not a terrorist. The Justice Department is flexing its power not for legitimate safety reasons but to control who in the news media covers their story.

But on this day, September 2, I'll get into the White House because I'm invited. A taxi drops me off on the corner of Pennsylvania and Sixteenth Street, where I make my way to the West Gate entrance. Reporters from the *Los Angeles Times*, the *New York Times*, and the *Washington Post* are there, too.

After clearing security, we're led through a maze of twists, turns, and hallways to a conference room in the Old Executive Office Building, adjacent to the White House.

White House spinmeister Schultz is offering us an advance look at some *Fast and Furious* documents the White House plans to turn over under demand from Grassley and from the House Oversight Committee. We get this preview in exchange for listening to their take on the material, which we're happy to do. As part of the deal, we're not allowed to report on the documents before the White House gives them to Congress. I don't know how long such arrangements have been taking place in Washington. I'm not usually among the journalists selected to attend any administration's invitation-only events.

We're each provided a folder containing printouts of selected White House emails. I scan my set to see if it reveals anything new. I ask, are these *all* the communications about *Fast and Furious*?

No, say the officials who are briefing us, *but they're "representative."* I ask why, then, can't we see the rest if they're just more of the same? They repeat that the documents we have are "representative." The problem is, they're supposed to turn over all the documents to Congress, not a representative sample. And for all the journalists present, the trust meter is running a bit low, considering the administration's track record to date.

After the special briefing, three weeks pass and the White House fails to meet a September 23 deadline to turn over the documents to Congress. Then, on September 30, 2011, comes a famous Friday Washington Document Dump. We know the drill. When the feds have to turn over potentially damaging documents, they like to do it late on a Friday when members of Congress are headed to their home districts and journalists are dreaming of our first icy cold beer of the weekend. And by Monday, the administration calls it "old news." After all, it's been out for *days*!

At exactly 4:28 p.m., Schultz emails me that the White House has finally turned over the documents to Congress. He indicates there's nothing particularly newsworthy in them. They're more of the same type of material we reviewed earlier in the month. At least that's what he says.

I obtain copies of the documents and start sorting through them. There are about one hundred pages of communications involving three White House national security staffers: O'Reilly, Senior Director Dan Restrepo, and counterterrorism and counternarcotics official Greg Gatjanis. Other administration names are copied on some emails. Jeffrey Stirling. Sarah Kendall.

Far from proving that the White House knew nothing at all, the documents show keen interest in the efforts of ATF's Gun Runner Impact Teams, or GRIT for short. GRIT was a surge in personnel and efforts from May 1 through August 6, 2010, to fight trafficking of firearms to Mexican drug cartels. In Phoenix, GRIT included eighty-four special agents, industry operations investigators, and support staff from around the country. And the largest case that GRIT had going—in fact, the biggest case of its kind in the country—was the one that would become *Fast and Furious*.

One of the relevant White House emails is dated the summer of 2010 and mentions John Brennan, who was then assistant to the president for Homeland Security. (At about this time in 2010, Brennan's name was being circulated as being "behind the witch hunts of investigative journalists learning information from inside the beltway sources." He would later be promoted to director of the CIA.) According to the House Oversight Committee, Brennan made a trip to Phoenix on June 28, 2010, to announce an Obama administration initiative described as a "multi-layered effort to target illicit networks trafficking in people, drugs, illegal weapons and money." National security staffers and Justice Department officials accompanied Brennan on the trip. Wouldn't this trek have necessarily included discussion of the biggest gun-trafficking case going at the time?

A month later, on July 28, 2010, the White House's O'Reilly emailed ATF's Newell that he wanted to share with his White House colleagues Restrepo and Gatjanis some of the gun-trafficking information that Newell had provided. About a month after that, on September 1, 2010, Newell emailed O'Reilly to say that he has "great stats and investigative stories to tout" on the subject of Southwest border firearms trafficking. O'Reilly answers, "Great-thanks. We want John Brennan well-prepared to talk GRIT with the Mexicans next Wednesday." An email from the White House's Stirling to O'Reilly the same day refers to preparing a PowerPoint presentation for a "high level" meeting coming up on October 5. It's clear that White House officials are paying attention to ATF's gun-trafficking cases.

Two days later, internal emails show, Newell sends more gun-trafficking case information and documents to his White House friend O'Reilly with the caveat, "You didn't get these from me." Attached are statistical charts and a map of the Mexican locations where suspect weapons were destined or "ended up." Newell is going around his ATF command chain in emailing directly to O'Reilly in the White House. Then, possibly referring to *Fast and Furious*, Newell writes, "Also, not mentioned in these docs but VERY relevant to Mr. Brennan's meeting next week is the fact that we and the [U.S.

attorney] were going to announce the indictment of a dozen 'straw purchase' cases addressing firearms trafficking by 30 individuals."

After reviewing all of these email exchanges provided by the White House in the Friday document dump to Congress, I have some questions. I go to the White House's Schultz for answers. He claims that because the emails don't explicitly discuss gunwalking, they *prove* that nobody in the White House knew of the controversial tactic.

It's a flawed leap in logic. It requires dismissing the unknown content of other emails and communications that the White House hasn't released. It requires forgetting about the phone conversations Newell acknowledged having with O'Reilly in testimony to Congress, for which no record is provided. On the question of who knew exactly what, the emails are definitively—inconclusive.

I also want to ask Schultz what did Brennan tell "the Mexicans" in his briefing referenced in the September 1 email. To what, exactly, was O'Reilly referring in another email on September 3, 2010, when he asked Newell about "last year's [Texas] effort"? And was the referenced upcoming indictment of a dozen "straw purchase" cases with thirty firearms traffickers actually *Fast and Furious*?

Schultz isn't happy with my questions. He begins arguing that the emails I'm asking about are "old news"—the common PR refrain—because I'd reviewed them at the White House four weeks before. I compare the two sets and tell him no, there are new ones in today's batch. And that's hardly the point. None of these emails had been reported on before.

We end up on the telephone to talk it out. After some editorial conversation, Schultz erupts into a middle school meltdown.

"Goddammit it, Sharyl! The *Washington Post* is reasonable, the *L.A. Times* is reasonable, the *New York Times* is reasonable, *you're the only one who's not reasonable!*"

He's screaming now. The tirade continues for several minutes, during which time I push a button and put him on speakerphone. A producer two doors down hears the outburst, walks to the doorway of my office, and mouths, *What the hell?*

"So, Sharyl Attkisson is the only reporter who knows what she's doing?" Shultz continues, sarcastically. "Nobody else thinks this is a story. Just you. You're the only one. Sharyl Attkisson is right and everybody else is wrong? God*dam*mit it!"

It's hard to know if Schultz is really that out of control or if he's just trying to be intimidating. It's not uncommon for administration officials to be sarcastic or even bully, berate, and raise their voices. But this full-blown screaming, cursing tirade does stand apart, in my experience. When Schultz takes a breath, I tell him he's clearly too upset to have a civil conversation and he should put anything else that he wants to say in an email. He accuses me of not being willing to listen. He threatens to call my bureau chief. I tell him to go ahead. He hangs up and that's the last time I can remember that we ever speak on the phone.

A couple of days later, I get the anger treatment from Justice Department flack Schmaler. She hasn't contributed one good piece of information in the months that I've covered the story. Ideally, as a public information officer paid with your tax dollars to answer questions from the press, her job is to facilitate interviews and release information in the public interest. But if that's ever how federal press officials saw their job, those days are long gone. Today, they're co-opted as personal press agents for their political bosses. Their goal is not to provide information, but to find out as much as they can about what *you* know.

Schmaler is obviously tasked with deflecting and denying. ATF refers my questions to her, then she refers me right back to them. I'm sent on an infinite loop that never produces coherent answers. When she talks to me at all, instead of answering my questions, she poses her own. For instance, early on, when I request interviews with Justice Department officials and ask who was involved in the case, Schmaler answers, "Who do your sources say was involved? And I can't believe you're listening to a bunch of disgruntled agents." When I ask if she'll confirm my information that Criminal Division chief Lanny Breuer authorized wiretaps in *Fast and Furious,* which were accompanied by lengthy affidavits explaining everything about it, Schmaler only asks, "Just because someone's signature is on an authorization, does it mean he read it?"

Her agency's spin has morphed from calling the whistleblowers liars, to acknowledging the gunwalking happened but saying it was the work of renegades in Phoenix, to admitting that ATF headquarters knew of it but that nobody at the Justice Department did, to conceding that people at Justice were involved but insisting the attorney general was kept in the dark. She bobs, she weaves, she shifts—and afterward pretends it's all consistent.

Based on the track record, I know that I can't count on getting the truth from Schmaler. But I still have to ask.

On this particular day in October, I'm asking about a statement Attorney General Holder made before the House Judiciary Committee on May 3, 2011. He was making his first round of congressional appearances since the *Fast and Furious* scandal broke. He'd testified to everyone's shock that he never heard of *Fast and Furious* until long after the public controversy erupted.

"When did you first know about the program officially I believe called *Fast and Furious*?" Representative Issa asked Holder.

"I'm not sure of the exact date, but I probably heard about *Fast and Furious* for the first time over the last few weeks," said Holder, then blinking his eyes in rapid succession.

The testimony seems incredible. The attorney general is telling Congress and the American public that nearly five months after Terry's death, four months after Senator Grassley began asking about the case, three months after the CBS News reports, he only just heard of *Fast and Furious* in the last couple of weeks?

Unfortunately for Holder, it wasn't long after his testimony that we obtained internal documents showing he was actually sent weekly briefings on *Fast and Furious* as early as July 2010, ten months before. The briefings came from the director of the National Drug Intelligence Center and from Holder's own Assistant Attorney General Breuer.

When I ask Schmaler to comment on the discrepancy, she, like Schultz, acts as though it's not the government's story that's out of whack, but the fact that I'm asking the question. First, she insists there's no inconsistency. When I persist, Schmaler grows irritated and locks in on an explanation: Holder didn't understand the question Congress asked.

I, for one, think Holder's a pretty smart guy. Schmaler's account would have us believe that the nation's top law enforcement manager, an attorney, misunderstood a simple, straightforward question posed by Congress. A question that everybody else seemed to understand. For clarity's sake, I ask her to put her explanation in writing. If I try to characterize what she's just told me, and it receives a poor reaction from the public, there's every chance she'll deny having said it or claim that I misunderstood her.

Schmaler doesn't want to put anything in writing. We go back and forth on the point. She's yelling now. Eventually, she reaches the position that Holder *did* know about *Fast and Furious* much sooner than he'd told Congress, but she says he didn't know the details about the gunwalking. (The Justice Department also later says that Holder never read any of the briefings that his deputies directly sent him regarding the case.)

The next day, I have an interview about *Fast and Furious* with conservative radio talk show host Laura Ingraham. In the past, CBS has given the okay for me and other correspondents to routinely appear on Ingraham's show and I perceive there's standing approval. CBS also allows correspondents to appear on liberal programs. These appearances reach broad audiences and could potentially work to improve CBS's third-place position among the three networks' morning and evening newscasts.

In the radio interview, I tell Ingraham the administration is sensitive and defensive on questions about *Fast and Furious*. I can tell by the yelling and screaming.

"So they were literally screaming at you?" Ingraham asks.

"Well, the [Department of Justice] woman was just yelling at me. A guy from the White House on Friday night literally screamed at me and cussed at me."

Ingraham is intrigued. The account of a White House official cussing me out is quickly picked up and circulated on conservative blogs. Many comment that the administration is behaving like bullies: unprofessional and inappropriate. But getting yelled at doesn't upset me. To the contrary, it makes me think I might be on to something.

Meantime, CBS has recently had a major change in top producers and management. Some of them are positively incensed over my providing this factual account of the White House official's behavior. Let me be clear: they're not upset with the White House, they're upset with me. One of them calls from New York to tell me that Ingraham is "extremely, extremely far right" and I shouldn't appear on her program anymore. I'm taken aback since Ingraham is a former CBS News correspondent and CBS has allowed several of us to be guests on her program for years. Reporters and anchors from all the networks make appearances on programs left and right. Programs hosted by Ingraham; Chris Matthews and Don Imus on MSNBC; on NPR;

Bill O'Reilly on FOX; Howard Kurtz on CNN's *Reliable Sources*; and more. In my view, appearances on these programs—regardless of the hosts' politics—give our reporting positive exposure before broad audiences. Isn't that good for CBS? I wonder if other on-air reporters are being given the same orders not to appear. I also wonder who at CBS decides which programs are "extreme" and which are not.

Meanwhile, the stream of internal documents leaked or officially provided to Congress continues and the Justice Department's plausible deniability is becoming more implausible.

In an email exchange dated October 18, 2010, two Justice Department officials are caught red-handed discussing gunwalking. They even use the g-word itself. The email references an earlier ATF gunwalking case, called *Wide Receiver*, which was started circa 2005 under the Bush administration and let hundreds of firearms walk. I learned about *Wide Receiver* from a confidential informant shortly after my early *Fast and Furious* stories and first reported on it in March 2011. It is reported that, in 2007, there was so much internal controversy over the fact that the government allowed gunwalking as part of *Wide Receiver* that prosecutors quietly abandoned the case. But after President Obama was elected, his Justice Department, seeking gun cases to prosecute, revived it.

This newly released email exchange from 2010 shows that one month before Brian Terry's murder, two of Holder's deputies are worried that their resumed prosecution of the old *Wide Receiver* case is potentially problematic. Deputy Assistant Attorney General of the Criminal Division Jason Weinstein and Deputy Chief of the National Gang Unit James Trusty share speculation about what the public's reaction might be if they learn that federal officials had let guns walk.

"[I]t's a tricky case given the number of guns that have walked . . ." Weinstein writes of *Wide Receiver*. Trusty replies hopefully, "I'm not sure how much grief we get for 'guns walking.' It may be more like, 'Finally they're going after people who sent guns down there.'"

Remember, three months after this blunt email exchange by Justice Department officials, the Justice Department told Congress in writing that gunwalking hadn't happened.

In October 2011, Assistant Attorney General Breuer is further mired in the mess. We already know that Breuer had sent Holder many briefings on *Fast and Furious* and that his Criminal Division signed off on the case wiretaps. But now, he acknowledges that he too knew of *Wide Receiver* and its gunwalking, even as the Justice Department denied to Congress it had ever occurred. He issues a public apology, as well as cover for Holder, claiming that he never thought to clue in the attorney general even after the controversy over *Fast and Furious* surfaced.

Meantime, Democrats seize on *Wide Receiver* as an opportunity to blame Bush for everything. Media outlets that largely ignored *Fast and Furious* eagerly dive into the story for the first time to cover *Wide Receiver* for the sake of implying that it's all Bush's fault. The Justice Department, which is mum on all my *Fast and Furious* questions, happily leaks all kinds of information about *Wide Receiver* and pushes the story to reporters who are sympathetic to its cause. Some of those reporters uncritically accept and report the spin. And while still withholding *Fast and Furious* documents from Congress, the Justice Department promptly gathers and turns over documents about *Wide Receiver*.

The Associated Press, apparently operating on information being pushed by the Justice Department, claims an exclusive: that gunwalking was used in the *Wide Receiver* case under Bush. (But it's seven months after I first reported it.) Left-wing bloggers sympathetic to the Obama administration, without checking the record, foolhardily accuse me of failing to report the Bush-era connection—I'd been first to report it and had repeatedly referenced it in subsequent stories.

Some CBS managers also circulate the "news" about the Bush connection, also apparently oblivious to the fact that, months ago, I aired a full TV report exclusively devoted to the case and referred to it many times since. It's news to them since they're not paying attention to our own coverage—only the administration's spin. When a preferred interpretation of a story I'm covering appears on a competitive news outlet or in a blog they like, they take that as gospel. Even if the competitor's story is inaccurate. Even when our sources and reporting are better.

The idea of a Bush connection is an alluring draw to liberal ideologues. One manager supportive of my coverage suggests I should fend off my internal critics—those who for ideological reasons just don't like my pursuing the story—by constantly referring to the "Bush" connection when writing any story about *Fast and Furious.*

While there's truth to the notion that the first gunwalking we know of occurred under President Bush, the attempts to pin the whole *Fast and Furious* scandal on Bush is disingenuous at best. *Wide Receiver* involved several hundred weapons, rather than thousands, and was abandoned. It was the Obama administration that vastly expanded the strategy, using it in multiple cases, states, and agencies. Incidentally, there's at least one common factor between the Bush-era *Wide Receiver* and the Obama-era *Fast and Furious* episodes: Bill Newell. He was ATF's special agent in charge of Phoenix during both.

Even amid the specter of Bush's *Wide Receiver,* Breuer's plight to defend himself and the Obama administration becomes more challenging. Additional internal documents show that during an official visit to Mexico in February 2011, just as the controversy over *Fast and Furious* was breaking loose, Breuer actually suggested that the United States and Mexico work together to allow cartel arms traffickers "to cross into Mexico," so that Mexican authorities could later prosecute and convict them. It sounds a lot like Breuer is proposing more gunwalking. The timing of Breuer's gunwalking suggestion is interesting because it happens as the Justice Department is swearing to Congress that such a tactic would never be used. Was Breuer attempting damage control? Trying to bring the Mexicans in at the eleventh hour and codify a tactic that had been used secretly for more than a year? Maybe Breuer figured if he hurriedly got the Mexicans on board, the sting of the unfolding public scandal would be less severe.

But according to documents, Breuer's idea was shot down by Mexico's then attaché, who "raised the issue that there is an inherent risk in allowing weapons to pass from the U.S. to Mexico; the possibility of the [government of Mexico] not seizing the weapons; and the weapons being used to commit a crime in Mexico." This common-sense objection turned out to be prophetic.

The Justice Department didn't hesitate to label the *Fast and Furious* whistleblowers as liars when they spoke out, while Breuer would have us believe that it never occurred to him to look more carefully through ATF's cases—like *Fast and Furious*—to see if the whistleblowers just might be telling the truth. He also claims he never thought to go to Holder, and say, *You know, we shouldn't be telling Congress there never was any gunwalking, because we've done it before . . . and, by the way, I just suggested doing something similar with the Mexicans.*

After all of the damning revelations, perhaps it's no surprise that the Justice Department declares it's done releasing documents. They're just feeding more controversy. To put a button on it, President Obama exerts his first-ever claim of executive privilege to withhold outstanding materials. That prompts the House to hold an historic vote to hold Holder in contempt.

Why can't we see any more documents if there's nothing more to see?

In September 2012, after a lengthy investigation, the Justice Department inspector general issues a scathing report about *Fast and Furious*. It finds no evidence "that contradicted Holder's statements to us" regarding his lack of knowledge about gunwalking. Instead, it faults more than a dozen officials who work under Holder. And it disproves the Justice Department's many claims along the way about its supposed utter lack of knowledge all the way up the line.

But as damaging as the IG's findings are, most of the press extrapolate only one thing: a headline that Holder has been "exonerated." A *New York Times* Web headline reads: "Holder cleared of Wrong Doing [*sic*] in Fast and Furious." Never mind the blame laid at the feet of his office and many in it, and the fact that he's in charge. Forget about how and why he could have been so clueless about such an important and controversial cross-border initiative. Disregard the evidence of the interagency cooperation on the gunwalking cases. Please ignore all of the qualifying language in the IG report, such as Holder telling the IG he did not *believe* he reviewed *Fast and Furious* weekly reports and that his acting deputy attorney general "had no recollection" of reviewing them.

Holder sure is lucky that so many in the media have such a generous interpretation of the facts.

Fast and Furious ends up being *the* investigative story of the next two years. CBS News CEO Jeff Fager later tells me that it's proven to be one of the most important stories for CBS News not just in recent history, but *ever*. In 2012, CBS News receives an investigative Emmy and an Edward R. Murrow Award for our reporting—the stories I was able to get on television before the internal appetite dried up. Then the Spanish-language news channel Univision picks up where I was forced to leave off with a special titled *Rapido y Furioso*. It chronicles the deadly toll on Mexican citizens hurt with the *Fast and Furious* firearms . . . a toll that's guaranteed to climb for years as the weapons remain on the streets. The Univision report is recognized in 2013 with a top award from the prestigious Investigative Reporters and Editors organization.

I can't think of another story that compelled the Justice Department to admit it gave Congress bad information and retract it; involved the brutal murders of two federal agents and countless Mexicans; forced the head of a federal agency, Kenneth Melson, to resign; led to the forced resignation of a U.S. attorney, Dennis Burke; resulted in a public apology from the Justice Department's criminal chief, Breuer; caused the reassignment of a half dozen other federal officials, including ATF's Chait, Newell, Voth, and Gillett, and Burke's assistant U.S. attorney Hurley; prompted an historic vote to hold the U.S. attorney general in contempt; and culminated with the president invoking executive privilege. For the first and only time of his presidency.

Yet much of the news media dismisses *Fast and Furious* as a Republican story and calls it a day.

| Green Energy Going Red |

The Silent Burn of Your Tax Dollars

In August 2012, CBS News producer Jennifer Jo Janisch and I make a surprise visit to an electric car plant in Elkhart, Indiana, that was supposed to employ four hundred workers churning out twenty thousand vehicles a year. It was near deserted.

Elkhart had lost jobs faster than any other city in 2009. It's where President Obama launched his $2.4 billion electric vehicle initiative and promises of new glories ahead. As a result, Norwegian company Think Global received $17 million in stimulus tax credits to build "Think City" electric cars in Elkhart.

But three years later, Think Global had declared bankruptcy and been acquired by a Russian investor.

I park my rental car and enter the facility, first without the camera crew. There are exactly two employees on site: Rodney and Josh. They have one car jacked up on a lift and are listening to country music on a transistor radio plugged into an electrical outlet with an extension cord. They tell me they're slowly finishing assembly on a few dozen 2011 models shipped in from Norway. Rodney and Josh let me drive a Think City car around inside the plant. There's plenty of room because the plant's so empty. It's a lot of fun to drive, indeed. Clean, quiet, maneuverable.

Just not much of a seller.

Think Global's lack of success should have been predictable: the company had a checkered track record, including three previous bankruptcies. One of its primary investors, Ener1, had also recently gone belly-up after spending $55 million of a $118.5 million federal grant to manufacture batteries for the Think City cars.

Then there's Fisker's Karma: a beautifully sleek, six-figure sports car—lean, mean, and green. Not to mention the darling of the electric car movement. But in March 2012, there sat Fisker's pride and joy: broken down and waiting for a tow on a flatbed truck after conking out in a *Consumer Reports* test.

"We buy about 80 cars a year and this is the first time in memory that we have had a car that is undriveable before it has finished our check-in process," wrote *Consumer Reports* in a devastating review.

It was a worst-case scenario for the reputation of the advanced vehicle, the company, and the Obama administration green initiative that generously supported it all with not just thousands of dollars. Or even millions. But *hundreds of millions* of your tax dollars.

But somehow it gets worse.

It turns out the Karma's failure was directly attributable to a second Obama green effort: a faulty lithium ion electric battery made by A123 Systems. A123 had managed to parlay the unbridled confidence of the Department of Energy into $249 million in stimulus tax money. Fisker, meanwhile, had gotten a $528.7 million taxpayer-backed loan. Now, less than three years after hitting the jackpot with Uncle Sam, both companies were on their way to bankruptcy. And President Obama was running for reelection.

It was October 27, 2009, that Vice President Joe Biden announced Fisker's ambitious production plans in his home state of Delaware, where the innovative electric cars were to be built. If we in the news media had examined things a bit more carefully on the front end, consulting independent analysts, we might have seen the disaster before us. Perhaps even the uninformed observer could have sensed the fantastical nature of the overenthusiastic projections. Before Fisker's first car was plugged in, Secretary of Energy Steven Chu declared the project "proof positive that our efforts to create new jobs, invest in a clean energy economy and reduce carbon pollution are working." He said the efforts were "reigniting a new Industrial Revolution." In Chu's vision, Fisker would single-handedly save hundreds of millions of gallons of gas; offset millions of tons of carbon pollution by 2016; and export more cars, by percentage, than any other U.S. manufacturer. There would be (not *might* be, but *would* be) 5,000 factory, vendor, and supplier jobs by 2014! And . . . (drumroll) . . . Fisker *will* build 75,000–100,000 cars a year by 2014!

In the end, a Fisker spokesman put the number of actual total car sales before bankruptcy at around 1,800.

How could the government experts have been so wrong? Were these failed enterprises alone among an overwhelming body of successful green energy initiatives funded by tax dollars? No.

Which raises larger questions of public interest. Was it appropriate for Secretary Chu to take on the role of venture capitalist? What do the failures say about our leaders' judgment and business acumen? Should the government have the right, whether motivated by political interests, ideology, or the best of intentions, to commit a great deal of tax dollars to projects on which few savvy private sector investors would gamble?

Substitution Game: Imagine a parallel scenario in which President Bush and Vice President Dick Cheney personally appeared at groundbreakings for, and used billions of tax dollars to support, multiple giant corporate ventures whose investors were sometimes major political campaign bundlers, only to have one (or two, or three) go bankrupt. At a cost to taxpayers of hundreds of millions of dollars. During a presidential election. When they knew in advance the companies' credit ratings were junk. News headlines would have been relentless with images of Bush and Cheney smiling and waving at one construction-start ceremony after another, making their invalidated claims about jobs and untold millions . . . contrasted with images of empty plants and boarded-up warehouses. And I would have been proposing those stories.

For example, the media didn't hesitate—nor should it have—to contrast Bush's 2005, "Brownie, you're doing a heckuva job" with his administration's disastrous handling of Hurricane Katrina. Seeming to be wildly disconnected from the facts, the president was prematurely congratulating his Federal Emergency Management Agency director, Michael Brown, for a job well done. Brown resigned ten days later amid the failures and devastation. The disparity was evoked time and time again—rightfully so—by the likes of the *Washington Post*, CNN, the New York *Daily News*, the *New York Post*, *Mother Jones*, *Huffington Post*, the *Weekly Standard*, *USA Today*, ABC, CBS, NBC, the *Daily Beast*: you name it.

But there isn't the same hankering to show the Obama-Biden contrasts.

Obama officials argued that it was no great scandal for some of these endeavors to prove to be poor investments: that the whole point was for the government to subsidize and encourage worthy projects that wouldn't otherwise merit private support. They argued that the losses weren't really losses because Congress had set aside $2.4 billion in a fund to pay for any failures.

Think about what they're really saying, in simple terms:

We're using $90 billion of your money to promote clean energy. Some of it will be loaned to companies that are so risky, nobody in their right mind (besides the government) would support them. But don't worry! When they default on the loans, and they will, we'll call it "even" by sub-

tracting the losses from a $2.4 billion fund we're setting up in advance. With your tax dollars. How's that sound?

If you're a consumer of ordinary news, you probably didn't hear much about any of this. You probably thought the clean energy money scandal began and ended with Solyndra.

I first began looking into green investments after Solyndra's death, complete with an FBI raid, in September 2011. Two years earlier, the Energy Department had granted the solar panel maker a loan guarantee backed by more than a half-billion tax dollars—*that's five hundred and thirty-five million dollars to a single company.* Within six months, accountant PricewaterhouseCoopers stated that Solyndra had fiscal problems that were so serious, there was "substantial doubt about its ability to continue." But when President Obama visited the company two months later, in May 2010, he remained publicly bullish on its future.

What would I find if I dug into other investments?

Following the green energy money was a natural outgrowth of the reporting I'd already done on boondoggles associated with the Obama administration's 2009 stimulus plan, which was a natural outgrowth of my reporting on the 2008 Bush administration's Troubled Asset Relief Plan, or TARP, which was a natural outgrowth of my investigations into wasteful congressional earmarks. The common denominator? Questionable spending of billions of hard-earned American tax dollars.

The numbers are staggering. As a presidential candidate, Obama campaigned on a $190 billion stimulus plan to revive the economy. Once elected, he decided vastly more money was needed: four times his original proposal. So in 2009, Congress passed his $787 billion stimulus package—and later upped it to $840 billion in 2012. For comparison, Bush's TARP started out with a massive $700 billion in funding but Congress reduced it to $475 billion in July 2010.

President Obama's stimulus was nearly double, and $90 billion of that was directly earmarked for green energy.

I began poring through the backgrounds of some troubled green ventures that benefited from federal tax dollars, whether under Bush or Obama. Documents filed with the federal Securities and Exchange Commission proved to be a gold mine of information that had not been widely reported. One after another, I discovered business plans built on flimsy foundations formulated by entrepreneurs who had little to no experience in the specialty. Millions upon millions of dollars were handed over to companies facing financial difficulties or with a history of making poor decisions. In some instances, the government secretly knew in advance that it was committing tax dollars to firms so risky, their bonds were rated as "junk"—below investment grade with a significant threat of default.

| MORE SOLYNDRAS?

My first investigation into the subject of green energy taxpayer waste aired January 13, 2012, during the debut week of the latest reinvention of CBS's morning broadcast. At the time, the program was looking for hard-hitting, original reporting and this fit the bill.

Among other facts, the story discussed what the Energy Department knew about green energy storage company Beacon Power before committing $43 million in tax money to it:

> Documents obtained by CBS News show Standard & Poor's had confidentially given the project a dismal outlook of CCC+.
>
> "[I]t is not even a good junk bond," said economist Peter Morici. "It's well below investment grade. This level of bond has about a seventy percent chance of failing in the long term."
>
> In fact, Beacon did go bankrupt. . . . We count twelve green

energy companies that are having trouble after being approved for more than $6.5 billion in federal assistance. Five have filed for bankruptcy.

As my research would reveal in the coming months, twelve troubled companies was only the beginning.

I presented the story live on the set in New York and was there after the broadcast when the staff celebrated the end of a successful first week of the new *CBS This Morning*. CBS News chairman Jeff Fager was on hand and had just signed me to a new three-year contract. He hugged me and held on long enough to whisper in my ear that the story was remarkably strong. "That's just what we're looking for," he told me. "We want as many as you can do . . . just like that."

Obama administration officials were still mired in damage control over my ongoing *Fast and Furious* coverage. Adding green energy to my portfolio apparently whipped them into a panic. My White House handler, Schultz, was now spinning on both stories.

The administration had declined my requests for on-camera interviews for the *CBS This Morning* investigation. But after the fact, its response was predictably multipronged and indefatigable. It included a long letter of objection replete with mistakes that largely argued points not addressed and claims never made in the report. When CBS replied that the story was entirely accurate so no corrections were warranted, the administration turned to its unwavering partner in uncritically advancing its agenda: Media Matters. The liberal blog printed the administration's error-riddled spin point by point repeating nearly the exact language and format that the administration had used in its letter to CBS.

As a news organization, we actively choose not to elevate the spinners and the media surrogates by publicly taking part in their propaganda games. But to disengage often means leaving the record muddled by their false information and innuendo, which tends to then miraculously place in the top result spots in subsequent Google searches, where less-informed readers might mistakenly believe they've located a legitimate news source.

I'm accustomed to the PR campaign. But not everyone is. I get the sense that some colleagues and supervisors in the story chain would rather not deal with it. They want to be patted on the back by the administration after a story, not criticized and taken to task. Some of them have friendly relationships with people connected to the administration and don't like catching flak from them after a story like mine. Frankly, that's what the White House counts on. It's why they do what they do.

Sometimes, we oblige by going so far as to give favored political interests special access.

During the 2012 presidential campaign, Obama Treasury secretary Timothy Geithner was afforded the chance to meet with and spin network news managers off camera. According to those who attended, Geithner pretty much blamed all of the nation's economic troubles on—the drought. His analysis became a basis for subsequent *CBS Evening News* story decisions that advanced the drought theory of economic weakness, helpfully pinpointing a factor outside the president's control and, therefore, one for which he could not be blamed. Naturally, this advanced Obama's case rather than that of his Republican opponent, Mitt Romney.

Corporate interests can rate access, too. In 2008, after word leaks out about the government's secret settlement of a vaccine-related autism injury in the Hannah Poling case, vaccine makers and their government partners are working overtime to controversialize and tamp down all news coverage of the facts. Their strategy includes a full-forced attack on me and my ongoing reporting. I'm especially dangerous to their interests because my reporting on medical issues cannot accurately be portrayed as fringe or lacking in credibility. After all, it's been cited in the *New England Journal of Medicine* and the *Columbia Journalism Review*. My reporting has received an Emmy nomination and a finalist award from the independent Investigative Reporters and Editors organization.

But I learn in June 2008, after the fact, that PR officials and a top attorney for vaccine maker Wyeth have managed to get a private meeting to spin two *Evening News* senior producers in New York about my reports. (One of the pharmaceutical PR officals is former ABC and CNN reporter Eileen O'Connor, who now works at the State Department under President Obama.) It's wrong on so many levels, in my opinion. Improper for the meeting to be conducted without my participation or knowledge. Unethical to offer the powerful corporate interests—who are also advertisers—special access, while those on the other side aren't given an audience to be heard. Inappropriate because the producers haven't been in the chain of command on any of my vaccine-related stories.

| THE BIG CHILL

After my first green energy investigation on *CBS This Morning*, which was so well received (except by the Obama administration and its supporters), the idea for my next report came from a CBS investigative producer in New York, Laura Strickler, who was also looking into government-funded green energy projects. She identified two companies that received a combined $300 million under the stimulus program to build electric car batteries at plants in Michigan. The money was supposed to grow the U.S. economy and level the playing field with foreign competitors. But most Americans probably didn't know that one of the companies, Dow Kokam, was a Korean partnership. The other, LG Chem, was Korean owned. The firms used their

American stimulus funds to buy Korean technology, equipment, and supplies, and they filled some of those sought-after American stimulus jobs with Korean workers. This so angered the local labor unions that they openly criticized the Obama administration for allowing foreigners to receive benefits that they felt were meant for Americans. On top of all that, the plants were already said to be behind schedule.

Unable to get the answers they sought from the Obama administration and their members of Congress, the local labor unions filed a Freedom of Information Act request asking for payroll records of contractors performing LG Chem's construction. The government's response named eighteen companies, and at least eleven of them were Asian firms.

By any neutral measure, this was a terrific story and illustrative of other cases we'd identified where green energy stimulus funds were benefiting players outside the United States, including China. So we went full speed ahead with producing the story.

Strickler accomplished the nearly impossible, convincing the labor unions to go on camera with their gripes about the Obama administration. And we worked for several weeks to obtain crucial visual components: undercover photographs and video of Korean workers inside the plants allegedly performing nonspecialized tasks that could be done by Americans. Nobody from the companies would agree to interviews or disclose how many Koreans they'd flown in altogether, but one had acknowledged in the local news that it had 150 of the foreign workers on site at one point, so we knew the number wasn't inconsequential.

The resulting story is a natural to be next in the series I plan to offer for *CBS This Morning*, since the first report was so popular. But when Strickler and I propose it, the broadcast takes a pass. Astonished, I push for an explanation why. I'm told it's too similar to my last story. It's an absurd notion. The previous story had recounted a litany of clean energy financial woes. This one explored the idea of foreign-owned companies benefiting from the stimulus funds, angering labor unions. The stories aren't remotely the same. There's some other dynamic at play. I'm left to wonder what.

Next, we approach the *CBS Evening News*. It's already widely understood that the current managers have a lack of interest in the investigative reporting that was once a staple of the broadcast. But this story is so powerful, we're hopeful that it will transcend that posture. Strickler hand-delivers the script to executive producer Shevlin in the New York newsroom. Afterward, Strickler calls me in Washington to report the response.

"I hardly know what to say," Strickler tells me.

Sounding perplexed, she says that Shevlin was unreceptive to the story, objecting, among other things, to the phrase "foreign workers."

"What are we supposed to call them?" I ask.

We brainstorm for a moment, wondering how use of the word *foreign* in this context could be seen as pejorative or politically incorrect. We decide that Shevlin could be looking to call the foreign workers something like 'non-American workers.'

"That's awkward. What else?" I say.

Shevlin also doesn't want us to call them "Koreans," Strickler tells me, suggesting that we go with something like "Korean nationals."

These are nitpicks that can be easily resolved.

"What's the real problem?" I ask.

Strickler says Shevlin really didn't have many suggested changes; she just hated the whole thing. She doesn't like the whole idea of the story. Shevlin feels that even if Koreans were given jobs, some Americans got jobs, too, so she doesn't think there's a story.

"Why not let people make up their own minds?" I argue rhetorically. "Some will feel the way she does; others may not. What counts is that we put the news out there and let people decide for themselves."

Strickler listens politely. But I know from experience that *Evening News* is a dead end.

Next, we offer the story to the *Weekend News*, which often draws a large audience and can be a great platform for diverse subject matter. The executive producer of that broadcast watches the video of our completed report and calls me on the phone from New York. She's effusive.

"First of all, I just want to say thank you for bringing me this story. It's *incredible*! Really brilliant! I mean, it's just so outrageous! *Weekend News* would *love* to have it."

She schedules it for that weekend. Before we hang up, she asks, "Why doesn't *Evening* want it? I mean, it's such a strong story!"

"You'll have to ask them," I say.

Apparently, she does.

A couple of days go by and nobody initiates the usual email traffic that precedes a story going on air. So I check on the status with the executive producer.

"We're going to rescreen the piece," she tells me.

Rescreen it?

That means she plans to view it again in the presence of unnamed advisors, even though she'd already watched it and said that she loved it. Again, from experience, this telegraphs a familiar signal: *somebody* doesn't want the story to air.

"Why would you rescreen it—unless you're thinking of not running it?" I ask.

On the spot, she grasps for reasons.

"It just feels a little *dated* and *old*, I mean they broke ground on these plants *months* ago."

I counter. "No, it's not old; it's current. The plants aren't even open yet. The controversy is happening now, with the unions objecting to Koreans being brought in to work. Who are on site. *Now*."

She tries another.

"It just feels a little . . . *boring.*"

I can't help but think of how excited she was after she initially viewed the piece. When did it turn dull?

"Besides," she continues, adopting the *Evening News's* line, "some Americans got jobs even if Koreans did, too. I'm just not sure there's an outrage factor."

"The point isn't to outrage viewers," I argue. "They're free to have any reaction they choose. But whatever their opinion, a huge component of our audience will find this story fascinating and something they didn't know about."

But as with all conversations of this nature that I've had in the past year or so, the executive producer's mind appears to be made up.

I call Strickler to tell her about the change in plans. She's equally puzzled. We both know this is a story of great public interest. We take the default position and publish the story on CBSNews.com. But what's behind the effort to keep it off television?

As I continue my reporting, I soon discover formidable internal opposition to the entire subject matter.

| INTERNAL OPPOSITION

"Internal opposition" can be a daunting obstacle.

In mid-2011, I'm at an airport on a shoot when my cell phone rings. On the other end of the phone is a New York assistant for our anchor, Katie Couric.

"Apparently you did a story a year ago on members of Congress and all the tax money they spent going to a junket at a climate summit in Copenhagen?" says the assistant.

"Yes," I agree.

"I need an explanation for why you included [Congresswoman]

Gabbie Giffords in the story. And what's the backstory as to why you did the story."

I don't understand the basis of the question.

"I'm not sure what you mean. I was assigned the story, and it was a good one. There's no backstory. Giffords wasn't singled out among the others. Her name was included along with the twenty congressmen who went on the trip. Why?"

"Well, Katie is trying to get the first interview with Giffords after her shooting. So I need to know the justification behind your story. Her [Giffords's] staff is still really mad about it and it's affecting Katie's chances of getting the interview."

I still don't understand how I can help. "Tell Katie just to blame me," I tell her. "Just tell them 'I have no control over what Sharyl does.'"

"Yes, but that's a little hard to do," says the assistant, "because it's Katie's face and name on the broadcast and she's managing editor. So you see, it's difficult. Apparently Giffords's opponent used a clip of your story in campaign ads and it made the election really close. Her staff is really upset."

When we hang up, I don't think she received an answer that helped her, but I'm not sure what she had expected me to say. *I'm sorry I did a truthful story and fairly included Giffords's name with all the others. It won't happen again. If you'll just give Katie this interview, there won't be any more nasty stories like that on the* CBS Evening News?

Diane Sawyer ends up with the first Giffords interview.

When it comes to green energy investigations, I conclude that the internal opposition I face has its origins in the personal beliefs of those who decide which stories go on the air and which are kept off. The purpose of the stories I propose isn't to examine the general merits or shortfalls of the technology, ideology, or movement. They're financial stories delving into possible waste, abuse, and questionable spending of tax dollars. What I didn't anticipate is that some colleagues and managers, unable to disconnect their personal viewpoints from their duty as journalists, would view this line of reporting as damaging to a cause about which they hold deep-rooted beliefs. Fearful that the stories would discourage rather than promote green energy, they want to prevent the public from seeing them at all. It's a paternalistic attitude that results in de facto censorship. Simply put: they decide that it's best for you to not hear a story at all rather than run the risk that you might see it and form the "wrong" opinion. (By that, I mean an opinion that differs from theirs.)

I turn to CBS News president David Rhodes, who had expressed interest in trying to rejuvenate the news broadcasts' interest in more original and investigative reporting. He agrees that the green energy topic is of significant public value. And though he's seen as predominantly laissez-faire in his management approach, he exerts influence in this case to encourage the *Weekend News* to run my future reports. So for a few months, we're on a serious roll.

First, it doesn't take a genius to figure out that if electric battery technology is experiencing so much difficulty, and if the demand for cars like the hybrid Chevy Volt is falling below projections, then the administration's entire electric vehicle goal could be in jeopardy. It's an important yardstick. In his January 2011 State of the Union address, President Obama had announced the objective of getting a million electric vehicles on the road by the end of 2015. And he earmarked $2.4 billion in tax dollars to help reach it.

Finding out where we stand on that continuum isn't easy. I search for records that will show how the White House projected its numbers. I find out that it counted on eleven models of electric vehicles to reach specific production figures year by year. All I need to do is compare those with the actual figures to date. Some of the automakers share their stats with me on background. For those that don't, I turn to trade publications and well-respected auto industry experts who have their fingers on the pulse of production.

What I find is that six of the eleven models either haven't made their first delivery, have stopped production, or are already out of business. Others are nowhere near the government's projections. Only one company, Tesla, is meeting or anticipates it will meet the administration's production goals. But in terms of getting to a million total by 2015, there's no way that'll happen.

For example, President Obama counted on 36,000 Fisker Karmas. But the newest projections say the reality will be closer to half that: 18,000. (In the end, as mentioned earlier, only around 1,800 were sold before the company went bankrupt.) Here's the outlook for a few others:

To reach one million electric vehicles by 2015	Original, Obama Administration Projections	New, Adjusted Projections	Fraction of Goal That Will Be Achieved	Solvent?
Chevy Volt	505,000	62,000	1/8	
Fisker Karma	36,000	1,800	1/20	Bankruptcy
Ford Transit Connect	4,200	500	12/100	Bankruptcy
Think City	57,000	263	>5/1000	Bankruptcy

Using the industry's most generous projections, I'm able to estimate that, at best, only around 300,000 electric vehicles will be on the road by the president's self-imposed deadline. Considering the $2.4 billion investment, that means American workers would be spending a total of $8,000 for each car put on the road. Meantime, the president is already pushing a plan to spend $4.7 billon more on electric vehicle incentives.

Meanwhile, my list of companies to watch is growing by the day. One dozen, then two. I circulate notes to colleagues and supervisors, updating the emerging concerns. It's clear there's a larger pattern—and billions of tax dollars are in play. I receive little direct internal feedback about my notes with the exception of sporadic comments from colleagues around the news division as well as the broader CBS corporation who say things like, *This seems like a really important story—why isn't it on* Evening News?

It's not as if we haven't dedicated ample airtime to positive clean energy coverage. We've done countless stories showcasing cool, next-generation electric vehicles; President Obama's election year appearances campaigning for green energy tax credits; and Vice President Biden announcing new clean energy ventures and touting all the jobs that will be created. Some of the stories read almost like press releases, without evoking the controversies or failures to date. One of them uncritically trumpets a "new era of green energy" featuring a government-backed solar energy project that received a $1.6 billion federal loan guarantee. There's an entire CBS News Web page called "powering the future," with uplifting stories about cutting-edge green batteries, solar power projects, the future of electric energy, and Toyota's futuristic hydrogen fuel cell cars.

There's plenty of room on the news table for these inspiring features. But surely there's also a fair place in journalism to examine other aspects, such as deficiencies in the taxpayer-funded programs. Yet too many news gatekeepers seem eager to push the positive stories and intransigent when it comes to any other kind.

A colleague provides me with this telling anecdote. *Evening News* executive producer Shevlin and a CBS News executive in New York were discussing those green energy notes I'd been circulating. Here's the account as told to me:

> **EXECUTIVE**   Attkisson's green energy stories are pretty signif-icant. . . . Maybe we should be airing some of them on *Evening News*?
> **SHEVLIN**   What's the matter, *don't you support green energy*?

The person relaying the conversation was concerned, as was I, that Shevlin appeared to be improperly judging the merit of this news story solely through the prism of her personal biases. We also felt consternation that she would use her position as gatekeeper to dismiss the story and prevent the public from hearing about it—as if it didn't exist.

Furthermore, it's preposterous to conclude that it's "anti–green energy" to question these tax investments. That's as silly as accusing a reporter of being against "medicine" because he reports on phar-maceutical company fraud, or opposing charities because he exposes a fraudulent nonprofit, or being anti-education because he covers a school shooting.

Though some view the green energy problems as a vulnerability facing Democrats, there's plenty of Republican responsibility for the deals gone bust. After all, there's bipartisan appeal to bringing federal tax dollars into local economies: politicians feel as if they're helping the folks at home by capturing a share of "free money." Sometimes, they receive campaign contributions and support from the special interests that benefit. And it can become all too conve-nient for the politicos to unquestioningly accept the positive prog-nostications.

The Obama administration promised that a solar panel maker called Abound Solar would create a thousand full-time jobs and generate "several hundred million dollars in revenue." So it received a $400 million federal loan guarantee and made the White House's list of "100 Recovery Projects That Are Changing America." Democratic backers included Senator Evan Bayh and Representatives Pete Visclosky, Baron Hill, Joe Donnelly, Brad Ellsworth, and André Carson. Republican boosters included Senator Richard Lugar and Representatives Dan Burton, Mark Souder, and Mike Pence.

But in June 2012, Abound Solar collapses—leaving behind dashed promises, toxic waste in some of its plants, and a taxpayer loss estimated at $40–60 million. It turns out that, like Beacon, the company had a dismal, junk credit rating before the administration awarded the loan guarantee. It became the third failure, after Solyndra and Beacon, in the Energy Department loan guarantee program known as "Section 1705." The green track record was beginning to look undeniably grim: more than one in seven companies that had won the enthusiastic full faith of the federal government had now gone bankrupt.

But you probably didn't hear much of this on the news. Nor did you likely hear that one of Abound's primary investors was a Democratic donor who bundled funding for President Obama's campaign. Or that emails later revealed that the White House allegedly had pushed for the Abound deal to go through even when the government's own analysts had expressed concerns about the company.

Could my judgment, and that of my producers on these stories, be exceedingly off the mark? Is this a phony scandal of interest only to anti-green energy forces? In 2013, peer judges in journalism validated the subject matter by nominating our series of reports for an investigative Emmy Award. As with *Fast and Furious* and Benghazi, this served as acknowledgment that, sometimes, the stories that meet with the most resistance are, in fact, the most significant.

| "I DID A GOOD JOB"

At a congressional hearing on March 1, 2012, Republican Paul Broun of Georgia evoked Solyndra, A123, Abound Solar, and Beacon when asking energy secretary Chu how he would grade himself on managing taxpayer investments. Chu answered that he felt he'd had a great deal of success.

"There's always room for improvement," said Chu. "Maybe an A-minus."

As 2014 dawned, Fisker's doomed battery supplier A123 had abandoned $120 million in untapped federal grant money and been bought out by a Chinese firm that renamed it B456, hoping for better days. And two Chinese companies were fighting over Fisker's scraps.

Odds are, you probably didn't hear much about any of that.

CHAPTER 4

| Benghazi |

The Unanswered Questions

It's July 29, 2013. I'm out somewhere in Northern Virginia leading my private life when a U.S. Special Forces officer approaches me unsolicited.

"We were ready," he tells me quietly, with no preface. No drama in his voice.

He assumes I know what he's referring to. And I do.

I've been approached the same way on a regular basis since I began covering the September 11, 2012, terrorist attacks on Americans in Benghazi, Libya. Approached by men affiliated with the secretive world of military Special Operations. Men who know firsthand the abilities and capabilities of our elite teams and in extremis forces—so-called Tier 1 assets.

They speak to me about the lack of an outside military rescue attempt as several dozen Americans were trapped, under attack, at a CIA annex about a mile from our unofficial embassy compound in Benghazi. Two Americans, U.S. ambassador Christopher Stevens and Information Officer Sean Smith, were already dead. Two more, former Navy SEALs Glen Doherty and Tyrone Woods, would die trying to help protect the rest of the Americans awaiting the U.S. military cavalry from outside Libya that never came.

These men who approach me won't speak on camera and can't be quoted by name. And if they say too much, they'll be arrested. They challenge the insistences made by the Obama administration, the military's top brass, and the Accountability Review Board (ARB) that nothing more could have been done to come to the rescue. They tell me there were military assets all over the place. Assets that should have been spun up and dispatched at the outset of the crisis when nobody knew how far it could spread or how long it would last—one hour? Eight? Three days?

They contend that for starters, a U.S. military plane should have gotten to Benghazi quickly and buzzed over the site. "The Libyans know that sound from the NATO missions" to oust Libyan dictator Muammar Qaddafi, says one source. "You should see 'em scatter when a plane buzzes in low! But we didn't even try."

They also tell me that every Special Forces Group (Airborne) includes an element trained for Direct Action-Counter Terrorism missions. This element is called a Combatant Commander's in-Extremis Force (CIF) company. The night of the Benghazi attacks, there was a Europe-based CIF a few hours' flight away. They had access to an AC-130 gunship. It's the same kind of plane special ops forces used to attack suspected al-Qaeda militants in Somalia and strike Taliban targets in the Afghanistan war.

But instead of being poised to respond on the anniversary of September 11, 2001, the CIF and its plane were off on a practice mission in Croatia. It's a sad irony: the CIF assaulters, breachers, and snipers were training for the very type of emergency unfolding that night but they couldn't get there. Well, at least, they *didn't* get there.

According to the Pentagon's timeline, Secretary of Defense Leon Panetta waited between two and a half and four hours before giving the order for the CIF to be ready to move. From Croatia, it's a three-hour flight to Libya on an AC-130 with several fuel options along the way. Or it's a two-hour flight to the U.S. Navy installation at Sigonella Naval Air Station in Sicily, Italy.

But according to the Pentagon's timeline, it was eighteen to twenty long hours from the time of Panetta's call until the CIF landed at Sigonella. From Sigonella, it's a relatively short five-hundred-mile hop to Benghazi, but they were far too late to help. It was all over.

Why did it take close to a full day for the CIF to pack up and fly two hours to Sigonella? No explanation is provided. But my sources say the team should have been spun up immediately, in the first uncertain moments of the attack. That they could have had the chance to reach Benghazi before Doherty and Woods were killed. In fact, these sources say the CIF should have been staged hours *before* the Benghazi attacks . . . up to eight hours earlier when a giant mob of attackers descended upon the U.S. Embassy in Egypt with attackers climbing the walls. That should've put all the wheels in motion. Even if the United States had unwisely let its guard down on September 11, 2012, the Egyptian attack should've been the wake-up call that put every possible resource on full alert, spinning up and positioning in case of trouble anywhere else in the region. But that didn't happen. Why didn't the smartest military strategists on earth see the Cairo violence as the possible beginning of a string of attacks? And when the second in the series occurred in Libya, what made them conclude there wouldn't be more in the region?

Special Operations Command deputy commander Lieutenant General John Mulholland later made a provocative statement about the CIF's movements that night. He seemed to introduce an entirely different explanation than the idea that the CIF simply couldn't get there in time. "Those forces worked as advertised, and they were in position," he tells a Special Operations conference in Washington, D.C., on November 28, 2012. "I'll leave it at that because other decisions came into play that perhaps aren't privy to [Special Operations Command]. . . . [O]ther decisions took place . . . that other commanders can speak to."

Other decisions. *What decisions?*

Obama administration officials insist there were no other decisions. Everything that could be done was done. Period. No one was ever stopped from moving. Nobody—not even a single U.S. military aircraft—could get to Benghazi over the course of eight hours.

Later, in secret closed sessions with Congress, there would be many qualifiers. General Carter Ham, the head of U.S. Africa Command (AFRICOM), would concede that assets *were* available. Just as my sources had said. But it was decided they wouldn't be used. And it was decided that a potential rescue of Americans under attack on foreign soil wasn't in line with the military's mission.

Speaking of the lull between the attacks in Benghazi, Major General Darryl Roberson, one of the principal military advisors to the president, told the House Armed Services Committee that

> the mentality of everybody was, it doesn't make sense to launch
> an F-16 now, given what we know about the situation. Now, in
> hindsight, 20/20, we know that there was another attack at 5:15
> in the morning. But again, given the environment, the circum-
> stances, what these systems are designed to do, the F-16s are not
> on a mission to respond. It is not like a fire station. We don't have
> assets to respond like a fire call, jump down the pole and respond
> for any American that is under fire anywhere in the world. That
> is not [Department of Defense's] role. Our role is to support the
> State Department, whose primary responsibility is for security of
> their mission.

Roberson acknowledged that aircraft could have buzzed the hostile crowd to try to scatter it. But that, too, was ruled out because it wasn't seen as a sure bet.

"So there is a potential you could have flown a show of force and made everyone aware that there was a fighter airborne," Roberson conceded. "Would it have changed anything? Certainly, we couldn't have gotten there before the ambassador was dead. We know that. But even if we had gotten there before the annex attack, in my experience, again, it doesn't necessarily stop the fighting, especially if they are conditioned to it. . . . And so I can't tell you if it would have been effective or not in Benghazi with a show of force."

Representative Jason Chaffetz, a Republican from Utah, responds, "And General, I guess what the shame is, we didn't even try."

These admissions in six months of closed hearings in 2013 wholly contradict the administration's public story line, which is still widely advanced to this day, with the assistance of many in the news media who frankly haven't dug deeply into the facts. After all, Benghazi is a phony, political scandal. And old news. And most members of the House Armed Services Committee are satisfied with what they hear. *Clearly*, they tell the military officers in sympathetic tones, *you did all you could. We hate to even have to be asking you these pesky questions. We thank you for your brave service*. Republicans and Democrats pat themselves on the back for their "rigorous oversight" and go home.

On May 1, 2014, yet another military general provides testimony that contradicts the Obama administration's we-did-everything-we-could-possibly-do posture. At a House Oversight Committee hearing, Retired Air Force Brigadier General Robert Lovell acknowledges to Chaffetz that there were military assets in the region but says that there was no attempt to move them.

"We had assets there in Europe. Did they actually go into the sound of the guns? Did they actually go into Benghazi?" Chaffetz asks.

"No sir, those assets did not," Lovell replies.

"Why not?"

"Basically, there was a lot of looking to the State Department for what they wanted and the deference to the Libyan people and the sense of deference to the desires of the State Department in terms of what they would like to have."

"Did they ever tell you to go save the people in Benghazi?" asks Chaffetz.

"Not to my knowledge, sir," says Lovell.

But none of this information is public yet when I begin posing my first questions to White House officials in mid-October 2012 and they push back. Hard. I'm on the phone with National Security Council spokesman Tommy Vietor and Deputy National Security Advisor (later White House chief of staff) Denis McDonough. They try to push my questions off track and won't give straight answers to most of them. And they won't provide an on-camera interview with anyone representing the administration.

On Saturday, October 20, I publish a report on *CBS This Morning* titled, "Could U.S. Military Have Helped During Libya Attack?" Although most of my sources can't appear on camera, I'm able to use their information and round out the report with additional on-camera experts.

The story says, in part:

The Pentagon says it did move a team of special operators from central Europe to the large Naval Air Station in Sigonella, Italy, but gave no other details. Sigonella is just an hour's flight from Libya. Other nearby bases include Aviano and Souda Bay. Military sources tell CBS News that resources at the three bases include fighter jets and Specter AC-130 gunships, which the sources say can be extremely effective in flying in and buzzing a crowd to disperse it. . . . Add to the controversy the fact that the last two Americans didn't die until more than six hours into the attack, and the question of U.S. military help becomes very important.

As is often the case, the Obama administration wishes to take issue with the story after refusing to provide the requested public information. The White House's Vietor begins an email exchange with me, criticizing the experts we consulted after the administration rejected our interview requests. I tell Vietor the main question remains: Why no outside military help?

"What options were considered by whom and what decisions were made for what reasons (which you guys won't say)," I ask via email. "Most of the questions I have, you folks haven't answered. . . . Would you like to reconsider putting someone on camera and answer more of these questions?"

Vietor writes back arguing that "forces were sent from Tripoli to Benghazi as reinforcements. . . . That's a relevant data point."

"How many military reinforcements were sent and what time did they arrive on site at the compound?" I ask that same question three times. Surely, Vietor knows the answers or can find them, but he doesn't budge.

"Why is the number required for you to include it?" he retorts. "I give up, Sharyl. . . . I'll work with more reasonable folks that follow up, I guess."

That remark makes me recall Vietor's colleague, Eric Schultz, telling me during *Fast and Furious*, "Goddammit it, Sharyl! The *Washington Post* is reasonable, the *L.A. Times* is reasonable, the *New York Times* is reasonable, *you're the only one who's not reasonable!*"

Maybe I'm on to something here, too.

The White House isn't filling in the blanks as to the commander in chief's actions that night so I have to brainstorm other ways to get pieces of that information. My mind turns to the White House photo office. Your tax dollars pay to have a professional photographer cover most every aspect of the president's work life. The positive images may be tweeted, posted, and sometimes autographed by the president

himself and sent as souvenirs to those who appear in them. Remember the dramatic picture taken in the White House Situation Room
during the successful raid on Osama bin Laden? It depicts the president and his top advisors as they watched the drama unfold in real
time. They're concerned. They're engaged. From the standpoint of
the administration, it's great publicity. But not all of the photos taken
by the White House photo office are released to the public.

Absent real information, I'm left to theorize. A photograph like
the one taken during the bin Laden raid might have been taken
during the Benghazi attacks. If not an image of the president in the
Situation Room, there might be images taken in other White House
locations. And they might give some insight into what the president
was or wasn't doing at what time.

For a few minutes, I try to think like a politician. There was a
time during the attacks before anybody knew that Stevens was
dead. When the administration might have thought there could be
a "hero moment." And, just in case the night would end positively,
and with the presidential election campaign in full force, wouldn't
this administration—wouldn't any administration—want to have a
photograph memorializing the president and his advisors on the job?
Concerned and engaged as the United States falls under attack in
Libya as they mounted the rescue effort?

Getting such a photograph from the White House photo office,
if it exists, should be easy. At least in a nonpolitical world. And when
my producer Kim first calls on November 1, 2012, and asks for all
photos taken that night, the office promises an answer by day's end.
But two months later, we still hadn't heard back. The White House
photo office ended up saying it needed permission from press officer
Josh Earnest at the White House, who never returned a single of our
phone calls or emails. No matter how many times we called the photo
office and explained that Earnest was nonresponsive, the photo office

would just send us back to Earnest, who wouldn't return our calls. (I'm pretty sure nobody's ever explained to him that he works for the public.)

My communications with the White House aren't much more fruitful when we discuss some issues to be raised in my next story.

"Why wasn't the Counterterrorism Security Group convened during the attacks?" I ask. Sources have told me that presidential directive requires the interagency Counterterrorism Security Group (CSG) to be convened in the event of a possible terrorist act. The CSG is made up of designated experts on coordinating assets and responses, the ones deemed best suited to brief agency leaders on what's possible and what's advisable. My sources tell me the CSG inexplicably wasn't called upon during the Benghazi attacks.

"What moron is pushing this?" Vietor shoots back when I ask the question. "They don't know what they're talking about."

He goes on to tell me that my information on the CSG "conjures up antiquated notions" and is "fake, a misimpression." He says the CSG wasn't needed because the principals were already engaged at a higher level and had access to all the advisors who make up the CSG. He says the CSG was used differently under the Bush administration, but now things have changed. Under Obama, the group is considered to be more policy analysts than emergency advisors.

Vietor will neither confirm nor deny whether the White House violated a presidential directive by the decision not to convene the CSG experts as a group. But considering the night's tragic outcome, it makes sense to ask whether the CSG might have been able to provide helpful information and advice. Or an outcome that was less tragic.

I move on to another topic.

"Why wasn't the FEST team deployed?"

FEST is short for Foreign Emergency Support Team, which is billed as "the U.S. government's only interagency, on-call, short-notice team poised to respond to terrorist incidents worldwide." Its members have hostage-negotiating expertise, something that it seems could have been potentially useful when U.S. Ambassador Stevens was reported missing shortly after the launch of the first attack.

To my surprise, Vietor and Deputy National Security Advisor McDonough indicate they haven't heard of FEST before. They also seem befuddled by my questions as to the status of "Tier 1 assets" and "in extremis" forces. Nonetheless, Vietor implies I'm the one who's ill-informed.

"I don't know what [FEST] is," he barks dismissively. "It sounds like a bogus, made-up effort. It's antiquated. . . . You're coming to me with low-level antiquated information . . . it's a fake story."

Moron. Bogus. Fake. Phony. The same kinds of words administration officials used to try to discredit *Fast and Furious.* Before they were forced to admit it was true. To me, this song has a similar tone and timbre. Their words and arguments aren't based in facts. They sound like petulant middle school kids.

Oh yeah!!?? Who says!?

After our phone conversation, Vietor asks around and gets briefed on FEST—he learns that, yes, it does exist—and he follows up with me the next day. But now he contends the team, based in the United States, wouldn't have gotten to Benghazi in time to help. Of course, since nobody knew at the start how long the crisis would last, it doesn't explain why FEST wasn't sent in the beginning.

Vietor doesn't see FEST as the on-call, short-notice team with hostage-negotiating expertise poised to respond to terrorist incidents worldwide, as the team is described on the government's website. The website also states FEST "has deployed to over 20 countries since its inception in 1986, [and] leaves for an incident site within four hours of notification, providing the fastest assistance possible." Apparently, Vietor has his own unique and much more limited definition of FEST as logistical experts "used in the past to re-establish infrastructure, communications, etc. after a devastating attack. . . . That wasn't the need here."

This is at sharp odds with FEST's own view of its training and mission. In fact, I later learn from an Obama administration source that FEST team members "instinctively started packing" as soon as they heard of the Benghazi attacks but that Undersecretary of State Patrick Kennedy advised against sending them. They wanted to go, but weren't allowed.

We also later learn in testimony from the Accountability Review Board that nobody from the administration tried to get air clearance from Libya for a rescue attempt. Nobody asked NATO for assistance. (The review board's Admiral Mike Mullen said there was "zero" likelihood that NATO could have responded, but I wonder who decided not to try to clear the way for all options—since the president said he had ordered officials to take all necessary actions.)

All of this information contributes to a report I publish on November 2, 2012. It states, in part:

> Without the Counterterrorism Security Group being convened, as required by presidential directive, the response to the crisis became "more confused."
>
> The FBI received a call during the attack representing Secretary of State Hillary Clinton asking for agents be deployed but the FBI agreed it "would not make any difference without security and other enablers to get them in the country and synch their efforts with military and diplomatic efforts to maximize their success."
>
> A hostage rescue team was alternately asked to get ready and then stand down throughout the night, as officials seemed unable to make up their minds.

A counterterror force official stationed in Europe said components of AFRICOM were working on a course of action but no plan was put to use.

"Forces were positioned after the fact but not much good to those that needed it," according to a military source.

"The response process was isolated at the most senior level," says an official referring to top officials in the executive branch. "My fellow counterterrorism professionals and I [were] not consulted."

The story is factually indisputable, with all opinions clearly sourced. But when it's published, Vietor fires off a lengthy email complaint calling the article "fundamentally inaccurate." He copies my bureau chief Chris Isham, as well as CBS News president David Rhodes and Rhodes's brother Ben. Ben Rhodes is a top national security advisor to President Obama. Also copied on the email are Pentagon spokesman George Little, secretary of state spokesman Philippe Reines, and Paul Bresson. (I don't know Bresson, but there's a Paul Bresson listed as an employee at the FBI's Terrorist Screening Center.) I do know Reines. He's a longtime Clinton confidant considered to be quite the character. About a month earlier, when reporter Michael Hastings had persisted with questions about Benghazi that were similar to mine, Reines emailed him to "have a good day. And by good day, I mean Fuck Off." Reines and other Clinton advocates would later form a Washington PR firm called Beacon Global Strategies. The same firm would hire CIA deputy director Mike Morell, who defended Clinton's State Department and bucked his own CIA boss, Director David Petraeus, in their internal dispute over the Benghazi talking points.

In his November 2012 email to me, Vietor repeats that the Counterterrorism Security Group didn't need to be convened because higher-level officials met, including "Denis McDonough, John Brennan, [Vice Chairman of the Joint Chiefs of Staff James] Winnefeld, [and] Deputy Secretary of State Bill Burns . . . And the notion that the individuals I listed and others in these meetings don't have decades of experience working these issues is wrong."

The thing is, the "notion" with which Vietor takes umbrage appears nowhere in my story. Nobody claims that he and his colleagues lack "decades of experience." But despite that experience, neither Vietor nor McDonough apparently knew FEST existed when I first asked them about it. And after they got briefed, they had a mistaken interpretation of its capabilities, as well as the Counterterrorism Security Group's mandate, according to some of the men who actually serve on and supervise the teams. Sometimes decades of experience don't add up to all that much.

Vietor's email complaint recommends that my report be "pulled down" from the Web "until the facts are corrected." Of course, since the story is entirely accurate, it remains on the Web and no correction is warranted.

I reply to Vietor via email: "I would point out that I included all of your on the record comments to me in my story and I would also repeat my request for an on-camera interview should you decide to provide someone from the administration to address these issues further."

After all the stonewalling, it borders on humorous when, at a press conference two weeks later, on November 14, 2012, President Obama incorrectly tells reporters that his administration has provided all information regarding what happened in Benghazi.

"We have provided every bit of information that we have," Mr. Obama tells reporters.

Does the president simply think that if he says it, people who don't know better will be convinced? Or is he disconnected—misled by his staff into thinking all the questions have been answered? From my perspective, very few answers or documents have been given. Some were still dribbling out for the first time in 2014 as a result of a Freedom of Information lawsuit the conservative watchdog group JudicialWatch filed against the State Department.

In January 2013, I'm still seeking answers. The trajectory of this story seems to be following a course similar to *Fast and Furious*. The administration has deflected attention from its missteps by declaring the Benghazi story a scandal manufactured by Republicans for political purposes. Many in the media adopt the narrative and lose interest. The stories they do publish are often written as political reports without a thorough examination of what I consider key apolitical issues at heart.

I send a list of my unanswered questions in an email to Vietor to jog his memory. In case he's forgotten.

What were the President's actions that night?

What time was Ambassador Stevens' body recovered, what are the known details surrounding his disappearance and death including where he/his body was taken/found/transported and by whom?

Who made the decision not to convene the Counterterrorism Security Group (CSG) the night of the Benghazi attacks?

We understand that convening the CSG is a protocol under Presidential directive (NSPD-46). Is that true? If not, please explain. If so, why was the protocol not followed?

Is the administration revising the applicable Presidential directive? If so, please explain.

Who is the highest-ranking official who was aware of pre-911 security requests from U.S. personnel in Libya?

Who is/are the official(s) responsible for removing reference to al-Qaeda from the original CIA notes?

Was the President aware of General David Petraeus' potential [sexual scandal] problems prior to Thursday, November 8, 2012? What was the earliest that any White House official was aware? Please provide details.

What is your response to the President stating that on September 12, he called 9/11 a terrorist attack in light of his CBS interview on that date in which he answered that it was too early to know whether it was a terrorist attack?

Is anyone being held accountable for having no resources close enough to reach this high-threat area within 8+ hours on September 11 and has the administration taken steps to have resources available sooner in case of emergency in the future?

A Benghazi victim's family member stated that Mrs. Clinton told him she would find and arrest whoever made the anti-Islam video. Is this accurate? If so, what was Mrs. Clinton's understanding at the time of what would be the grounds for arrest?

If true, what is the administration's view regarding other videos or future materials that it may wish were not published, but are legal?

What is the administration's criteria in general for requesting removal of a YouTube or other Internet video?

Vietor, like Josh Earnest, apparently hasn't been given the you-serve-the-public talk, either. He replies to me that he has no intention of giving answers unless I "correct all the stories about how we didn't act fast enough to send troops to Benghazi when the [State Department's Accountability Review Board] clearly said it wasn't possible."

"Our stories were entirely accurate and no correction is warranted," I answer.

I then point out that the law doesn't permit him to hold public information hostage to his demands for a certain behavior on the part of the media.

"[T]he info I'm asking for is public information, and you guys work for the public. We pay your salaries."

"Thanks for paying my salary," Vietor replies. "Your stories were terrible, misleading and did a disservice to all who read them."

"Tommy, we're not looking for thanks. We're looking for the information that we own that you're keeping secret. Politicians, government employees and their staff are not entitled to limiting the release of public information only when they like reporters or stories."

"Thanks for the note," writes Vietor. "I thoroughly reject your rationale for the response. I would point you to the [Accountability Review Board] report and hours upon hours of testimony for your answers."

Of course, the answers to my questions aren't in the Accountability Review Board's report or the "hours upon hours of testimony."

It's spring 2014. An impeccable source who cannot go on camera tells me that Special Operators from the Commander's in-Extremis Force (CIF) were launched on a C-130 airframe and headed toward Benghazi during the attacks. They traveled for about an hour before having to turn around and return to base. A second aircraft attempted to depart, but the pilot was late arriving and an argument ensued between the pilot and U.S. Special Operations Command Africa Commander Brigadier General James B. Linder. The general wanted an immediate departure but the pilot was objecting to gear that was being loaded. The pilot was concerned that the equipment had a lot of hazardous and unstable material. Apparently the pilot refused for long enough that the second aircraft never actually departed before the mission was canceled.

The administration has repeatedly denied that any such happenings occurred.

It's another day. I'm somewhere out of state living my private life when another source affiliated with Special Forces approaches me. "We should've gone in to help," he tells me. "We *could* have. We were ready. Someone at the highest level stopped us."

| DYING FOR SECURITY

The entire Benghazi debacle begins with security threats ignored and security requests denied. But for me, the story begins three weeks after September 11, 2012.

Our correspondents have already broken some major news. There's a feeling that much is yet to be uncovered. On the morning of Wednesday, October 3, I walk into the Washington, D.C., bureau newsroom and drop my bag near an empty desk and computer. The senior producer for *Evening News* is on a telephone conference call. He spots me and puts the call on mute.

"Pick up, they're talking about you," he says.

I join the call. The subject is the Benghazi story. On the phone are CBS News journalists conferencing in from New York, Washington, D.C., and London who are already working various angles. They share the latest about what they know and review the unknowns, inconsistencies, and controversies. The head of the CBS News investigative team in New York, Len Tepper, suggests I join in and see what I can dig up.

Rumors are circulating that the State Department denied the U.S. diplomats in Libya security they requested leading up to the brutal attacks. But there's no proof. The witnesses and survivors are being kept secreted away. Nobody has seen or heard from them in public. It's as if a strangely tight clamp is being kept on the information and people who hold the truth.

I start reading up on the public info and calling my contacts and sources. Two days later, I'm lucky to connect with the man who would provide the biggest break in the story to date: Lieutenant Colonel Andrew Wood. When I first contact him, Wood is in the middle of nowhere in Utah working in his civilian job to keep the nation's dams secure from terrorist threats. Cell phone coverage is spotty. He tells me he'll call back later.

I'm reaching out to Wood because my sources tell me that he led the last U.S. military security team in Libya. One that left just a month before September 11. What's the story behind his team's withdrawal? What was the security profile before and during the attacks? Most important, will he talk about any of this with me off or on camera?

Wood is a patriotic, mild-mannered Mormon family man. A longtime M-day soldier in the Utah National Guard. *M-day* is slang—short for "man day," meaning he serves normal Guard duty one weekend a month and two weeks a year. But he's no ordinary M-day soldier. He has thirty years of Special Forces experience: a highly decorated officer with expert training in counterterrorism. He wouldn't blink if he needed to crush an enemy's throat to save an American life. His National Guard duty has taken him on assignment in Afghanistan near the Pakistan border as part of Operation Enduring Freedom (2003–2004) and on a dangerous counterterrorism deployment in the Philippines (2006–2007).

In the Philippines in 2006, Wood's expertise was applied to the insurgency and terrorism that have dominated the southern region for years. Terrorists exploit the area as a transitional route for entry into the United States and elsewhere. Planning for the September 11, 2001, attacks on the World Trade Center was conducted against the glorious backdrop of the Philippines' coral-filled ocean and tropical forests. In fact, shortly after 9/11, President George W. Bush quickly opened a second front in the War on Terror in the Philippines. When Wood and his hundred-member team of specialists arrived on the volcanic island of Jolo in the Sulu province, it was ground zero for the Muslim extremist violence. They joined five thousand Filipino marines and soldiers in Operation Ultimatum, targeting an Islamic separatist movement linked to al-Qaeda called Abu Sayyaf. The Abu Sayyaf fighters proved to be proficient in the deadly arts of improvised explosive devices, bombings, and kidnappings. In 2006 and 2007, they murdered 53 people and injured 270. They're also suspected in the November 2007 bombing of the Philippine House of Representatives, which killed a local congressman and four staffers. Wood's men trained Filipino forces how to sniff out roadside bombs and take on the bad guys themselves. By February 2007, Jolo was deemed to be clear of terrorists.

Five years later, on February 12, 2012, Wood hit the ground in Tripoli, Libya, to be the commander of a sixteen-member counterterrorism military team put into place a few months before. The element was a joint force primarily made up of senior noncommissioned officers from Army Special Operations and Navy SEALs. His arrival rounded out a thirty-four-member elite security contingent that also included three U.S. State Department six-man SWAT-style Mobile Security Deployment teams.

I'm still waiting for Wood to call me back from Utah after he finishes the day's fieldwork. Hours pass and I'm worrying that I might not hear back from him, when my cell phone finally rings. It's Wood. He tells me he's seen the news reports about Benghazi and heard a lot of speculation. He says that much of what the government is saying simply isn't true. He's grown increasingly agitated as no one steps forward to correct the information and fill in the blanks. I can tell he's eager for the truth to be told, even though he's not terribly eager to be its public face.

He agrees to talk to me about his assignment—and what went wrong. It's Friday and there's a sense of urgency for me to check out his story and, if warranted, get him on camera. If I've managed to locate him, other reporters can't be far behind. If I try to fly out to him in Utah, it's a day out and a day back with a day in the middle for the actual sit-down interview. The travel would cost me valuable research time on a fast-moving story. It would also require me to find a good camera crew in Utah. Getting that ball rolling late on a Friday night isn't ideal. My regular producer, Kim, would normally help, but it just so happens that she's off.

But I have an idea. If Wood will come to Washington, D.C., I can continue my research while he flies. I can easily get a camera crew here. So I check flights from Utah, run the idea by him, and he agrees to fly to D.C. the next morning. Next, I book him a hotel room close to his airport in Utah so that he can get an early flight out with no worries about battling traffic. Putting him in a hotel also gets him away from his house, where other reporters might otherwise be able to find him. Meanwhile, I work to check him out further. In addition to my own reliable sources, the Pentagon verifies Wood's identity to our military correspondent David Martin, and one of our foreign correspondents happens to know Wood from a previous assignment overseas. He's the real deal. By Sunday morning, Wood and I are sitting down in the CBS bureau in Washington, D.C., for a one-on-one interview.

"My assignment there was to command what they call SST, or Site Security Team, to assist the State Department with security in Libya," Wood tells me. "It was a military organization put together to assist [the State Department] in their ability to reestablish the embassy after it was evacuated during the revolution."

This SST is a unique arrangement, with the military loaning forces to help the State Department mission on the ground. The United States had abandoned its embassy in Tripoli just a year earlier at the start of the uprising against Qaddafi's regime. Pro-Qaddafi forces obliterated the embassy to retaliate for a NATO bombing that killed Qaddafi's son. With the bad guys officially "out," the State Department was anxious to cut through the chaos and normalize the post-Qaddafi relationship between the United States and Libya. Wood and his team were part of the effort to help make sure no Americans died in the process. They were tasked with supporting whatever the State Department regional security officer needed, whether it was help right there on the embassy compound in Tripoli or mobile security for travel by the principal officers and the ambassador himself. It was a flexible assignment that changed day to day, which made it both exciting and dangerous. And it demanded a heavy dose of knowledge about terrorism.

Wood had a nagging sense of déjà vu. As in Afghanistan and the Philippines, Libya was suffering under an unstable and deteriorating security situation. Terrorists and antigovernment forces had found a firm foothold among the disorganization and chaos. There was potential danger around every corner.

Many Libyans appreciated the fact that Americans were there. Others did not. The Americans never knew exactly how the locals would react. For Wood and his team traveling between neighborhoods, they could run into the same friendly guys for four days and then, on the fifth, have one of them point a loaded pistol at their head. It took a lot of diplomacy just to move about. It took a lot of explaining about who they were and why they were there.

Wood didn't know it at the time, but a major terrorist plot had been thwarted in December 2011, not long before his arrival. It was a chilling foreshadowing of the September 11 attacks. In what was called Operation Papa Noel, pro-Qaddafi elements had planned to launch a sophisticated attack on foreign diplomatic missions and oil fields in Libya. Fortunately, the plot was exposed when several insurgents responsible for the planning were arrested before it was executed. Some details were later disclosed in the written emergency-evacuation plan for the U.S. mission in Benghazi, which warned, "the majority of Loyalist insurgents tasked with carrying out this plan are still active and free in Benghazi" and "Islamic terrorist elements do exist in this area of the country, and have been reported by open sources to be gaining operational capability." Islamic terrorist elements . . . gaining operational capability.

The current security status in Libya was precarious at best, in Wood's view. There were no organized services and there was no real government infrastructure. No police on the street, no trash pickup. Litter was strewn everywhere. The lights didn't work. In an attempt to instill some sense of safety and order, civilians had established their own neighborhood watches. Most any Libyan man with a gun could form a self-standing militia. And plenty of them were wary of Americans.

Partnering with Wood in the security mission was Regional Security Officer Eric Nordstrom, who requested additional security help from headquarters in March 2012, but got no response. It was becoming clear to everyone on the ground that as things grew more dangerous, they were going to have to do more with less.

On April 10, an explosive device is thrown at a convoy traveling in Benghazi carrying United Nations envoy Ian Martin. On May 22, a rocket-propelled grenade (RPG) hits the Benghazi offices of the International Red Cross and the agency decides to pull out. As the incidents pile up, they become more troublesome. They're dissected, documented, and digested into reports sent regularly to State Department headquarters. Hundreds of pages. Week in and week out. There can be no doubt about the dangers in Libya. The security officers live with persistent concern. What's the threat to the ambassador? To the embassy staff? To themselves? It's work day and night. If they're awake, they're on duty. If they're asleep, they're on call.

Even more alarming, in an online posting, al-Qaeda had stated its intent to attack the Red Cross, the British, and then the Americans in Benghazi. With the first two promises fulfilled, the attack on Benghazi was the last outstanding threat. It seemed just a matter of time.

"This isn't Afghanistan or Iraq," the State Department's Charlene Lamb at headquarters in Washington would tell the Libya contingent.

The guys on the ground were made to feel as if they were being melodramatic, maybe even a little cowardly in asking for more resources to protect the U.S. mission and its diplomats. Wood couldn't believe the disconnect. How little the bureaucrats in D.C. understood about the reality that he and the rest of the Americans were living in Libya. A disintegrating country that, in some respects, *was* as dangerous as Afghanistan. He knows because he's been there, too. Washington seemed to have no concept of prevention. It was all about reacting.

Nordstrom later testifies before the House Oversight Committee, "It was abundantly clear we were not going to get resources until the aftermath of an incident. . . . The question that we would ask is, again, 'How thin does the ice have to get before someone falls through?' "

Even before Ambassador Stevens's time, the warning signs were clear. In 2009, Gene Cretz became the first U.S. ambassador to Libya in more than thirty years. He had to be temporarily pulled in December 2010 after embarrassing documents posted on WikiLeaks recounted Cretz describing Qaddafi's fear of flying over water, and Qaddafi's proclivities, which included a "fondness for flamenco dancing" and reliance on a "voluptuous blonde" Ukrainian nurse. When Cretz returned to Tripoli in 2011, he knew the security situation was perilous. Al-Qaeda was in town to exploit Libya's unsettled status and to try to obtain some of the thousands of missing MANPADS (man-portable air-defense systems): shoulder-fired missiles seized by rebel forces that stormed Qaddafi government bases. Cretz realized there were seriously dangerous tensions among anti-Qaddafi factions: Islamists and secularists. "I think there is a genuine cause to be concerned that things could go wrong," he told reporters. It was a premonition.

Ambassador Cretz was the first U.S. diplomat in Libya to be faced with the prospect of relinquishing much-needed security. The State Department pulled one of its six-man Mobile Security Deployment teams. Cretz gave up the team begrudgingly and not without objection. Then, in April 2012, he was chosen to be the next ambassador to Ghana and Stevens was picked to replace him.

"Was Ambassador Stevens one of your primary concerns?" I ask Wood.

"Yes he was. As the chief of mission he was the primary concern there as far as security is concerned. He's a man that has to get out and see and be seen. So that makes security difficult. And it makes it extraordinarily difficult in an environment such as Tripoli and the rest of Libya."

Stevens had already served as the deputy chief of mission from 2007 until the start of 2009, during a period when there was no U.S. ambassador. Later, during the Libyan revolution in 2011, he was appointed to be America's special representative to the National Transitional Council, the anti-Qaddafi rebel government headquartered in Benghazi. His friends say this is when Stevens developed a deep affection for Benghazi.

Almost from the moment he became ambassador, Stevens spoke of his desire to revisit Benghazi, where he had forged many friendships and relationships the year before. It was a top priority. In some respects, Benghazi was home for Stevens, at least when it came to his comfort zone in North Africa.

Wood and Stevens developed a fast friendship. They ate dinner together almost every night and became close confidants. They talked a lot about the diminishing security and how to overcome it. Stevens wasn't one of those diplomats to stay holed up in the office even if it's dangerous in the field. A big part of his job was to be seen out in public. Interact with the locals. To visit local stores, run at the local track, portray a sense of confidence in the community. Never let them know about the private concerns discussed with the security specialists at the embassy. About cables quietly dispatched to headquarters documenting the threatening environment and making the case for better security. The public face has to be confidence and smiles. That's an ambassador's mission. And nobody did it better than Stevens.

At one point, the U.S. State Department's regional security officer in Libya, Nordstrom, asked for a dozen additional security agents, and he says the State Department's regional director told him, "You're asking for the sun, moon, and the stars." Nordstrom replied, "You know what makes it most frustrating about this assignment? It's not the hardships, it's not the gunfire, it's not the threats. It's dealing and fighting against the people, programs, and personnel who are supposed to be supporting me. . . . For me, the Taliban is on the inside of the building."

Not only was Nordstrom's request for additional help refused, but headquarters also broke the news to Stevens that he'd be losing a second Mobile Security Deployment team.

"Did Ambassador Stevens or the regional security officer fight losing another team?" I ask Wood.

"Yes."

"How did they do that?"

"It was quite a degree of frustration on their part," Wood says. "They were, I guess you would say, clenched-fist over the whole issue."

Meanwhile, Stevens planned to visit Benghazi in June but the trip never came to fruition. On June 6, an improvised explosive device detonated just outside the Benghazi consulate compound. June also saw an al-Qaeda demonstration right smack in the middle of Benghazi. The terrorists advertised out in the open in advance: a three-day rally for all their supporters.

"A rally for al-Qaeda supporters out in public?" I ask Wood incredulously when he explains this to me. The last I'd heard, al-Qaeda was "on the run." President Obama said so.

"Oh yes," Wood says. "They had a parade down the streets. They raised their flag on one of the county buildings. And people came from different parts of Libya as well as outside of Libya for that event."

Wood tells me that many Libyans do not support al-Qaeda and made sure the terrorist group didn't feel welcome for the rally. "The people of Benghazi themselves surrounded that crowd and told them of their disgust for that type of thing and shut down the operation. They had one day of a three-day rally and they were pushed out of town."

"On the other hand," I ask, "isn't that sort of a red flag for the security situation that you have al-Qaeda supporters rallying in the streets of Benghazi in June of 2012?"

"Yes, that was another indicator to watch, to be aware of, and to try to compensate for as well."

Then, on June 11, a rocket-propelled grenade hit a convoy carrying the British ambassador in Benghazi. Wood happened to be in the city when the assault occurred.

"I was there to perform some additional work for the defense attaché in receiving some equipment for the Libyan army," Wood says. Within minutes of the attack, he and other U.S. personnel were called upon to help. "We received a request from the security people in Tripoli stating that [the British ambassador] had been attacked and [they] asked us to go for assistance, which we responded to immediately. They had a security officer injured severely and we got over there as quickly as we could."

After the attack, the United Kingdom decided Benghazi was too dangerous and closed its consulate there. But the United States stayed in place and continued its security drawdown. Not only a reduction in men with a very specific set of skills but also an important piece of equipment: a DC-3 fixed-wing prop plane that had been reengineered to play a security and support role. The DC-3 was used for resupply trips around the Mediterranean and offered a way for U.S. personnel to travel between Tripoli and Benghazi on short notice in the span of a little more than an hour. It transported all kinds of equipment, including weapons that can't be taken on commercial flights.

"For security personnel, that was a great asset," Wood says. But on May 3, Stevens was copied on an email from the State Department's Libya post management officer. It said that Undersecretary of State Kennedy "determined that support for Embassy Tripoli using the DC-3 will be terminated immediately."

"It was a loss again. It was 'okay, now how are we going to compensate for this?' Again, sub-optimizing to do the same thing you were trying with less resources," says Wood.

Despite the multiple warnings about the dangerous circumstances in Benghazi, Kennedy later testifies that it just wasn't enough to trigger alarm bells at the highest levels. Not the foiled terrorist plot in December 2011 and the warning that Islamic terrorist elements are gaining operational capability in the Benghazi region. Not the April 10 IED attack on the UN envoy's convoy in Benghazi. Not the May 22, 2012, RPG attack on the Benghazi offices of the Red Cross. Not the June 6 IED explosion just outside the U.S. compound in Benghazi, nor the June al-Qaeda rally in the streets of Benghazi, nor the June 11 RPG attack on the British ambassador in Benghazi. The Red Cross pulls out. The United Kingdom closes its consulate. One wonders what it would have taken to trigger alarm bells at headquarters.

"We had no actionable intelligence . . . about this threat in Benghazi," Kennedy testified a year later before Congress. "And therefore . . . I never went to the secretary of state and told her it was time to leave Benghazi."

Two months before the attacks, on July 9, Stevens sent a cable asking headquarters to keep Wood's sixteen-man military team and retain the last Mobile Security Deployment team at least through mid-September. His request said that benchmarks for a drawdown had not been met. However, the teams were not extended.

"We were fighting a losing battle," Wood says. "We were not even allowed to keep what we had."

State Department officials would later blame the Defense Department when asked why Wood's team wasn't allowed to stay. But Wood says that's patently untrue. His team was on loan from U.S. Africa Command, commanded by General Ham.

"There was a great understanding reached where General Ham made Ambassador Cretz fully aware that as long as he needed Site Security Team or the security force from [the Department of Defense], he could have them there," Wood tells me.

"You were told that?" I ask.

"Absolutely, yes," Wood answers.

"By whom?"

"General Ham. I heard him on a number of occasions, personally as well as across videoconferencing."

"So there was no pressure from the military to pull your team out?"

"No, none whatsoever."

On August 2, six weeks before Stevens died, he made still another security request of headquarters. This one was for "protective detail bodyguard positions," to "fill the vacuum of security personnel currently at post who will be leaving within the next month and will not be replaced." He called the security condition in Libya "unpredictable, volatile and violent." On August 8, as Wood's special Site Security Team terminated its duty, Stevens dispatched yet another cable telling headquarters that "a series of violent incidents has dominated the political landscape," and calling them "targeted and discriminate attacks."

As he departed Libya, Wood was haunted by a lingering discomfort. He knew he was leaving behind embassy staffers—friends and colleagues—who were worried about their own safety. "I didn't feel good about it. They asked if [they] were safe. They asked what was going to happen. And I could only answer that what we were being told is that [State Department headquarters is] working on it."

On August 27, the State Department issued a travel warning for Libya, citing the threat of assassinations and car bombings in Benghazi and Tripoli. Then, when Stevens embarked upon his trip to Benghazi in September, he was guarded by two rookie Diplomatic Security guards who joined three already at the U.S. compound in Benghazi. They're not military forces. They're not counterterrorism experts. On September 11—the last day the ambassador was to awake on earth—he sent headquarters a weekly report that, in part, described Libyans' "growing frustration with police and security forces . . . too weak to keep the country secure." The agents guarding him didn't even have their weapons and gear with them when they fell under attack. They had to rush to a storage area to retrieve their M-4 carbine assault riles after the terrorists used diesel fuel to set the compound on fire. The agents never fired a shot in defense. All of this confounds Wood.

"*We* slept with our rifles," he says of the contrast between his own team's standard operating procedure and that of the Diplomatic Security guards left to protect Stevens. "You never separated yourself from your weapon."

Later, in a classified Senate hearing in December 2012, Kennedy is repeatedly challenged on the question of why no defense shots were fired.

"Were there orders for them not to shoot?" asks Senator Dianne Feinstein, a Democrat from California.

"No," testifies Kennedy. There were no such orders. They just didn't shoot.

Maybe there was no point. Maybe all they could do was to hide as best they could. They were so far outnumbered. The enemy swarmed the compound like bees.

The administration seemed pleased with how the closed hearing had gone. When the hearing adjourned, a CIA representative and State Department official who had been inside were practically "high-fiving," says one observer present, "like they had pulled something over on the committee."

In defending the substandard security, State Department officials would incorrectly tell reporters and Congress that even if Wood's military team had been allowed to remain in Libya, it was tied to Tripoli and would never have been located in Benghazi to help. "It would not have made any difference in Benghazi," Charlene Lamb, deputy secretary for Diplomatic Security, tells Congress on October 10, 2012.

Could it be that Lamb and other officials at State Department headquarters are ignorant of the plain facts even as they testify to Congress? Or are they using misinformation to spin? The truth is that Wood and his team members *did* travel to Benghazi for their official duties. Anyone who bothered to ask could have found that out. Heck, anyone who saw my recent interview with Wood knew it. Remember, he was in Benghazi when the British convoy was attacked and he helped with the rescue. He also planned to include members of his team on Stevens's trip to Benghazi in June, had it not been postponed. "It was a security marathon, if you will, to encompass or try to provide security for that type of a movement," Wood tells me. Wood describes other instances in which his team members went to Benghazi to protect a top U.S. diplomat. "At times there [was] a need for us to go out to Benghazi to perform those same static as well as mobile security functions for the principal officer that was out there. . . . So twice I sent [Site Security Team] members out there to support the security functions there," Wood says.

With so many security questions, administration officials engage in their predictable strategy of deflection. State Department officials who don't want to be quoted by name begin whispering to reporters that Stevens was partly at fault for his own demise. They imply he was a renegade. "I'm not even sure we knew he was going to Benghazi. Why would he go there on 9/11?" one official asks me rhetorically, quickly adding, "That's not for attribution." They also claim that Stevens had the final say-so in matters of his own security in Libya. Of course, if that's true, then why did the State Department not grant his security requests? But State Department sources spread this spin to so many reporters that it's repeated back to me with similar wording by a number of colleagues. They wander into my office or strike up a casual conversation and ask, *Why would Stevens choose to go to Benghazi on 9/11? . . . I hear he was kind of a renegade. . . . I'm not even sure the State Department knew he was going to Benghazi. . . . You know, he was in charge of his own security and had final say.* Others who knew Stevens bristle at the whispers and implications, telling me it's the worst kind of violation to blame a dead man, who can never tell his own story.

The State Department's Accountability Review Board continues to lay the groundwork for blaming Stevens in its December 2012 report. It says that Stevens's "status as the leading U.S. government advocate on Libya policy, and his expertise on Benghazi in particular, caused Washington to give *unusual deference to his judgments*" (emphasis added). The clear implication is that Stevens's misfortune was somehow a product of his own miscalculation or poor judgment. That the professionals in Washington deferred to his wishes and didn't know any better. But it can't be both true that Washington deferred to Stevens and that Washington also rejected his security requests. We know factually that the latter is true; so the former simply cannot be.

The Accountability Review Board also implies that Stevens was acting as a freelancer in arranging his schedule without the knowledge of headquarters or even his colleagues in Tripoli. "The

Board found that Ambassador Stevens made the decision to travel to Benghazi independently of Washington, per standard practice," reads the report. "Plans for the Ambassador's trip . . . were not shared thoroughly with the Embassy's country team, who were not fully aware of planned movements off compound."

I note that the wording in the report uses a lot of qualifiers. It attempts to imply one thing but, if examined, may say quite another. When it comes to Washington politicians, investigations by appointed boards, and other such matters, I've learned that you have to carefully consider every word they choose. Often, lawyers and politicians construct phrasing that may be technically and legally defensible but is intentionally misleading. So what does the Accountability Review Board's report *really* say? What does it leave unsaid? What can one discover reading between the lines?

FROM THE REPORT   "The Board found that Ambassador Stevens *made the decision* to travel to Benghazi independently of Washington."

ANALYSIS   This sentence implies that Stevens was acting on his own. But a careful reading leaves open the possibility that headquarters was well aware of his travel.

FROM THE REPORT   "Plans for the Ambassador's trip . . . were not shared *thoroughly* with the Embassy's country team. . . ."

ANALYSIS   This implies Stevens kept his plans secret. However, it really seems to indicate the plans *were* shared with the embassy's country team, just not "thoroughly" shared, whatever that means.

FROM THE REPORT "[The embassy's country team members] were not *fully* aware of planned movements off compound."

ANALYSIS This implies Stevens didn't tell his colleagues about his plans off the compound. But in actuality, it seems to indicate they *were* aware, just not "fully" aware, whatever that means. Additionally, the supposed lack of knowledge about Stevens's "planned movements off compound" is irrelevant since he was *inside* the compound when attacked. But perhaps it's included to add to the implication that Stevens wasn't keeping his colleagues clued in.

Later, Stevens's number two, Gregory Hicks, tells me that Stevens did not secretively freelance his own schedule: quite the opposite. Hicks says that Stevens's daily plans were routinely circulated within the State Department. Specifically, his planned travel to Benghazi was shared with headquarters via email several weeks in advance of the visit and in regular staffing reports during the trip. Headquarters "knew Chris was going to Benghazi for five days during a gap between principal officers until Benghazi's new principal officer arrived," Hicks tells me with certainty.

I'm not even sure we knew he was going to Benghazi, State Department officials had told reporters.

On a difficult assignment in Libya, Stevens wasn't the kind to whine or complain when his security requests were denied. Given the choice to go to Benghazi with the protection he had or not go at all, he would always have chosen the former. To sit behind the relative safety of the walls of the posh embassy in Tripoli would be no kind of job for a guy like him. It wouldn't be a job worth having.

Stevens served only three short months as the U.S. ambassador to Libya before being murdered by terrorist thugs.

On February 26, 2013, President Obama meets with a small group of senators at the White House and makes a brief reference to Stevens's presence in Benghazi on September 11. "We screwed up," Mr. Obama reportedly tells the lawmakers. "Chris shouldn't have been there."

| THE LIGHT SWITCHES OFF

There's a saying some of us have: The news broadcasts are in *love* with a story, until the day they aren't.

This refers to the mysterious popularity cycle many stories seem to follow. Developments on the same story may air night after night with the lead producers wanting more, More, *MORE*. So you keep digging. You work your sources. You get plugged in. Day and night. Then one day you come to work and they don't want to hear it anymore. Like a light switch. Like you entered an alternate universe where they would never be interested in such a story. They look at you as if to say, *Why are you still talking about this?* From that point on, it can be a mighty battle to convince the broadcasts to air a development, even when it's more significant than developments they aired just a few days before. In the other universe. Back when they were giddy over the story.

I can't fully explain it; I can only tell you this is how it is. As the correspondent, you never really know why the interest falls off. Maybe a bigger story emerges. Maybe viewer feedback indicates the audience has tired of the subject. Maybe the White House and Democrats' phone calls, emails, and blogs are taking a toll. You don't ask and the bosses don't explain. This is just part of the job.

But if you're me, you keep pitching developments because the good ol' University of Florida–trained journalist in you doesn't allow herself to be steered away from a legitimate story that's still unfolding. Your job is to keep following the leads no matter where they go. It's what I'm trained to do.

For that reason, I suppose, two of my former *CBS Evening News* executive producers have independently referred to me as a "pit bull." Jim Murphy was first to use the metaphor and I wasn't quite sure initially whether he meant it as a compliment or insult. When one of Murphy's successors, Rick Kaplan, also called me a pit bull, I settled on the idea that it was a compliment. (Why not?) Once a pit bull chews into something, it doesn't let go. I think one of the shortfalls of journalists is our short attention span. Our tendency to cover a story, get stonewalled, and quickly move on to an easier target. We also lack follow-through. We raise questions and don't stick with the story long enough to find the answers. Chewing in and not letting go—as long as there's more meat—is what I love to do most.

Yet when you keep pitching a story they've grown tired of, it makes them uncomfortable. Colleagues say, *Why don't you just move on? You're wasting your time. You know they don't want that story anymore.* You get the feeling that some of the managing producers are thinking, *Why can't you just make it easy on us and shut up?* They don't *say* that. But you can tell by the way they act. They don't want to know what you've learned. They argue against the story without knowing the facts. Or they may say they *love* the story but there's just no time for it in the broadcast. There's that big weather story we have to cover. And more fires out west. You get the picture. They're dug in and not going to change their mind.

A personal favorite is the attempt to squelch by labeling all new developments "incremental." As in, *the story you're offering is just an incremental development.* Or *it's too incremental.* I first heard the term used in this context just a few years ago. Once a managing producer uttered it, it really caught on and it seemed everyone began to parrot it. Like the first time an executive said a story was "a bridge too far." Pretty soon, all the senior producers around him were saying every story development they didn't want was "a bridge too far." Everybody's got their own. NBC talks about stories not having "enough uplift," as in they're not positive enough. I was originally so stumped by the application of the term *incremental* that I looked it up in the dictionary. *Incremental* simply means an increase or decrease in a series on a fixed scale. What's wrong with reporting a story development that's incremental? If I can advance a story by reporting a development that's 50 percent better each time, in fixed increments, isn't that a good thing? But what these producers are really trying to imply—however inartfully—is that the development is too small or meaningless to merit a place in the broadcast. I found the word used in this context by broadcast producers dating as far back as January 15, 1994, in a story about how long it took the networks to begin covering the Clinton Whitewater scandal. In the article, an *NBC Nightly News* executive producer was quoted as using two of my favorite catchphrases often invoked to stop a story: "piling on" and "incremental." In covering Whitewater, the producer stated that, "The caution for us is to make sure we are not piling on . . . not just another incremental nag." Today we routinely hear "incremental" and "piling on" invoked as excuses for stories they really don't want, even as we observe that developments on stories that they like are aired in the tiniest of increments. The phrase would rear its head again as I covered HealthCare.gov.

When this happens, I continue publishing online, where the thirst for great stories is insatiable and space is, thankfully, unlimited. There are always niche followers who will seek out the material online that they can't find anywhere else.

The height of popularity for the Benghazi story inside CBS is when I get Colonel Wood on camera in October 2012. But even then, not everybody is happy. I happen to be in New York City, where I've just picked up an investigative Emmy for *Fast and Furious*. It's the first New York visit that my producer on the Benghazi story, Kim, has made with me. She quite correctly detects that she's getting the cold shoulder from New York colleagues she's never met before. I'm getting it, too. I tell her I call it the Big Freeze and not to worry. There's no point in trying to figure it out; their response isn't logic based. It's visceral. Having worked at CBS for nearly twenty years, I tell Kim that there are groups of people who are so ideologically entrenched, they literally see you as the enemy if you do stories that contradict their personal beliefs. They may not even consciously understand why it is that they hate you—and I do mean hate—but they do. "It has nothing to do with you," I explain to Kim. "They don't like you because you work with me." She thinks it's crazy. I'm used to it.

Through mid-October, I and my CBS News colleagues in Washington, D.C., including Jan Crawford, Margaret Brennan, and David Martin, break a number of important stories. So do our foreign correspondents. But as things look worse for the Obama administration and the election draws near in late October, the light switch turns off. Most of my Benghazi stories from that point on would be reported not on television, but on the Web.

| DYING FOR THE TRUTH

In the early days after the Benghazi attacks, high-ranking Obama administration officials seem to be on the very same page. But it's a page pulled from a work of fiction.

First, here's the nonfiction version.

Americans on the ground in Libya believed from the outset that it was an act of terror. And Libyan officials immediately concluded that it was terrorism. A State Department Operations Center alert issued mid-attack stated that the al-Qaeda–linked "Ansar al-Sharia Claims Responsibility for Benghazi Attack." The first interagency talking points read " . . . Islamic extremists with ties to al-Qaeda participated in the attack."

But before any of that information became public, the Obama administration painted a very different picture.

White House spokesman Carney doesn't refer to the attacks as "terrorism" in briefing reporters on September 12. President Obama also avoids the t-word when speaking in the Rose Garden the same day. He calls what happened "an outrageous and shocking attack," "senseless violence," and "brutal acts" but never possibly the work of terrorists. He refers to the assailants as "killers" and "attackers." Only when he segues to evoking the World Trade Center attacks does the president use the phrase "acts of terror."

As luck would have it, *60 Minutes* correspondent Steve Kroft is at the White House on this day for a previously scheduled interview and asks the president about his wording on Benghazi.

> **STEVE KROFT** Mr. President, this morning you went out of your way to avoid the use of the word *terrorism* in connection with the Libya attack.
>
> **PRESIDENT OBAMA** Right.
>
> **STEVE KROFT** Do you believe that this was a terrorist attack?
>
> **PRESIDENT OBAMA** Well, it's too early to know exactly how this came about, what group was involved, but obviously it was an attack on Americans.

That brief part of the interview isn't big news at the time and doesn't even make the air on CBS News. But weeks later, there's a reason to take another look at it when President Obama is debating the Republican candidate for president, Mitt Romney. In that debate on October 16, Mr. Obama claims that in the Rose Garden on September 12, he definitively called Benghazi an act of terror.

Remember, that's not what he said in the interview with Kroft. *Too early to know.*

Then there's Secretary of State Clinton. Like Carney and President Obama, she avoids calling Benghazi a "terrorist act" in her September 11 public statement, her September 12 public statement and her September 14 speech at the ceremonial return of the bodies of the four American victims. Instead, she refers to it as an "attack." "Assault." "Rage and violence . . . over an awful Internet video." She refers to the terrorist attackers as "thugs," "killers," and a "mob." The only nod she gives to the notion that it might be something different is when she quotes a foreign official who called the event "an act of ugly terror."

But administration officials being on the same page means a lot more than just tiptoeing around use of the word *terrorism*. They also steer public attention toward the idea that an anti-Muslim YouTube video turned ordinary protesters into violent attackers. "Some have sought to justify this vicious behavior as a response to inflammatory material posted on the Internet," Clinton says the night of the attack. "The United States deplores any intentional effort to denigrate the religious beliefs of others."

Family members of two victims say that Clinton and other administration officials personally consoled them at the return of the bodies by saying, *We'll find whoever made that awful video.* Why focus the families' attention on the producer of a perfectly legal video instead of the actual killers? Why not instead say, *We'll find whoever killed your loved one?*

Meantime, the Sunday political talk shows were just a few days away and on September 13, the White House asks Clinton to take the hot seat and make the TV appearances. She has zero interest. One source tells me: "She'd rather chew tin foil." So it's decided the job of appearing on television will be assigned to the U.S. ambassador to the UN, Susan Rice.

On Sunday, September 16, Rice makes the rounds on TV and seems to be on the same page as Carney, the president, and Clinton.

On *Face the Nation with Bob Schieffer*, even when she follows an appearance by a Libyan official who declares that the Benghazi attacks were "preplanned" and many of those arrested are linked to al-Qaeda and its affiliates, Rice sticks firmly to her own talking points, which differ. She says the attacks were "spontaneously" inspired by protests at the U.S. Embassy in Cairo.

It's still unclear as to how an untrue story about protesters and a YouTube video grows to such prominence in the Obama administration's initial narrative. But we do now know the genesis of Rice's infamous talking points. Shortly after CIA director Petraeus gave a classified briefing on September 14 to the House Intelligence Committee, the lead Democrat on the panel, Maryland's Dutch Ruppersberger, asked, "What can I say on TV"? Later, an administration source says to me, "How cynical is that? All he cares about is what he can say on the campaign trail." In his defense, Ruppersberger said he simply wanted clarity on what material was classified and what could be shared with inquisitive constituents. In any event, Ruppersberger's question got the ball rolling.

There's interagency disagreement over how much should be disclosed. Should the public really be told about suspicions of terrorism? Is it wise to let Americans hear that the CIA had issued warnings in advance? As the various agencies duke it out, Mr. Obama's deputy national security advisor Ben Rhodes intervenes and emails that there will be a deputies' meeting the next morning, on September 15, to work out the issues. One official involved later tells me, "That's polite code for 'let's not debate this on email for eighteen hours.'" After the Saturday morning meeting, the talking points emerge drastically reduced and finessed. (As mentioned earlier, Ben Rhodes is the brother of CBS News president David Rhodes.)

Four days after Rice's Sunday talk show appearances, on September 20, a team of Obama administration officials agrees to brief the House and Senate in closed sessions with the freshest information. There, Director of National Intelligence James Clapper removes any doubt as to the origin of the assaults and tells members of Congress that Benghazi "had all the earmarks of a premeditated attack." No longer is it peddled as "spontaneous." Upon hearing this news, Senator John McCain, a Republican from Arizona, storms out of the room while Senator Lindsey Graham of South Carolina utters an expletive to a colleague sitting next to him. They feel they'd been misled until this point. An Obama administration official who was present later calls this moment a turning point. "Something just snapped. [Senators] started yelling and screaming, 'Why did Susan [Rice] lie?' . . . Susan was done."

Meanwhile, another controversy is waiting to boil over within the Obama administration: a sex scandal involving the CIA's Petraeus. The timing is—intriguing. Only after the Benghazi attacks, as Petraeus's loyalty to the administration falls into question, does everything turn sour for the spy chief.

In the immediate aftermath of the Benghazi attacks, Petraeus first draws ire from some administration colleagues for not reading from the Carney-Obama-Clinton-Rice book of fiction. While *they're* pushing the spontaneous protest narrative, *he's* disclosing full information on the suspected al-Qaeda links to House Intelligence Committee members at a classified briefing, according to those present. Then the talking points his agency approves for public dissemination on September 14 say that the CIA provided warnings on September 10 that the U.S. Embassy in Cairo, Egypt, could come under attack and that Benghazi was in a precarious state. Clinton's state department sees the inclusion of that damning information in the CIA's original proposed talking points as a "knee-jerk cover-your-ass moment" on Petraeus's part. One official later tells me, "We thought, *Why are you guys [Petraeus's CIA] throwing us under the bus? . . .* They made it seem like the State Department was given a warning they ignored. [But] no specific warning was given."

Emails indicate that on September 15, 2012, a CIA representative sent Petraeus the final version of the talking points that had been revised "through the Deputies Committee" after "State voiced strong concerns with the original text." The CIA's references to terrorism and early warnings had been removed.

Petraeus expresses disapproval of the final version, writing that he assumes that they not be used. But his deputy, Morell, and the White House give them the green light.

Is all of this the beginning of the end of Petraeus's career as CIA director?

Let's look at a timeline constructed primarily using government accounts:

In November 2011, Petraeus, who's married, allegedly begins an affair with his biographer, Paula Broadwell.

The following summer, of 2012, the FBI discovers the affair and FBI director Robert Mueller is notified on a date the government won't disclose. Also, at some point, the FBI interviews Petraeus and Broadwell and concludes national security hasn't been breached. But the FBI continues investigating whether Petraeus had any involvement in sending harassing emails to a third party.

In late summer, on a date the government won't reveal, Attorney General Eric Holder is notified of Petraeus's troubles. Supposedly, the White House is kept in the dark. Apparently, Holder doesn't think President Obama needs to know that one of his top cabinet-level officials is under FBI investigation (not to mention part of a potential sex scandal). No one starts developing a strategy in the event the Petraeus scandal blows up before the election. And, we're to believe, not a soul worries that President Obama could get hit with a surprise question about Petraeus on the campaign trail.

Odd.

Then comes September 11.

Some Obama administration officials become frustrated if not downright angry with Petraeus and his post-attack behavior. His deputy, Morell, is given authority over the talking point edits and sides with the State Department against Petraeus's desires. In late October, as Petraeus's interagency relationships become increasingly strained over Benghazi, some FBI agents suddenly reach out to Republicans in Congress to disclose Petraeus's dirty laundry. They eventually land at the office of Republican majority leader Eric Cantor. About that same time, the week of October 29, the FBI interviews Petraeus and Broadwell a second time.

Now, normally in Washington, D.C., this would be about the time the scandal goes viral. Republican leaders, alerted to a sensitive issue that they could argue has national security implications, could be expected to at least leak to the press. Especially with less than two weeks to go until the presidential election.

But strangely enough, that doesn't happen. On October 31, in a move that seems to defy everything that defines Washington, the chief of staff for Congressman Cantor keeps publicly mum about the administration's burgeoning scandal and instead confidentially contacts the FBI's chief of staff about the Petraeus rumors. Even with the news having reached the president's most ardent political opponents and with the election just a week away, the entire White House is still, somehow, for some reason, uninformed.

Fast-forward a week to November 6, the day of the election. Someone at the Justice Department, we're told, has finally decided to tell Director of National Intelligence Clapper about Petraeus. (How good of a chief intelligence officer are you if you don't know the head of the CIA has been under investigation by your FBI for months? And Republicans on the Hill know before you do?) Clapper calls Petraeus the same day and urges him to resign. It's a stark reversal of the FBI's pre-Benghazi determination that there was no harm in Petraeus staying on the job.

On Wednesday, November 7, according to the government's accounts, somebody finally notifies the White House about all of the above. And when is the president himself finally looped in? Not until Thursday, November 8, say officials. The president accepts Petraeus's resignation on Friday, November 9.

If President Obama was indeed kept out of the loop regarding one of his most important political appointees, it adds to the perceptions created during *Fast and Furious* when the president and his staff say they had no idea that a federal agency conducted a cross-border weapons operation that helped arm killer cartels in a foreign country. It adds to an image evoked after the Benghazi attacks when the president directed his staff to do everything they could, but didn't speak to Libyan officials or personally keep in close touch with the secretary of defense. It builds upon the theme when the president said he didn't know his own spy agency was monitoring friendly world leaders, and when his people insisted Obamacare was ready—only to have the website crash on opening day.

Then again, the timing of Petraeus's departure could be purely coincidental. Maybe it had nothing to do with his supposed disloyalty to the administration after Benghazi. But one thing is certain: his inelegant and abrupt exit from the CIA ended the interagency resentments that he sparked in the aftermath of Benghazi. As for Petraeus's insight into all of this? He's not talking.

Though the administration and its supporters would repeat the mantra time and time again that the accusations were solely generated by politically motivated, conspiratorially minded, witch-hunting Republicans, the truth is that most of the damaging information came from Obama admnistration insiders. From government documents. From sources who were outraged by their own government's behavior and what they viewed as a cover-up. From loyal Obama administration officials who testified truthfully under oath. From the State Department's own employees. From military officials and rank-and-file.

Some of them were self-described Obama and Clinton support-ers. One relayed to me how he had enthusiastically contributed to Obama's first presidential campaign.

But all that was before Benghazi.

| MORE ON THE TALKING POINTS CONFUSION

Shortly after the talking points were constructed, there seemed to be endless secrecy and confusion surrounding them. But eighteen months later, called to a congressional hearing on the topic, former CIA deputy director Morell seems to have grown amazingly clear on the whole thing. Though he hadn't offered up the information early on, he now tells Congress that *he* was the primary editing force be-hind the talking points. And that there were no political motivations behind removal of references to terrorism and prior warnings given to the State Department. *That's just the stuff of conspiracy theorists and right-wing crazies.*

As I watch the testimony, my head spins with all the inconsisten-cies. I open the mental filing cabinet storing what's been said over the many months and can't help but notice that much of it doesn't match up with what Morell is saying today. Today, he's so bent on convincing Congress and the public that he, alone, made the substan-tive changes in the talking points, and that no politics were involved, that he's in the awkward position of defending his mistaken reliance on bad intelligence as if he would do it all again the same way. Bet-ter for the false narrative to have been the result of poor intelligence analysis than politics.

The reason Morell is brought before the House Intelligence Com-mittee is to answer for evidence unearthed in subpoenaed documents allegedly indicating he misled members of Congress by withholding what he knew about the genesis of the talking points.

First, he has to explain an email he received on September 15, 2012, from his own station chief on the ground in Libya stating that the attacks were "not an escalation of a protest" over a YouTube video. Morell says he and his Washington analysts disregarded the information as unreliable and didn't pass it along to other agencies.

"I did not hide nor did I downplay the station chief's comments as some have suggested, in fact I did the opposite," Morell said.

Next, we finally learn the answer to the simple but much-dodged question: *Who removed references to al-Qaeda from the talking points*? Morell now says it was the CIA. Not him, personally, but "[t]he group of officers from our office of Congressional affairs and our office of public affairs." (Previously, when I had reported the involvement of federal public affairs officials in editing the talking points, based on documents and my sources, government officials had vehemently denied the fact.)

Morell tells Congress it was his decision to remove the word *Islamic* from the phrase *Islamic extremists* and says he did it for two reasons: so as not to further inflame passions in the Islamic world and because "what other kind of extremists are there in Libya?"

Morell also explained that he opposed his boss, Petraeus, and removed language disclosing that the CIA had provided "warnings" in advance of the attacks.

"I thought it was an effort on the CIA's part to make it look like we had warned and shift any blame to the State Department," Morell testifies. "I made a decision at that moment I got the talking points I was going to take the . . . language out." I wonder why Morell was calling the shots, subordinate to his boss. I wonder why he seemed to be watching out for the best interests of Clinton's State Department over his own agency, the CIA.

As the hearing closes, I review the evolution of the talking points narrative.

On Friday, November 16, 2012, Petraeus had told members of Congress that it wasn't the CIA that revised the talking points. And another CIA official told reporters that the edits were made at a "senior level in the interagency process" so as not to tip off al-Qaeda as to what the United States knew, and to protect sources and methods. Soon thereafter, another reason was given. A source from the Office of the Director for National Intelligence (ODNI) said that office made the edits as part of the interagency process because the links to al-Qaeda were deemed too "tenuous" to make public. Then, later in November 2012, Morell provided yet another account in a meeting with Republican senators John McCain, Lindsey Graham, and Kelly Ayotte: he said it was the FBI that removed the references "to prevent compromising an ongoing criminal investigation."

But it was just a matter of hours before there was yet another revision. A CIA official contacted Graham and stated that Morell "misspoke" in the earlier meeting and that it was, in fact, the CIA, not the FBI, that deleted the al-Qaeda references.

Morell is so clear today on his recollection that changed the talking points. Why was he so unclear right after it all happened?

| HISTORY REPEATING?

The Accountability Review Board's investigative report on Benghazi begins with a quote attributed to Spanish philosopher George Santayana in 1905.

Those who cannot remember the past are condemned to repeat it.

The inclusion of the quote is ironic because, in some ways, history *has* repeated itself with Benghazi. Back in 1998, there was another tragic story of embassy security requested and denied. Lack of money was blamed. An Accountability Review Board was convened. It made recommendations to prevent something similar from happening again.

But it did happen again.

In 1998, Clinton was in the White House as first lady. And who was at State Department headquarters? None other than Susan Rice, Patrick Kennedy, and their boss, Ambassador Thomas Pickering, future head of the Benghazi Accountability Review Board, where he will be tasked with impartially investigating his longtime friends and former colleagues.

In 1998, the terrorist targets were U.S. embassies in Nairobi, Kenya, and Dar es Salaam, Tanzania. Two hundred twenty-four people, including twelve Americans, were killed by car bombers and more than five thousand were injured. The U.S. ambassador to Kenya, Prudence Bushnell, was among those hurt. Bushnell had warned eight months before that security at her embassy was inadequate. Twice she requested a new building.

"Unfortunately, we lacked the money to respond," Kennedy explained to reporters at State Department headquarters in the immediate aftermath in 1998. "[O]ther embassy projects had a higher priority than Embassy Nairobi for our limited funds. We just did not have the funds to meet all our needs."

As with Libya, the State Department also had declined the U.S. military's offer of assistance in Kenya. Kennedy told reporters that months before the East Africa bombings, "the U.S. military Central Command expressed to the Department its concern over the vulnerability of the Nairobi chancellory," and was also worried that "the embassy was close to the street at a busy intersection." The military offered to do a survey of the embassy but "the [State] Department . . . declined the offer of the military to send one of their teams, because we had already scheduled a security assessment team to visit the post in March of this year," said Kennedy.

The spring before the bombings, Bushnell tried to sound alarm bells at State Department headquarters as Stevens later did in Libya. She fired off an emergency cable to Secretary of State Madeleine Albright. It said that resource constraints "were endangering embassy personnel" and "expressed concern about crime, administrative matters and safety." State Department headquarters replied that "a new building was ranked low in relative priority, compared to the needs of other embassies."

| TWO QUOTES

On January 23, 2013, Secretary of State Clinton appears before the Senate Foreign Relations Committee and takes fire from Republicans on the Benghazi issue. Senator Ron Johnson, a Republican from Wisconsin, is probing Clinton's initial blame of the YouTube video. Clinton gets testy and makes a statement that may haunt her for some time.

"With all due respect," responds Clinton, raising her voice and appearing angry, "the fact that we had four dead Americans, was it because of a protest or was it because of guys out for a walk one night who decided that they'd go kill some Americans? . . . What difference at this point does it make? It is our job to figure out what happened and do everything we can to prevent it from ever happening again, Senator."

What difference at this point does it make?

To me, as a journalist, it certainly makes a difference. For one reason, it makes a difference if it turns out that anyone in the administration intentionally deceived the American public. And there are clues that point in that general direction. It also makes a difference if Benghazi was a well-planned attack long in the making amid warnings from Americans on the ground: it makes the poor security decisions even more egregious. Furthermore, as I listen to Clinton at the hearing, I can't help but think that she's continuing to pose scenarios in her controversial, passionate response that never happened. And she knows it. The Benghazi attacks were neither "because of a protest" nor were they the result of "guys out for a walk last night who decided to kill some Americans." Why is she still evoking those spontaneous images when there have now been official acknowledgments that it was a preplanned terrorist attack that required a great deal of coordination and practice? From knowing when and where the ambassador would be, to the incredibly skilled mortar hits that landed on the CIA annex—too precise to be lucky or spontaneous.

Kennedy likewise seems out of touch with the public when he testifies to Congress on September 18, 2013, a year and one week after the attacks. When pressed by Representative Ted Poe, a Republican from Texas, Kennedy acknowledges Benghazi was the work of terrorists. But, as if reading from the same page as Clinton, he indicates it doesn't really matter.

"I know that this was a terrorist attack and it doesn't matter to me whether it was Ansar al-Sharia or al-Qaeda or whoever," Kennedy testifies before the House Committee on Foreign Affairs. "These were terrorists and whatever organization they belong to, they are enemies of the United States and they must be brought to justice.

Republican Adam Kinzinger of Illinois replies, "I think it does matter . . . because ultimately, it gives us a blueprint on who we need to kill or capture, which I think is very important and I hope that's done."

| MRS. CLINTON'S BENGHAZI CHAPTER

Earlier, I described the propaganda strategies employed by the powers that be to shape public opinion. Astroturf tactics. Controversializing stories and those who report them. Use of trademark catchphrases.

No power or political party holds a monopoly on these techniques. But Clinton's use of them in the case of Benghazi is instructive.

In a June 18, 2014, interview with Greta Van Susteren of FOX News, Clinton said that her own assessment of the Benghazi attacks "careened from the video had something to do with it, the video had nothing to do with it . . . I was trying to make sense of it." She also spoke of being confused in the "fog of war," a phrase that Obama officials first evoked in the weeks after the attacks—and often repeated—to help explain why it didn't mount an outside military rescue of the trapped Americans that night.

The thing is, there's little sense of "careening" assessments or the "fog of war" in the documentary evidence recorded at the time.

It was the night of September 11, 2012, and at 5:55 p.m. Eastern time, while the attacks were still under way, a State Department email included a report that "the extremist group Ansar Al Sharia ha[d] taken credit" and U.S. officials had asked Libyan officials to pursue the faction. A few minutes later, an alert from Clinton's State Department Operations Center stated that the U.S. Embassy in Tripoli also reported that the Islamic military group Ansar al-Sharia had claimed responsibility and called for an attack on the embassy in Tripoli.

But four hours later, in her first public statement on the attacks at 10:07 p.m., Clinton spoke of none of that. She did, for the first time, introduce the connection to the video.

"Some have sought to justify this vicious behavior as a response to inflammatory material posted on the Internet," Clinton's statement reported. "The United States deplores any intentional effort to denigrate the religious beliefs of others. Our commitment to religious tolerance goes back to the very beginning of our nation."

If Clinton wasn't part of an effort to steer the narrative, then why didn't she report that terrorists *might* be involved, as many behind the scenes had already concluded? Or at least say what the administration has so vigorously claimed since: that there was wild uncertainty? Or that assessments were—foggy? And if they *were* so foggy, then why was she careful not to evoke terrorism—yet quick to finger the video?

We later discovered that President Obama telephoned Clinton during the attacks around the time that she issued the statement. White House spokesman Carney had, in the past, declined to answer whether that call came before or after. The obvious question is: Did the president and Clinton consult over her statement blaming the video?

Twenty-one months later, in an interview with FOX News anchor Bret Baier, Clinton was fuzzy on details and, apparently, hadn't bothered to refresh herself on them even though she had just authored a new book that included a whole chapter about Benghazi—which is why she was now giving interviews.

Baier found Clinton vague when he asked about the timing of her statement and the president's call.

"The statement went out, you know, I don't know the exact time, it, my recollection is it went out before [the call with the president]," Clinton said. And she wouldn't give a yes or no when asked whether they discussed the video: a fact she surely should know considering the controversy over that very issue.

"I don't know that I talked about it with him at that conversation," Clinton said.

Documents revealed in spring of 2014 cast further doubt on Clinton's description of fogginess. In a State Department email the morning after the attack, her then-assistant secretary of state Beth Jones told Libya's ambassador that "the group that conducted the attacks—Ansar Al Sharia—is affiliated with Islamic extremists." Period.

In a September 20, 2012, appearance on Univision, with Congress and the media chipping away at the video narrative, President Obama seemed to take a stab at blending ideas: retaining the video story but merging it with one that matched more closely with the terrorism reality.

"What we do know is that the natural protests that arose because of the outrage over the video were used as an excuse by extremists to see if they can also directly harm U.S. interests," Mr. Obama said.

The same day, there was a new spin from Carney who told the press that there was no reason to *say* there was a terrorist attack because everyone *knew* that, silly!

"It is, I think, self-evident that what happened in Benghazi was a terrorist attack. Our embassy was attacked violently, and the result was four deaths of American officials. So, again, that's self-evident," said Carney.

Except, perhaps, to Clinton, who says she was careening.

Carney's remark reminds me of a comment Morell made in April 2014 when he finally admitted to Congress that he removed the word *Islamic* from the phrase *Islamic extremists*. He did it not to obfuscate, he told Congress, but because, "what other kind of extremists are there in Libya?" *Everyone knows that. We don't have to* say *it.*

And on September 25, a full two weeks after the attacks, the president addressed the U.N. General Assembly and continued to refer to "killers" rather than "terrorists," evoking the "crude and disgusting video" that "sparked outrage throughout the Muslim world."

Why was the conversation with the American public so starkly different than the one taking place behind the scenes—the accurate one—unless the narrative was being seriously manipulated?

Clinton now freely embraces in her book what she and the White House so carefully avoided saying in those early days. In fact, she's decided to own it, if one can glean anything from the first sentence in her Benghazi chapter: the American victims, she writes, "were killed in a terrorist attack." It's almost as if she wants to convince us that she said so all along. In what looks like a striking attempt to rewrite her post-Benghazi narrative and speeches, Clinton goes heavy in her book on recounting instances in which she used terms such as "heavily armed militants," "violent attackers," or "extremists," but she conveniently omits how she repeatedly pointed to the YouTube video.

For example, she writes in her book that on September 12, "I laid out the facts as we knew them" to the press corps, reporting that "heavily armed militants" had assaulted the compounds. She fails to mention that, for the second day in a row, she pointed to the video. Same with the statement she made on September 13 when she appeared with Morocco's foreign minister. Same with the statement she made on September 14 when she met with the victims' families at Andrews Air Force Base.

Of that meeting, Clinton writes in her book, "All you can do is offer a human touch, a kind word, a gentle embrace." She leaves out the part about her speech at that same event in which she stated, "We've seen rage and violence directed at American embassies over an awful Internet video that we had nothing to do with." And she doesn't address the reports from victims' family members who said that Clinton privately promised them that she would hunt down the maker of the YouTube video—never mentioning that she intended to hunt down the terrorists who actually killed their loved ones.

With the passage of time and the release of more facts and documents, Clinton appears to be evolving her position from "the attackers were motivated by an awful, disgusting YouTube video" to "the video *played a role.*"

Clinton writes in her book, "I know there are some who don't want to hear that an internet video played a role" in the September 11 upheaval in the Mideast, such as the attacks on the U.S. embassy in Cairo. She says it "would have been strange not to consider . . . that [the video] might have had the same effect [in Benghazi], too. That's just common sense."

The problem with that defense is that, at the time, Clinton hadn't set forth the video scenario as "commonsense" musings. She falsely portrayed it as a fact, as if exclusive to the scenario of preplanned terrorism. We now know that this was contrary to the facts she and other Obama officials had in hand and contrary to what her own representatives were privately telling Libyan officials.

In her book, Clinton employs other techniques to deflect. She ridicules those pursuing unanswered questions as "fixated on chasing conspiracy theories." It's similar to the way in which Democrats reject allegations about the IRS's targeting conservative groups and the conveniently missing emails as "conspiracy theories." They seem to think that evoking the word *conspiracy* will lead some voters to dismiss the concerns. They controversialize the legitimate reporting of their self-generated controversies by using the language of propagandists.

Throughout her Benghazi chapter, Clinton inadvertently highlights contradictory characterizations that the Obama administration has switched between, depending upon which was needed for expediency.

For example, the administration advanced the narrative that it couldn't have predicted the Benghazi attacks. (That was to explain why it denied security requests and had no military help accessible.) Yet Clinton also argues that they were vigilantly prepared. (That was so as not to appear to be out of touch with the well-documented dangers.)

To be specific, Obama officials have stated that there was no reason to put the military on special alert on the 9/11 anniversary because there had never been a repeat attack on that date. But in her book, Clinton states that, prior to the Benghazi attacks, the 9/11 anniversary added a "potentially combustible element" that "like every year . . . prompted our intelligence and security officials to proceed with extra caution."

We're left to wonder what extra caution was supposedly exercised, since examples are lacking. Stevens and his team weren't granted the extra security that they said was necessary. Nobody dissuaded him from making the trip to Benghazi on September 11. The military says nobody was on a short leash for quick action the night of the assaults and that no assets were in place. And even when the assault on the U.S. Embassy in Cairo foreshadowed the Benghazi attacks, nobody seemed to "proceed with extra caution" to evacuate the Benghazi staff. Everything about the scenario seemed to telegraph a lack of extra caution.

Two more opposing narratives involve the administration originally indicating that it believed the attacks were going to be short-lived (to explain why they decided not to deploy outside military rescue teams at the outset), while Clinton claims, in her book, that they expected the violence to continue and spread (to give the impression that they were on top of it).

To be specific, Clinton writes that, during the Benghazi attacks, "I did not believe this crisis was over. We could expect more unrest to come." She says she warned Libya's president not to "assume the threat had passed . . . We also had to get ready for the possibility of other assaults elsewhere. We had to assume and plan for the worst—the possibility of further attacks against U.S. interests in the region."

If the administration anticipated an indefinite spate of attacks and violence, as Clinton states, then why did they conversely argue there was no point in spinning up military resources because they "couldn't get there in time"?

Further, Clinton seems to contradict her own assertion that they expected additional unrest when she writes that there was no point sending special operations forces standing by in Fort Bragg, North Carolina, because that they would take several hours to muster and were more than five thousand miles away. Why wouldn't one go ahead and muster them if they were truly assuming and planning for the worst, and if the administration were doing everything possible (as the president says he had ordered)?

Regarding the talking points used by Ambassador Rice— Clinton appears to attempt to revise the facts by stating something that simply isn't the case:

"The extensive public record now makes clear that Susan was using information that originated with and was approved by the CIA."

In my opinion, that's just plain wrong.

In fact, the "extensive public record" indicates that then-head of the CIA Petraeus expressed great disapproval of the talking points Rice used. Also, the "extensive public record" shows that White House officials and the State Department had significant input into editing the talking points into their final, scrubbed version.

Perhaps the most glaring section of Clinton's Benghazi chapter that deserves analysis is the analogy she applies to those investigating Benghazi.

"If somebody breaks into your home and takes your family hostage," she writes, "how much time are you going to spend focused on how the intruder spent his day as opposed to how best to rescue your loved ones and then prevent it from happening again?"

It strikes me that she and other administration officials who went to a great deal of effort to steer the public toward a false narrative now are spending equal effort asking why the narrative matters at all.

To expand on Clinton's clumsy analogy, one might counter that:

If somebody breaks into your home and takes your family hostage, are you going to decide, somehow in advance, that the hostage rescue team can't get there in time so there's no point in trying? And if there are policemen in the next neighborhood who want to help, are you going to order them to stay put to protect the neighbors instead of helping the family that's in danger now?

The fact is, the controversies over Benghazi don't surround questions about how the terrorists "spent their day," as Clinton implies. Those asking questions want to know why the landlord failed to secure the house when the family had asked for help in so many different ways, and when the landlord had been warned that a dangerous intrusion was imminent. They want to know the intruder's motivation: did he act alone or is he part of a dangerous ring that could strike again? They want to know why the police were told to do everything they could to help, yet didn't come to the rescue. They want to know why the police weren't better placed to provide assistance. They want to know if the police attempted a cover-up after the fact. They want to make sure that the truth is fully aired and that those responsible for any missteps or cover-ups are held accountable to help avoid a repeat occurrence in the future.

Throughout the chapter, Clinton laments "a regrettable amount of misinformation, speculation and flat-out deceit by some in politics and the media." On that point, many would agree. They just might disagree on who's responsible for perpetuating the deceit.

| CBS HIRES BENGHAZI FIGURE

In January 2014, Morell, the ex-CIA deputy director was hired as a consultant for CBS News. At the same time, the government was still very much embroiled in controversy over its monitoring of citizens and journalists, targeting of whistleblowers, and the handling of Benghazi. The hire drew immediate commentary from some of my sources.

CBS is employing one of the most controversial figures in the Benghazi controversy. Are you comfortable with that? one asked.

Once in the CIA, always in the CIA, said another. *And now he's in your newsroom.*

I felt that Morell was hired to spin rather than spy. But regardless,

CBS was presenting him on the air to viewers as though he were a neutral observer, without disclosing his political and financial ties. This risked opening CBS to criticism that, in my view, we simply couldn't afford. Network news operations are huge enterprises and it's impossible to prevent every mistake. But it's foolish not to prevent the obviously preventable ones.

About a month before CBS announced Morell's hiring, he'd also been hired at that PR firm dominated by Hillary Clinton loyalists: Beacon Global Strategies. I also got a tip that Morell was the target of new congressional allegations that he hid or gave false information about Benghazi. To protect CBS's reputation and interests, I felt it was urgent that we disclose Morell's financial and political ties when he made his on-air appearances.

On February 18, 2014, I sent an email to the CBS ethics czar to express this concern. I said that for our own protection at CBS, we had a responsibility to disclose Morell's relationships each time he appears. Putting it out front avoids criticism and gives the public the crucial information it needs to decide how much weight to give Morell's opinions on various topics. Disclosure is our friend. It protects us.

I instinctively knew that my email would further my reputation as a troublemaker rather than that of a loyal employee watching out for CBS interests. But I hit the SEND button.

Before long, the ethics czar called me. He didn't agree that we had an ethical duty to disclose Morell's financial and political ties each time he appears. He did acknowledge we should reveal them if Morell were asked a question specifically about Hillary Clinton.

"Well, the problem with that," I countered, "is that people who initiate propaganda are pretty clever. They steer public opinion in less obvious ways than in answers to direct questions. He may not be asked about Hillary, but can still subtly steer opinion in a certain direction. If we disclose his connections each time, we don't have to worry that somebody will later accuse us of hiding them."

I wondered if CBS even knew, prior to my pointing it out, that Morell worked for the company largely composed of ex-Clinton and Obama officials.

"Did you even know he worked for Beacon before I told you?"

"No," admitted the ethics czar.

The next morning, Morell appeared on *CBS This Morning*. There was no disclosure of his financial or political ties.

MORELL'S CONTRADICTIONS

On May 3, 2014, I have left my job at CBS and am now fully free to write on my own website about yet another contradiction in the administration's Benghazi narrative. Morell is at the center of it.

The contradiction surfaces when Vietor, former spokesman for President Obama's National Security Staff (NSS) gives an interview to FOX News anchor Bret Baier. In it, Vietor acknowledges that, while at the White House, he made at least one substantive change to the talking points. That change was to add a line that seemed to advance the notion that the attacks were born from spontaneous demonstrations.

It's a stark one-eighty from the story the administration has told to date.

"According to the e-mails and the time line, the CIA circulates new talking points after they've removed the mention of al-Qaeda," Baier says to Vietor, "and then at 6:21 the White House, you, add a line about the administration warning of September 10th of social media reports calling for demonstrations. True?"

"Uh, I believe so," answers Vietor.

Both Morell and White House spokesman Carney had previously

insisted that White House officials only made a single edit, changing "consulate" to "diplomatic post."

Carney said it at a White House press briefing on May 10, 2013: "[T]he only edit made by the White House or the State Department to those talking points generated by the CIA was a change from— referring to the facility that was attacked in Benghazi, from 'consulate,' because it was not a consulate, to 'diplomatic post.' . . . But the point being, it was a matter of non-substantive/factual correction."

On April 2, 2014, Morell repeated the claim under oath before Congress.

"To be very clear the White House did not make any substantive changes to the talking points."

He was even more specific and adamant in the written testimony he submitted in connection with the hearing.

"No one at the NSS [where Vietor worked at the time] suggested or requested a single substantive change. That is a simple fact, and calling it a myth doesn't change the reality," wrote Morell.

With Vietor feeling chatty in the FOX News interview, Baier continues to press.

"Did you also change 'attacks' to 'demonstrations' in the talking points?" Baier asks.

"Uh maybe. I don't really remember," answers Vietor.

"You don't remember?"

"Dude, this was like two years ago . . ."

"The key part is 'attacks' to 'demonstrations . . .'" continues Baier.

"Yeah," says Vietor.

"Did you do that?"

At this point, Vietor appears to rethink the wisdom of the conversation. Perhaps he recalls that Morell had provided a different account to Congress a month before.

"No . . . what did we—what was the question?" says Vietor.

"The CIA talking points," Baier repeats. "It was edited from 'attacks' to 'demonstrations.'"

"No," says Vietor. "Michael Morell testified to what he changed and what was changed in those, in those emails, the whole process of that, Michael Morell testified that he took them back, didn't like them and changed them."

Vietor's new contradictions create a turning point.

After more than a year of resistance, House Speaker John Boehner at last gets behind the idea of convening a special select committee to investigate Benghazi, replacing the piecemeal efforts of four separate committees.

About this time, a member of Congress sends me an email titled, "You see this? First question I have is, was this speech really delivered Sept. 12?"

The email links to a speech that CBS president Rhodes delivered to the San Antonio Chamber of Commerce the day after the Benghazi attacks. In it, Rhodes told the audience, "Our government thinks that, you know, there's a really good chance this was not just a spontaneous mob reaction to what some thought was an offensive film but actually a coordinated effort timed to the 9/11 anniversary."

Why were the Rhodes brothers giving their respective audiences opposing accounts at the same time? The CBS Rhodes seems to know right away that the government suspects a 9/11 terrorist attack. Did he know this from his brother at the White House, who then ended up steering the talking points toward the YouTube video narrative?

On May 8, 2014, my phone rings. It's Senator Graham. He tells me he's just had a conversation with the CBS Rhodes.

"He's really worried about that speech he made," Graham says.

"How do you know?" I ask.

"The sound of his voice."

Senator Graham says he wanted to give Rhodes the benefit of the doubt. He told Rhodes that he assumed his information came from his own CBS reporters and "not your brother."

"That's absolutely true," Rhodes replied, according to Graham.

"So how did it go from what you said on the twelfth based on good reporting, to what Rice said on the sixteenth? What happened during those days that fundamentally turned the story around?" Graham asked Rhodes.

"Therein lies the question," Rhodes replied, according to Graham.

Graham also told Rhodes that he didn't think his brother alone could have been responsible for the spontaneous protest narrative.

"Probably not," Rhodes said, according to Graham.

| FACT-CHECK

If one compares the Obama administration's first accounts of the Benghazi fiasco—the pages from the novel, if you will—to the facts that have trickled out since, the contrasts are stark.

CLAIM Nobody ever denied security requests for Libya.

FACT A long-documented trail of denied security requests was produced.

CLAIM The Defense Department pulled out Wood's team.

FACT The Defense Department offered Wood's team at no cost for the State Department's use as long as they wanted it. It's the State Department that ended its mission.

CLAIM Wood's team never left Tripoli so wouldn't have helped in Benghazi had they stayed.

FACT   Wood and his team had been to Benghazi on numerous occasions and would have helped guard Stevens there.

CLAIM   The administration didn't even know Stevens was going to Benghazi on 9/11.

FACT   Stevens's trip and schedule were widely distributed in advance and during the trip.

CLAIM   Stevens went to Benghazi independently and nobody really knew why.

FACT   Headquarters was informed Stevens was filling the Benghazi post while it awaited arrival of a new principal officer and he was also said to be on a personal tasking from Secretary Clinton.

CLAIM   The attackers were spontaneous protesters inspired by a YouTube video.

FACT   Extensive eyewitness testimony and documents reflect terrorism from the very start. Nobody thought it was spontaneous or YouTube inspired.

CLAIM   Security in Benghazi was adequate on 9/11.

FACT   Security in Benghazi was sorely lacking on 9/11.

CLAIM   The White House photo office will answer our CBS News photo request by the end of the day.

FACT   The White House photo office never fulfilled our request.

CLAIM   The FEST team doesn't have any expertise relevant to the Benghazi attacks.

FACT The Benghazi attack scenario fits precisely what the team says it's trained for.

CLAIM President Obama called the Benghazi attacks "terrorist attacks" in the Rose Garden the day after they happened.

FACT President Obama acknowledged in a *60 Minutes* interview that day that he had intentionally avoided calling them terrorist attacks.

CLAIM Everything that could be done was done to attempt an outside rescue.

FACT No rescue airspace clearance from Libya was sought, no aircraft was sent to buzz the crowd, the nearest Special Forces team was not immediately dispatched, a special FBI team in the United States was stood up and down throughout the night but never left the States, President Obama did not call Libyan leaders for assistance, NATO was not contacted seeking possible help, one of the small teams in Tripoli that planned to fly to Benghazi was ordered to stay in Tripoli, the specialty FEST team in the United States was prevented from responding, the Counterterrorism Security Group tasked with providing advice on options was not convened even though it's required by presidential directive.

CLAIM The White House made no substantive changes in the talking points.

FACT The White House made substantive changes in the talking points.

| BENGHAZI SELECT COMMITTEE

In June 2014, I'm on Capitol Hill to meet with Democrats and Republicans about the upcoming Select Committee on Benghazi.

I have little doubt that, as the committee spins up, there are meetings going on not far away. Meetings of PR officials strategizing how to delegitimize the Select Committee and its work, even before it's begun. PR officials who are digging for dirt on the chairman of the committee, Trey Gowdy, a Republican former prosecutor from South Carolina.

These PR officials may not be the smartest kids on the block. But they have money. They have access to powerful people. And best of all, many in the news media are on their side.

| EPILOGUE

WOOD   I heard about it in the evening, that there had been an attack on the compound in Benghazi. And I heard that there was a fatality. I didn't find out till the next morning—when I woke up my son informed me—that the compound had been attacked and Ambassador Stevens had been killed.

ME   Your friend.

WOOD   Yes. (pause) I took it pretty hard. He was a great boss and a great man to know. The United States lost a lot when they lost him. He was a great diplomat. He was the president's personal representative. It was an assault on the United States. It was a loss to the Libyans as well.

ME   From a security standpoint, what are the thoughts that went through your head as you heard what happened?

WOOD   We just lost, we lost big. . . .

ME   Did you wonder if your team might have been able to do something to prevent that from even happening?

WOOD Yes, those thoughts go through your head. You do wonder. I won't know. That's one thing I guess we'll never know. . . . But I do wonder about that from time to time. What could have been done differently. I think in the military you're taught to war-game things a lot and you do wonder if different pieces had been on the ground what might have happened, what might have there been to avoid, perhaps.

| The Politics of HealthCare.gov |

(and Covering It)

It's Thursday, October 31, 2013, and it's about to be a very scary Halloween for the Obama administration. I'm working the monstrously frightening Obamacare launch.

The administration is withholding most of the relevant public information, whether it's regarding HealthCare.gov's tenuous security, failed tests prior to the rollout, or dismal enrollment figures. The key to getting real facts is going to be the congressional committees that have the power to demand documents and issue subpoenas.

Republicans must sense an advantage. This is the most self-assured and aggressive I've seen them behave since Senator Obama became president. Previously, Republican house speaker John Boehner has tempered many of his colleagues' attempts to exploit the administration's vulnerabilities. He slow-walked their demands for a joint select committee to investigate Benghazi. He delayed subpoenas on *Fast and Furious*. But the Republican response to the HealthCare.gov susceptibilities is different. *Full speed ahead.*

Of course, if history accurately predicts the future, the Obama administration will thumb its nose at Congress and its document demands for as long as possible. There are few repercussions to this approach. Republicans usually wring their hands but don't do much about it. The media shrugs its collective shoulders but stays mute.

And the only true enforcement authority is the very administration that's committing the offenses.

But there are other keepers of revealing information: government contractors that worked on HealthCare.gov. Some of them aren't so cavalier about ignoring requests from Congress. Some of them will turn over relevant materials. I need to stay close to the essential congressional committees that stand the best chance of getting information that can be released to the public. They're all in the House: Oversight, Ways and Means, and Energy and Commerce. My producer Kim Skeen and I hit them up with phone calls and emails. Ways and Means and Energy and Commerce have good background material and context to balance all the information the Obama administration is releasing, but there's nothing particularly noteworthy from them . . . yet.

But I haven't heard back from Oversight. Four days pass and they still haven't responded to my emails and calls. Sometimes that means they've got nothing. But it can also mean the opposite. I'm left to guess.

Everyone wants to know what the early Obamacare sign-up figures are. They're significant because trusted experts I've consulted, including well-informed insiders, say the business model relies on two simple factors: the number and quality of customers. First, there needs to be seven million enrollees by March 31, not counting Medicaid customers. That's roughly 38,000 a day. Second, there needs to be the right mix: plenty of healthy, young enrollees—"young invincibles," in insurance industry jargon—to balance the cost of older and sicker customers. If either measure falls short, it could jeopardize the entire program. At the very least, premiums skyrocket.

There should be nothing secretive about how many Americans are enrolling: the figures belong to the public. And unlike Benghazi and *Fast and Furious*, the government can't withhold the information on the grounds of national security or "ongoing investigation"—two of their favorite stonewalling excuses.

Nonetheless, the administration simply says it's not going to announce enrollment numbers until it's good and ready, and then will produce them once a month. They justify this methodology by saying it's how the government handled the release of Medicare Part D figures. It's an invalid argument for the government to claim that statistics for HealthCare.gov must be disseminated the same way they were for the Medicare Part D prescription drug benefit when it started back in 2006. That's akin to declaring that everything in the future must be done the same as it was in the past, for no particular reason. If we all operated that way, we'd still be chiseling on stone tablets. Because that's how things used to be done.

But more important, the administration insists there *is* no enrollment data, yet. Experience, knowledge, and common sense lead me to suspect they're telling a fib.

So, on Halloween at about 3 p.m., I finally get a return call from Republicans on Oversight. It seems they've obtained so-called War Room notes taken by a HealthCare.gov contractor during emergency meetings convened when the website first failed at the start of October. The notes refer to a "dashboard" that's tracking enrollment and is apparently working better than the rest of the website. What does it reveal? On the first day of Obamacare, six people enrolled.

Six.

For a moment, I'm at a loss for words. No wonder the administration wants to run and hide. Everyone thought it would be bad. But not this bad.

"Did you say *six*? Are you sure?" I ask my contacts who are listening on speakerphone.

"Yeah," they say. "It's pretty clear."

I look at the documentation myself and consult additional sources for context. Then I call my senior producer, Linda Prestia.*

---

* Not her real name.

"I have some enrollment figures for the first day."

"And . . . ?"

"Apparently, six people signed up."

Pause.

"Six?" she asks. "How can that be?"

As I prepare to report this revelation on that night's *CBS Evening News*, I contact the Department of Health and Human Services (HHS), the primary government agency overseeing implementation of the Affordable Care Act. I already know the drill. The press spokesman will use the opportunity to attempt to pump me for what I know without giving up a shred of information.

Until now, HHS spokeswoman Joanne Peters has largely ignored questions I've raised in emails and phone calls. But the moment I ping her that I need confirmation on enrollment figures, I have her interest. My phone rings. It's Peters.

"I need to know how many people enrolled on the first few days," I tell her.

"We'll be releasing those figures in mid-November," she answers, repeating from the talking points that HHS has used for weeks.

"So if I were to give you numbers that I have, you couldn't confirm them?"

"There are no numbers," she insists. "They don't exist."

We go back and forth. I tell her that I know enrollment numbers are being collected and I have some of them. She continues to say there aren't any. I've long dealt with government officials who beat around the bush when they don't want to give an honest answer. Lately, it seems they're bolder. They say things that are provably false. And they say these things with conviction. Indignation. We're not getting anywhere and I draw the call to a close.

"Wait," says Peters. "I'd like to know what numbers you have."

"I'm sure you would. And I'd like you to give me your enrollment numbers but it looks like neither of those things is going to happen."

"There *are* no numbers," Peters shoots back once more. She's sticking to script—but sounding worried now. She needs to report back to her superiors. They need to prepare their spin. It's a game whereby they constantly modify their story as contradictions surface, necessitating formulation of an evolved position that's more consistent with the newly unearthed facts. *We didn't mean that, I'm afraid you must have misunderstood. Here's what we meant. . . .* The game is tedious but pro forma.

"You're going to go on the *Evening News* and report numbers, I'd like to know what they are!" Peters tries one last time, sounding testy.

She's got it backward. She gets a public salary and her agency is collecting information about the public that belongs to the public. She's the one who's obligated to provide information.

"I was looking for help from you to confirm enrollment numbers," I say. "But there's no point in telling you what I have since you say you have no numbers, right?"

We hang up and I grab my files and notes to head over from my office to the main CBS building, up the street. As soon as I enter the newsroom, I swing by Prestia's desk and tell her to expect a call from the White House. My chat with Peters has set the machine in motion. There's some comfort in knowing the routine. So predictable.

It's not long before I overhear Prestia arguing on the telephone. I walk toward her desk, and she looks up and smiles as if she doesn't mind the battle on the other end of the phone line. She scribbles on a piece of paper as she continues talking and hands it to me.

"*White House.*"

Fulfilling my prediction, a White House press officer has called to complain, and to try to find out what we know and how we know it.

Prestia pushes back. Why would we discuss details of our reporting with them when they insist no enrollment figures exist?

She hangs up. "Really? That's the best they can do is sic *him* on us?" referring to the White House press flack who had called.

"Somebody higher up the food chain is probably calling Isham [our bureau chief] and David [Rhodes, president of our news division]," I tell Prestia. She hasn't been in her position long enough to know the whole routine. Their normal strategy is multipronged. They hope to reach *somebody* at CBS who might be intimidated or sympathetic. It just takes one. But today, it doesn't work.

At 6:30 p.m., we air our report. It reads, in part:

> The website launched on a Tuesday. Publicly, the government said there were 4.7 million unique visits in the first 24 hours. But at a meeting Wednesday morning, the War Room notes say 'six enrollments have occurred so far.' . . . The notes leave no doubt that some enrollment figures, which the administration has chosen to keep secret, are available. . . . But head of [the government's Centers for Medicare and Medicaid Services] CMS Marilyn Tavenner would not disclose any figures when Rep. Dave Camp, chair of the House Ways and Means Committee, asked earlier this week. "Chairman Camp, we will have those numbers available in mid-November," she said.

It's big news.

Six-people-enrolling-the-first-day becomes an instant meme reflecting the HealthCare.gov disaster. It's fodder for a song written and sung on the Country Music Awards on November 6 from Nashville: "*Obama-care by Morn-ing . . .*" croon Carrie Underwood and Brad Paisley on ABC, " *. . . over six peop-le served . . .*"

Jay Leno pokes fun on his late-night comedy show: "According to CBS News, only six people enrolled in Obamacare on the first day of the rollout. Six! That means more people have walked on the moon than have signed up for Obamacare."

And casual observers can't help but note that the number six happens to jibe with a skit that *Saturday Night Live* had performed five days before. In the parody, an actress portraying Secretary of Health and Human Services Kathleen Sebelius tells Americans, "Millions of Americans are visiting HealthCare.gov, which is great news. Unfortunately the site was only designed to handle six users at a time."

The next morning, a CBS News producer shares with the rest of us that White House officials are unhinged—"out of their minds"— over the media coverage, and are on a mission to excavate information to exploit to their advantage. They're asking, *Which reporters are working on the story? What are the names of their producers?* There's a hint of more desperation than usual as they execute their PR game plan, which looks something like this:

KNOW YOUR ENEMY   Get to know the reporters on the story and their supervisors. Lobby them. If they don't adopt your viewpoint, try to discredit them.

MINE AND PUMP   When asked to provide interviews and information for a story, stall, claim ignorance of the facts, and mine the reporter for what information he has.

CONTROVERSIALIZE   Wait until the story is published to see how much the reporter really knows. Then launch a propaganda campaign with surrogates and sympathizers in the media to divert from the damaging facts. Controversialize the reporter and any whistleblower or critics to try to turn the focus on personalities instead of the evidence.

The Obama administration's downhill PR trajectory may have been a fait accompli from the moment Secretary Sebelius's handlers scheduled her to appear on Jon Stewart's Comedy Central program October 7, 2013. She cleared a spot in her tight schedule for the political comedy show after refusing Congress's "invitation" to testify because she supposedly didn't have time. It's a classic Obama administration move: bypass the traditional news media. Circumvent Congress, if you can. Go straight to the popular media. There you'll get friendly banter with no tough questions and no serious follow-up.

It usually works.

But Sebelius was ill-equipped for Stewart's brand of political humor, which exploits real-life observations to construct blistering satire. He begins the segment by opening a laptop computer on his desk.

"I'm gonna try and download every movie ever made," says Stewart as Sebelius chuckles nervously, "and you gonna try to sign up for Obamacare and we'll see which happens first."

"Okay," says Sebelius as the audience laughs.

Later in the segment, she's befuddled by Stewart's persistent bemusement over why the administration granted businesses, but not average Americans, a year delay in meeting Affordable Care Act requirements. After Sebelius repeatedly attempts an explanation, Stewart says, "Let me ask you this: Am I a stupid man?"

Stewart's treatment of Sebelius and the HealthCare.gov story seems to buoy some in the news media. We pass around the link and marvel at how he so skillfully shed light on the controversy. We're forced to look in the mirror and ask if we've grown accustomed to being overly deferential to some political figures. (Answer: We have.) Maybe we should be asking tougher questions and demanding full answers. Not accepting the usual runaround. If the liberal comedian finds fault with HealthCare.gov and the government's response, then perhaps some of us should be taking a more critical look.

| THE "GLITCH"

It's about two weeks later that the Affordable Care Act story falls into my lap, in much the same way that Benghazi did. There hadn't been any interest by the *Evening News* lately in my investigative reporting. But mid-morning, I get a phone call from a New York colleague who tells me that, as of right now, the network powers that be want me to focus on Obamacare. In twenty years at CBS News, I rarely know who it is and how high up who decides that we—or I—should be hot on a particular story or why. And when interest later suddenly dissipates, as it usually does, I rarely know exactly how that comes about, either.

Invited into the health-care story, I join a group of CBS News producers and correspondents who are already on the case, and we begin daily conference calls to discuss developments and unanswered questions. We share information and divide responsibilities.

As I'd watched the rollout of HealthCare.gov, much like an average consumer, it seemed as if some in the news media were hesitant to call a spade a spade. Or in this case, afraid to call a debacle a debacle. Many had adopted the administration's chosen term for what's going wrong: *glitch*.

It reminds me of how the media often perpetuates a propaganda lexicon rather than critically examining whether it's accurate. For me, detecting and resisting disinformation is an avocation: I'm always on the lookout for signs that we're being worked, whether it's by Democrats, Republicans, corporations, or other special interests. I've become so keen at detecting the techniques, they stick out like a sore thumb.

In the case of HealthCare.gov, the media has adopted the administration's understatement of the website's massive complications as a "glitch." While it's perfectly fine to quote administration officials who want to call it a glitch, we should not promulgate the notion as if we journalists have independently concluded it's the case. Yet the *Washington Post, USA Today,* the *Wall Street Journal,* and all the networks—have all used the g-word long after the troubles proved to be far beyond what can be fairly described as a glitch.

I look up the definition of *glitch.* TheFreeDictionary.com defines it as "a minor malfunction, mishap, or technical problem." Merriam-Webster.com says it's "an unexpected and usually minor problem; *especially*: a minor problem with a machine or device (such as a computer)."

I then look up *disastrous*: "very bad or unfortunate . . . terrible: *a disastrous report card.*"

HealthCare.gov's failed launch is much closer to being "a disastrous report card" than "a minor malfunction."

There is, at least for the moment in late October, an appetite for more aggressive coverage of the president's signature initiative. The problems are proving to be too big and persistent to downplay. Americans are just beginning to suffer a wave of insurance cancellations as a result of Obamacare. The president is taking live fire for the many iterations of assurances, at least thirty-seven, in which he or another top administration official said, "If you like your health-care plan, you can keep your health-care plan." One can almost feel sorry for him as the news media play montages of his past on-camera statements belying today's reality. But it's hard to feel sorry for too long, considering written evidence that shows his administration knew all along—and even worked into its formulations—the prediction that millions would, indeed, lose their insurance. It's figured into Congressional Budget Office projections over the years as well as internal CMS analyses.

Eventually, the administration will acknowledge the cancellations and instigate fixes. But for now, it's in denial mode. *It's the insurance companies' fault,* they say, and *plans aren't being canceled; people are being automatically switched to "better" plans.* Spinners fan out in the press and call it a "kerfuffle" of "manufactured Republican outrage." But for once, the spin falls flat: even Democrats in Congress are in a lather. Some of them will soon be facing tough reelection campaigns. And they know from their constituents that there's a groundswell of grassroots anger.

Further proof that government proclamations should be viewed askance, no matter how confidently they're made, comes from a White House–produced video posted in August 2009 as the Obama administration pushed Congress to pass the Affordable Care Act. It's one of those PR outreaches that bypassed the newsman and went straight to the public: unfettered and unquestioned. The video featured communications director (and former CBS News correspondent) Linda Douglass of the White House Office of Health Reform debunking "the myth that reform will force you out of your current insurance plan. . . . To the contrary, reform will expand your choices, not eliminate them." The article slammed critics saying that they "may find the truth a little inconvenient." Now, in 2013, we know that the "critics" were correct all along—millions *are* being forced out of their current insurance plans. Despite the conviction with which that White House video attack on health-care opponents was delivered back in 2009, it has proven to be either misinformed or dishonest. Ironically, the title on the banner that introduced the 2009 video, most unfortunate in retrospect, was *Facts Are Stubborn Things.*

As CBS News moves to get more aggressive on the story, there's palpable tension and no universal agreement on what our coverage should say. Key managers criticize another correspondents' health-care report for referring to insurance cancellations occurring under Obamacare.

"Customers aren't being *canceled*, they're being automatically switched to *better* plans with *better* coverage," argues one manager vehemently, adopting the administration's verbiage, "because they had *substandard* plans!"

Undoubtedly, there are some previously uninsured customers who will benefit from the Affordable Care Act. But it's paternalistic for us to claim to know that all of those switched against their will are better off, and just don't know better.

"We might be able to report they're getting *more* coverage, but it's not up to us to say it's *better* coverage," I say. "If it's coverage they didn't want or need and it's more expensive, it's not necessarily better for *them*."

Another manager voices concerns that to continue our watchdog reporting could give the appearance that we're "piling on" the beleaguered White House. It sounds like another argument from the administration's supporters: spinners often accuse us of "piling on" when they want us to ease up on negative coverage. As I've mentioned, broadcast producers have adopted the vernacular when they don't want a story. It's not a substantive argument and I'm not sure why it ever works, but it does. I'm unsympathetic. We should follow the story where it leads, not be deterred by red herrings.

Other reporters have shared with me experiences about meeting similar roadblocks at the hands of managers using similar language. Pulitzer Prize–winning investigative journalist Jeff Gerth disclosed in a footnote in a book he coauthored in 2007, *Her Way: The Hopes and Ambitions of Hillary Rodham Clinton*, how his *New York Times* bosses killed one of his articles about the Clintons. According to the footnote, "an editor in Washington told [Gerth] the editor in New York decided a second piece [about the Clintons' Whitewater controversy] would be viewed by readers as 'piling on' and spiked it."

If anyone is to blame for the cascade of critical reports on Health-Care.gov, it's not the news messengers: it's those who screwed things up. During my conversation with managers who are worried about "piling on," I point out that for many months, the news media produced plenty of glowing stories about the Affordable Care Act. We profiled countless individuals and families who would supposedly be helped, and uncritically accepted the promise that people would be able to keep their plans and doctors. If the new reality is less positive, so be it.

As journalists, we must have a tin ear for the propaganda campaigns that swirl furiously around us. We need to be cognizant of the many attempts to influence or manipulate by spinners and their media surrogates: bloggers, authors of letters to the editor and opinion pieces disguised as news articles, and social media engineers.

By the first week of November, insurance cancellations have reached critical mass and public outrage is so strong, the White House decides it's time for a mea culpa. It won't happen at a press conference. It won't be given during an interview with an adversarial reporter. And an appearance with Jon Stewart is obviously out of the question. Instead, the president's handlers call one of the friendliest guys on the block for a taped one-on-one: NBC/MSNBC's Chuck Todd. I don't blame Todd for answering the call. If they'd called me, I would've gone, too. Funny thing is, the White House never calls me for an interview.

The interview airs on November 7. The president doesn't offer an apology off the top. But when Todd presses the point about people losing their insurance, Obama says, "I am sorry that they are finding themselves in this situation based on assurances they got from me."

| PUSH-ME-PULL-YOU

Covering this story continues to involve push-me-pull-you when it comes to navigating internal politics. One conflict surfaces when I prepare a story about growing worries that the Obamacare business model could collapse. One Obama administration source has confided in me that the breakdown of the website poses a fundamental and perhaps insurmountable enrollment challenge. Several insurance experts tell me the same thing. It's the talk of the industry right now. In short, they believe that the coveted healthy customers won't waste their time trying to log in over and over. Only the sickest, most motivated patients will. And they will skew the risk pool. The experts explain it using the phrase "death spiral," an industry term of art to describe the fatal business phenomenon that results. Not enough low-cost customers to help pay for the expensive ones. The death spiral could defeat the Obamacare model.

"That's the road we're headed down," says one expert flatly.

As I write my report, my producer and I already know that some of our managers in New York will have a visceral repulsion to the phrase "death spiral." Their response is emotional and makes no logical sense, but through experience over the past two years, we've become adept at predicting what they'll try to keep off the news. Such battles used to be rare or unheard-of but now they're ingrained: the heavy-handed reshaping of scripts; the banning of certain words, phrases, views, and topics. Even so, we try to resist the inclination to self-censor in advance. So I write the story the way it should be written and submit it.

Sure enough, I immediately get one initial response: "One thing to avoid . . . the term 'death spiral.'" I'm told that all the relevant managers are "in agreement we don't want to be that inflammatory."

I begin the process of fighting this piece of censorship. I explain that "death spiral" is not an inflammatory or opinionated term; it's a widely known, accurate insurance industry term describing the fact pattern at issue. What's their real problem with the phrase?

I argue that it isn't appropriate for us to censor facts or terms of art. And I submit a scholarly reference to support my stance.

Death spiral. The term is found in the academic literature at least as early as Cutler and Zeckhauser's 1998 paper "Adverse Selection in Health Insurance" which refers explicitly to an "adverse selection death spiral."

—Cutler, David M.; Zeckhauser, Richard J. (1998). "Adverse Selection in Health Insurance." Forum for Health Economics & Policy 1 (1). doi:10.2202/1558-9544.1056.

After much ado, I bring upper management into the discussion and it's finally agreed that the piece should air complete with the term *death spiral*. But I know not everybody inside CBS is happy about it.

My next HealthCare.gov story won't make them any happier.

As I move forward with my research, I pinpoint a significant vulnerability that the news media hasn't explored to any meaningful degree: security. And judging by the administration's reaction, it's an Achilles' heel for them.

I begin by poring through an inspector general report and congressional testimony given months before the website went live on October 1, 2013. They reveal that crucial security-related deadlines kept slipping as HealthCare.gov's development fell desperately behind schedule. This prompted great concern from the inspector general as well as some Democrats and Republicans. As I get up to speed, I'm struck by how many warning signs there were throughout 2013. But we, the media, were largely disinterested. Asleep on the job.

The security issues don't just involve the personal information that a user enters on a HealthCare.gov application, though that's a serious matter. They also extend to the vast hub through which HealthCare.gov exchanges data to link to the IRS, Department of Homeland Security, Department of Veterans Affairs, the Defense Department, the Office of Personnel Management, and the Peace Corps. Even if you're not a Health-Care.gov customer, the system's security shortfalls could compromise information stored about you in these colossal government databases.

I learn that the deadline for final security plans to be formulated slipped three times from May to July 2013. Security assessments that were supposed to be finished in early June slid to mid then late August. And the final, required end-to-end security tests never got done prior to the launch. This presented the Obama administration with a dilemma: delay the rollout of the website—political disaster—or grant itself a waiver to go ahead and launch October 1 and hope for the best. Four days before the launch, it issued the waiver. The way we know is because Congress obtained an internal government memo, despite the Obama administration's best efforts to keep it secret.

The waiver memo was dated September 27, 2013, and it's a blatant red flag. In it, HealthCare.gov's lead project manager, Henry Chao, and a colleague tell their boss, head of CMS Marilyn Tavenner, that because major parts of the website are still under development, no "end-to-end" security testing can be conducted. This, says Chao's memo, poses "a level of uncertainty . . . deemed as a high [security] risk." Nonetheless, the memo shows Tavenner signed off on the required Authority to Operate the website, accepting the liability without notifying Congress or the public.

This is the same government that would likely squawk out objections and issue regulatory threats if it learned that certain private industry websites were doing the public's business without passing basic security assessments. But here, for the sake of forcing an unfinished website to launch by a certain deadline, the government secretly exposed Americans to a mandate with giant security holes. Notably, there were no disclosures on the website, not even in fine print. No terms for users to acknowledge and agree upon that divulge the site's true security status. In private industry, such a lapse could be seen as grounds for a lawsuit.

As the Obama administration frantically attempts to brush off the Chao memo and the risks, my inside sources are doing the opposite.

242 · | STONEWALLED |

One of them tells me that the decision to launch the website with such precarious security was so contentious that people threatened to quit over it.

Kim and I consult a range of cybersecurity experts who tell us it's "shocking" and "unacceptable" that the website was allowed to become operational with its vulnerabilities. However, nobody wants to say so on camera. I even turn to a major cybersecurity firm suggested by a CBS executive who has contacts there. Our communications begin cordially and I describe the issue at hand. A few minutes later, the contact at the firm calls back and tells me in a frosty voice that its executive will absolutely *not* address *that* topic on the record.

Let's face it. Many of these experts do lucrative contract work for the federal government. Or they're connected to universities that get a great deal of government funding. Whether by accident or design, it's almost as if the would-be critics have been bought off with tax dollars. Who can blame them? Why should they bite the hand that feeds them? It's yet another illustration of how information can be censored and manipulated in ways the public can't imagine.

I've begun familiarizing myself with the arcane security rules that the government is supposed to follow. The Federal Information Security Management Act (FISMA) requires federal government websites to meet standards developed by the National Institute of Standards and Technology (NIST). NIST defines a high risk as a "vulnerability" that "could be expected to have a severe or catastrophic adverse effect on organizational operations . . . assets or individuals." If a federal website goes forward with known risks, the law requires that a designated official with the agency formally acknowledge and accept the risks, and devise a written plan to mitigate and fix the hazards down the road.

HealthCare.gov's risk status is a very big deal, indeed.

Kim manages to locate one credible expert who will speak about the security problems on camera: Affordable Care Act supporter and Georgetown law professor Lawrence Gostin. Gostin is an especially valuable figure in this context because he helped craft the Affordable Care Act so that it would stand up to constitutional challenge. His criticisms can't be dismissed as partisan. When we tell him about the September 27 memo and waiver, he's disturbed that the Obama administration signed off and moved forward.

"Nothing can undermine public confidence more than the fear of a security and privacy breach," Gostin tells me in an interview. "You could have somebody hack into the system, get your Social Security number, get your financial information."

Adding to the security questions is a strange addendum to the September 27 memo. It's signed by three of Chao's colleagues: fellow managers at CMS. It states that while the government's mitigation plan would reduce the security risk to the overall operation, it "does not reduce the risk to the [Federally Facilitated Marketplace] system itself going into operation on October 1, 2013." For all the effort the administration has put into trying to convince the public otherwise, evidence of the persistent threat is codified in black and white, signed by the government's own experts.

I wonder: Is the addendum a "cover your ass" document? Did these security officials who signed it suspect that disaster might strike? Were they making sure that if people later asked, *Who the hell approved the website to go forward with such risks?* the record would reflect they had raised flags?

I also know from my research that CMS chief information officer Tony Trenkle—not Tavenner—was originally the authorized official who should have signed the website's Authority to Operate. Instead, he signed the odd addendum noting the risk. This seems like a clue. I consult my inside sources, who tell me this whole arrangement is unusual, if not unprecedented. I wonder if it's proper or legal. I ask

HHS to explain. But like most of my inquiries, these fall into the bottomless pit where unwanted questions to federal agencies go, never to be answered or addressed again.

| CHAO'S AWKWARD POSITION

Some Democrats as well as Republicans are now questioning the security status of the website and on November 13, 2013, Chao is called to testify before Congress. His demeanor couldn't be more different than what I expected based on the descriptions from some of his acquaintances. They said that he was a good guy to work with. A competent, straightforward man who always had a kind or encouraging word when he saw you in the hallway. But when Chao appears before Congress in a suit that's too big and a collar that's too tight, he appears uncomfortable, shifty, and sarcastic. He puts a great deal of effort into backpedaling from his September 27 memo. Now he tells Congress he never really had any serious security concerns and was confident the website would perform well on its debut. That the only reason he *sounded* so worried in internal emails is that he's an overly cautious kind of guy.

It's an awkward scenario for Chao, to say the least. HealthCare.gov is an unmitigated mess. For him to now claim that he didn't have a clue may advance the interests of the Obama administration, which wants America to believe there were no real warning signs, but the tradeoff is that Chao comes off as ignorant. Yet as long as Chao wears the mask of the ignorant but stays in synch with the White House, his job is safe. It's moving off that script that could jeopardize his government career.

In short, Chao must convince the public that the true Chao isn't the worried Chao revealed in the documents; the true Chao is the one who didn't foresee impending disaster and is, therefore, the incompetent Chao, but the Chao who's in harmony with the administration.

Democrats coalesce behind the incompetent version of Chao; Republicans prefer the concerned Chao who foresaw the train wreck. As for me? Do I believe Chao 1.0 from documents prior to the PR crisis, or the updated version, Chao 1.1, prepped by his HHS minders in advance of a potentially damaging congressional hearing? After the hearing ends, one government insider tells me he's shocked at how evasive, if not downright dishonest, his colleague Chao seemed at the hearing.

"I wouldn't have guessed he'd be like that," says the source. "He must be under a lot of pressure."

| ALTERNATE UNIVERSES?

To hear the opposing views of HealthCare.gov's security status, you might think you were in alternate universes: one where the system is invincible: another where it's frighteningly vulnerable. Never is the contrast more absolute than on Tuesday, November 19, 2013, during dueling hearings on Capitol Hill. It's Chao's second appearance before Congress since the website's launch; this time it's Energy and Commerce. Democrat John Dingell of Michigan asks a series of rapid-fire questions intended to dispel the security concerns.

> **DINGELL** Is HealthCare.gov safe and secure for my constituents to use today with regard to protection of their personal information and their privacy? Yes or no?
> **CHAO** Yes.
> **DINGELL** Is there any evidence at all to the contrary?
> **CHAO** No.

At the precise moment that Chao is giving those reassurances, four security experts are barely a stone's throw away giving the opposite assessment before the Science, Space and Technology Committee.

Republican Chris Collins of New York asks, "Would any of you have launched HealthCare.gov, recommended the launch, given the factual known status of the website on October first?"

"No," answer the four security experts.

"Do any of you think today that the site is secure?" Collins asks.

"No," they reply.

"In your opinion, do any of you think the site will be secure on November thirty?"

"No," say all four.

Back at Chao's hearing, Chao testifies that no identified vulnerabilities have been exploited by an attack and "the American people can be confident in the privacy and security of the marketplace."

At the security expert hearing, Morgan Wright, CEO of Crowd Sourced Investigations, testifies that "only in the government could such a gaping hole be allowed to exist without fear of consequence. . . . [There is] a massive opportunity for fraud, scams, deceptive trade practices, identity theft and more."

Democrats ask choreographed questions to try to make the Chao hearing go their way. But Republicans have their own preplanned strategy and get Chao to confess that up to 40 percent of the website systems remain unfinished more than seven weeks after it went live. On top of that setback, Chao once again pleads ignorance. He says as project leader he never saw a damaging independent consulting report that foreshadowed many of HealthCare.gov's problems. Even after the report was leaked to the *Washington Post* and published the morning of the hearing, Chao testifies he still hasn't bothered to review it.

These two hearings should be of great interest. A poll released the same day shows that more Americans are following the HealthCare.gov rollout than the monster typhoon in the Philippines that killed more than six thousand people. Yet the hearings receive scant attention in the mainstream media. CBS is alone among the big three to mention them at all on the evening newscasts. It seems as though the temporary surge in aggressive coverage on the topic is now waning.

NBC leads with a positive story for the Justice Department announcing JPMorgan Chase will pay $13 billion in the mortgage crisis. ABC leads with the stabbing of a Virginia state senator by his son. There are also stories on pilot obesity, insomnia, the JFK assassination anniversary (still three days away), Caroline Kennedy becoming U.S. ambassador to Japan, and a feature on penguins. But no time for the news topic that interests more Americans than most anything else.

Among the news wire services, Reuters does cover the security expert hearing. Interestingly, the article calls it a "Republican sponsored Congressional hearing." It's the first time I remember noticing an official congressional hearing described as being "sponsored" by a political party. It's as if readers are being cued to skeptically view the expert witnesses who criticize the Obama administration. If the article considers the hearing to be Republican-sponsored because Republicans hold the majority in the House, then—Substitution Game— shouldn't we describe all hearings in the Democratic majority Senate as "Democrat sponsored congressional hearings"?

It's an example of the disparate treatment the media may give to different political interests.

As a young journalist, I once had a supervisor who required us to label conservative analysts in our news stories as "conservatives," while the liberals were simply referred to as "analysts." And if a conservative analyst's opinion really rubbed the supervisor the wrong way, she might rewrite the script to label him a "right-wing" analyst. The implication is that when a conservative says something, the opinion needs to be qualified and perhaps discounted. But the liberal? He's just an independent, fair guy giving an everyman's opinion.

Often, this type of bias isn't thought out: it just comes naturally.

One day, to make a point, I called a conservative in my story a "right-wing" analyst and labeled the liberal a "left-wing" analyst. When the supervisor read "left-wing," she sputtered out a spontaneous objection. I argued that we could label both analysts similarly, or label neither, but that it wasn't logical to label one without the other. She leaned back in her chair as if the thought had never dawned on her, and I'm pretty sure it hadn't until that day. After a moment, she looked at me and said, "You're right." From then on, we applied equivalent labels to conservative and liberal analysts.

Many others have faced their own challenges. A network news writer recently told me he that he was forbidden to refer to President Obama as "Obama" or "Mister" on second references, which had been common style for other U.S. presidents. "When I questioned this," says the writer, "I was told it was because 'the office of the President demands respect.' I asked, 'Did you always say "President' Bush?" I was told 'No, he didn't deserve respect.'"

The writer says that when he reported on the Defense of Marriage Act, "the part about President Clinton signing it into law was taken out every time (thirty-five times, I counted)." When he reported on same sex marriage, "any reference to President Obama having opposed same sex marriage while serving in the Senate was taken out of my scripts." When reporting on HealthCare.gov, any reference to the government releasing sign-up figures but not actual enrollment "was taken out."

I think of all of this when I read the article about the "Republican sponsored Congressional hearing." Was there an editor somewhere up the line who, like my old supervisor, felt compelled to put a Republican label to qualify opinions he didn't like? To be clear, there's nothing wrong with applying a label if it's accurate, if there's a journalistic reason to do so, and if it's equally applied under similar circumstances. In other words, the same news outlet should refer to all Senate hearings as "Democrat sponsored."

| THE PUSHBACK

The news organizations that have been covering HealthCare.gov's troubles now face intense, daily pressure from the White House and its supporters, who are desperate to turn things around. The fervor with which they pursue their attacks on the stories and the journalists reporting them is directly proportional to the importance of the subject matter. Judging by the response, we've done some pretty impactful stories. At the same time, many in the media are wrestling with their own souls: they know that Obamacare is in serious trouble but they're conflicted about reporting that. Some worry that the news coverage will hurt a cause that they personally believe in. They're all too eager to dismiss damaging documentary evidence while embracing, sometimes unquestioningly, the Obama administration's ever-evolving and unproven explanations.

On Monday, November 11, we break news of another damning internal security document: a memo dated September 3, a month before HealthCare.gov went live. It's bad. It delineates specific "high risk" security problems—the most serious kind. Vulnerabilities that "could be expected to have a severe or catastrophic adverse effect."

It's pretty difficult to spin or sugarcoat "severe or catastrophic." Pretty much everyone knows that's serious.

The memo says the risks are posed to the "Federally Facilitated Marketplace," or FFM for short. Exactly what is the FFM? It's the entire support structure for HealthCare.gov and, says the memo, is what handles the flow of "financial, demographic, and (potentially) health information." (Remember this part, because Democrats will later falsely claim to an unsuspecting public that the described catastrophic risks didn't apply to the FFM and could not have jeopardized any personal information.)

The single most worrisome finding uncovered by independent security testers in the memo states that "macros enabled on uploaded files allow code to execute automatically. . . . The threat and risk potential is limitless."

Limitless.

Why? Because a malicious macro can do almost anything: transmit viruses, execute a program, gain access to other parts of the system, set up connections to outside computers, and search for passwords, personal data, and financial data. One cybersecurity expert I consult says it's impossible to overstate how potentially damaging this is.

"Anyone who downloads those documents with macros enabled can open a pathway for their computer to be hacked," he says. "Even a government computer."

He adds that criminals have been able to embed macros into documents and use them to hack an entire company.

Furthermore, according to the security memo, the independent testers uncovered another extremely serious issue: software that may produce functional errors was being deployed. That's "a very big red flag for security folks," says one expert, "and can introduce unknown, new security flaws into the system." It's a risky practice known in the industry as "cowboy coding."

There are other risks revealed in the memo: it appears there's "an inappropriate E-Authentication level" in the system that "contains financial and privacy data." One expert explains to me that means people could access sensitive information without proper authentication, for example, without logging in. Or one customer might be able to see the log-in and documents from another's health plan.

As I consider the memo's enormous implications, I assume the government is addressing these risks, but the fact that they arose so close to the website's deployment is troublesome. Experts agree that forcing the October 1 deadline jeopardized security.

Even more important, I learn that once again, the project's lead manager was in the dark about all of this information. Chao-the-Ignorant says he knew nothing of the security risks. He'd made that confession in a secret closed-door interview with House Oversight staff on November 1, a month after HealthCare.gov launched.

"I just want to say that I haven't seen this before," Chao tells Oversight staff when they show him the security memo outlining the "limitless" and possibly "catastrophic" security risks.

"Do you find it surprising that you haven't seen this before?" asks a Republican staffer.

"Yeah . . . I mean, wouldn't you be surprised if you were me?" He later added, "It is disturbing. I mean, I don't deny that this is . . . a fairly nonstandard way" to proceed.

Even more disturbing, Chao tells the committee that his own team had led him to believe the opposite was true.

"What I recall is what the team told me, is that there were no high [risk security] findings," Chao testifies.

Not only were the high-risk findings unearthed by security testers, but another government document indicates they persisted, unresolved, weeks after the September 3 memo. Why would Chao's team have kept him in the dark about all of this? Shouldn't he have had a better grasp on the big-picture items of concern and the supposed remedies?

As I prepare to write up the story for that night's *Evening News*, I contact Oversight Democrats and HHS asking for comments and context. The information on the security problems is particularly incriminating because it's not from political opponents; it comes from the government's own files. If the administration now contradicts it, it's undercutting its own documents and Chao's testimony.

Specifically, I ask HHS how and when it addressed the security holes outlined in the September 3 memo. I also ask to see the paper trail providing proof of any fixes. (I asked for all the website's security documents weeks ago by filing a Freedom of Information Act request, but it apparently got lost in the bottomless pit.) The most important question I ask now: How could Chao have been so far out of the loop on security? What else doesn't he know? What else haven't *we* been told?

The way I figure it, the government should already have its response to these questions prepared. After all, HHS has had the damaging security assessment memo for two months—it's *their* document. And Oversight Democrats were present for Chao's closed-door testimony ten days ago when he said he'd never seen the security memo and was completely blind to its findings.

However, both HHS and Oversight Democrats react to my queries as though I'm probing mysterious, new territory. In fact, both ask *me* for copies of the relevant materials. I point out that the documents originated with them, and that they've had the facts much longer than I have.

They're employing the Mine and Pump Strategy. Stall, claim ignorance of the facts, and mine the reporter for what info he has.

Hours tick by as Oversight Democrats tell me they have no information or comment. At 3:56 p.m., the spokeswoman for the Democrats, Jennifer Hoffman, emails me, "still waiting to see if our team has any insights on your questions." Then at 5:58 p.m.: "Nothing yet . . ."

Shortly before air, I get a brief email statement from HHS that fails to answer any of my questions but says that privacy is of the utmost concern and there's no reason for HealthCare.gov customers to worry.

We air our report on the *CBS Evening News,* after which Oversight Republicans issue a full press release providing the September 3 memo about the high security risks and the transcript from Chao stating that he didn't know about it.

The vehemence with which the Obama administration reacts shows how near the story hits to a nerve. Their hysteria is heightened because other media, including the *New York Times* and the *Hill*, pick up the story. It becomes more difficult for Democrats to credibly label the reporting as partisan.

But still, they try.

Long after the story airs, Democrats provide their first hint of response in the form of spin rather than answers. They spread it through media surrogates who publish it nearly word for word and, judging by the factual errors, without doing any research or asking for documentation.

Their first talking point is to falsely claim that—contrary to what the government's own memo states—there was never any true security risk to HealthCare.gov. They say that's because the implicated parts of HealthCare.gov are no longer in use.

The second talking point falsely holds that there was never any threat to customer privacy data because the implicated parts of HealthCare.gov don't transmit personally identifiable information.

And for good measure, the Democrats also circulate an on-the-record quote that, predictably, is devoted to the continuing campaign to controversialize Oversight's Republican chairman Issa.

"Controversialize," as in the PR tactic that involves launching a propaganda campaign using surrogates and sympathizers in the media to divert from the damaging facts. They try to turn the focus on personalities instead of the evidence.

Even the *Washington Post*, which has done some strong reporting on HealthCare.gov, gets snookered on this one. In a fact-check blog, the newspaper incorrectly states, "upon close examination of the [security-risk] memo, it had nothing to do with the parts of the Web site that launched on Oct. 1. Instead, the memo dealt with modules of the Web site that would not be operational until spring of 2014 . . . [and] will not submit or share personally identifiable information."

Yes, that's the Democrats' spin pretty much word for word. But it's factually incorrect.

The *Post* presents the Democrats' take without attribution, as if it's true, seemingly without proper fact-checking. Otherwise, the reporter would know that the security-risk assessment explicitly stated that sensitive, personal information *was* at risk because "inappropriate controls" exposed "financial and privacy data" that are part of the "entire enterprise." The memo also stated explicitly that the risks applied to the entire Federally Facilitated Marketplace supporting HealthCare.gov, not—as Democrats incorrectly state—small, dormant pieces of it. And although the Democrats' press release implies that there was never any danger because the dormant pieces where the problems were found won't go online until the following spring, it fails to mention that they were already operational, exposing the HealthCare.gov system to the high-risk threat. Taking them off line until the spring doesn't remedy that.

"Just taking [the suspect components] out of the system doesn't remove the threat," one cybersecurity specialist tells me. A second agrees and adds that to remove the "limitless" threat created when enabled macros on uploaded files allowed code to execute automatically, "the government would have had to audit every document already uploaded for malicious content." He says there's virtually no chance the government has been able to accomplish that massive job but goes on to say that "by law, all this audit work must be tracked and written down, so [if it's been done] they should be able to provide a record of it." Again, I ask HHS for such records but none are provided.

Now, the administration is in full pushback mode and Chao is indispensable to its PR recovery effort. The day after the *Evening News*, the *Hill*, and the *New York Times* reports, Chao testifies before Congress again and desperately attempts to revise and recast his closed-door testimony that looked so bad. Providing the Big Assist is a lead Oversight Democrat: Gerald Connolly of Virginia. In a pre-prepared exchange straight from the Democrats' talking points press release, Connolly prompts Chao to testify that he and that September 3 security-risk memo were entirely misunderstood by the incompetent media, who succumbed to the persuasions of the corrupt Issa. *There was never any security risk! Don't believe that internal government memo. Listen to what we're telling you now.*

This is neither unexpected nor out of line with what Democrats have every right to do in their defense. It's the media's job to sort through and get at the truth. The problem is, in today's environment, some in the media present political spin as if it's fact—even when it runs counter to the evidence.

I liken some of the media's behavior to a gullible jury hearing the case of the burglar who's confessed on video after getting caught on surveillance tape. At trial, the burglar insists he didn't really confess. His lawyer says the videotape recording of the confession is wrong. As for the surveillance tape showing the crime? Well, the defense says that's mistaken, too. *Who are you going to believe: me or your lyin' eyes?* The jury acquits, treating the implausible defense as fact rather than a position to be considered with appropriate skepticism.

Like the jury in the analogy, some in the media report the Connolly-Chao spin as if it sets the record straight. *They said it at a hearing! So now, we know the truth!* Never mind that it contradicts the evidence and that the administration refuses to provide the documentation that would theoretically support its version of events. Some just want to believe.

The administration's surrogate bloggers ask whether CBS and the *New York Times* are going to correct our reports now that Chao says it's all wrong—as if we're to believe Chao's latest spin instead of his previous sworn testimony and the actual documents. And in my case, I have the added supporting evidence from experts inside and outside the government who have explained the computer security risks, the memo, and its context.

Obama officials join in the effort to get me to "update" the Web version of my original report with their follow-up spin. They become incensed when I reply that I still need them to answer some basic questions and show documentation of their claims, which should all be public record. My reticence interferes with another of their PR strategies: they decline to provide information for the original story, then wait for it to publish, issue their spin, and ask that it be added to the Web version of the report. That way, they get their unchallenged statements printed verbatim and don't have to answer any pesky questions. Then, they and their surrogates portray the "update" as a correction to try to discredit the original story premise.

It's not much trouble to add an after-the-fact statement to a Web story, and most of the media usually go ahead and do it because it's the path of least resistance. But the administration has a well-established history of misrepresenting facts on this story and it would be irresponsible to unquestioningly accept and print their spin when they've refused to answer basic questions of public interest and when their spin contradicts the available evidence.

So, ever predictable, White House press secretary Carney begins nagging my bureau chief, Isham, hoping to sway him into a sympathetic position. And Oversight Democrats call my senior producer, Prestia, to complain. I think about how much of the public's time and money these federal employees are spending to execute their PR efforts.

Sadly, the propaganda effort takes hold and persists among a complacent media that fails to check its own facts and instead relies on partisan sources and blogs for background research, parroting what it reads or hears. A good eight months after my report on the security risks, in July 2014, NPR reporter David Folkenflik asks me about the Democrats' complaints for a profile piece he's producing about me.

To try to condense or expect anybody to quickly digest the research I spent many hours performing, and to ask them to immediately comprehend the jargon, background, documents, and expert sources isn't realistic. That's why I'm an investigative reporter: I put in the time and understanding to present the facts to others who don't have the time or ability to do the same on a given topic. I sure couldn't absorb all the research in ten minutes, I can't explain the research process and details in ten minutes, and I don't think it would be easy for anybody else to understand in ten minutes.

Nonetheless, I spent a great deal of time with Folkenflik summarizing the evidence—documents, expert opinions, inside sources—in the simplest way I knew how. He seemed satisfied or at least didn't question it further.

Not a word of describing my efforts made it into Folkenflik's NPR report. In fact, he didn't summarize or represent anything I told him. Instead, he mischaracterized my reporting as if my entire research for the HealthCare.gov security-risk story consisted of relying upon "a partial transcript" of a witness: Chao. That's false and entirely contrary to the content of our interview. He also treated Chao's contradictory testimony as if it should be accepted uncritically as the final word on the matter. This from an administration that repeatedly provided provably false information on this very topic. In the end, Folkenflik simply called the facts that I presented in my story "difficult to prove." That's wholly false. They may have been difficult for him to understand. They might have been time-consuming to explain. But they certainly weren't difficult to prove.

After Watergate, few would have predicted today's dynamic in which some journalists view their job not as questioning the powers that be, but undermining those who *report on* the powers that be. In this instance, journalists misreporting the HealthCare.gov security story accept, at face value, the word of the very government officials implicated in the mismanagement even though it's contrary to their own prior testimony and documentary evidence. At the same time, these journalists portray my reporting, which culls from independent experts and documentary evidence, as "difficult to prove."

| WANING APPETITE

If there's a moment that's emblematic of the political low point in the HealthCare.gov catastrophe, it might be the release of a CBS News poll on Wednesday, November 20, 2013. The president's overall approval rating has fallen to the lowest of his presidency: 37 percent. His handling of health care has also hit bottom: just 31 percent approve. Fifty-seven percent disapprove of the job he is doing: the worst ever for President Obama in CBS News polls. And he's lost ground on personal qualities like honesty.

How can the administration reverse the momentum? With help from the media.

Kim and I finish three weeks of strong coverage on the *CBS Evening News*, often breaking exclusives. It's the kind of momentum that serves both our audience and the network.

But then, the light switch goes off.

Just as we edge ever closer to exposing more of the facts the government is trying to keep hidden—it's a process and our mission—

there's a sudden loss of interest, internally, in my hard-hitting stories on the topic.

It begins, as it often does, with New York requesting that I work on a story that ultimately never airs. In this case, they want me to explore Chao's wild inconsistencies. As the day-to-day manager of HealthCare.gov's development, he's the public face on its failures. We've all noticed the many contradictions in his positions and explanations, including those prior to HealthCare.gov's rollout.

One example is found in a July 16, 2013, email I recently obtained from congressional investigators. In it, Chao worried about prospects for the website and contractor CGI: "I just need to feel more confident they are not going to crash the plane at take-off," Chao wrote.

But he gave a very different impression publicly the next day when he and Tavenner testified to the subcommittees of the House Homeland Security and Oversight committees. Republican Scott DesJarlais asked about unfinished tasks.

> **DESJARLAIS** So both of you are testifying today that [the website's shortfalls] are going to be one hundred percent complete on October first?
> **CHAO** Correct.
> **DESJARLAIS** Ms. Tavenner?
> **TAVENNER** Yes, sir.

A few days later, the worried Chao was back. He emailed colleagues the video link to his congressional testimony, saying, "I am not sharing this with you because I think it's entertaining and informative" but rather "so you can see and hear that both Marilyn and I under oath stated that we are going to make October 1st . . . please share this up, down, and wide."

Another contradiction comes from Chao on November 13, 2013,

after the website's launch, when he testifies before Congress and tells Republican Cynthia Lummis that he didn't talk to White House officials before HealthCare.gov went live.

LUMMIS Did no one brief the White House about the status of the website before October first? Mr. Chao?

CHAO Not me personally, but our administrator, Marilyn Tavenner, certainly is representing the agency. So you might want to ask her.

In other words, Chao is helping shore up the Obama administration's narrative that nobody at the White House knew the website was in trouble.

But internal government emails I've recently obtained indicate Chao personally met with White House chief technology officer Todd Park prior to the rollout of HealthCare.gov.

"One of the things Todd conveyed was this fear the [White House] has about [HealthCare.gov] being unavailable . . ." wrote Chao to colleagues after their discussion. "Todd does have a good point. . . ."

Drilling down on Chao's conflicting positions is important. Public officials have a responsibility to be truthful in matters of their public duty, and part of our job is to pursue accountability. But my New York managers who originally assigned the story have a change of heart and delay it from one day to the next, and then it just fades away altogether.

Another story I propose that *Evening News* passes over is the discovery that CMS and the Congressional Budget Office predicted for years that the Affordable Care Act would cause millions of Americans to lose their work insurance. This directly contradicts recent statements from the White House's Carney. In his frenzy to deflect attention from all the individual insurance cancellations, Carney had repeatedly insisted before TV news cameras that Americans who get insurance through their workplace will not be affected: "They don't have to worry about or do or change anything."

This is as stark and important a distortion as the president's if-you-like-your-health-care-plan-you-can-keep-your-health-plan, only more audacious since Carney is making it after all the flak over the president's misstatements. As I write in my script, Carney has given repeated assurances that nothing will change for those insured through work. But in 2010, it turns out, the Centers for Medicare and Medicaid Services estimate Obamacare would "collectively reduce the number of people with employer-sponsored health coverage by about 14 million."

The prospect of 14 million workers getting dropped is at least as significant as the news of several million individuals being canceled—and *that* made big headlines. But the *Evening News* is oddly disinterested. The producers say it's too soon to do the story about workers. Maybe we'll revisit it next year when their insurance actually gets canceled.

I disagree with the premise of waiting: when you discover new facets of a story, you don't keep them secret. You don't wait to report them after the fact. *Yes, we knew this disaster was coming all along but didn't think you needed to know until it was too late.* Under that mentality, we wouldn't report that the government *might* shut down or a wildlife species *might* die out or a political candidate *might* win or a suspect *might* be guilty of a crime or a hurricane *might* strike a region: we'd just wait until it happened and then report that it did.

But Kim and I know that this dynamic has little to do with logic or what the audience wants or even the significance of the particular story. When I receive these kinds of signals, the writing's on the wall. Stop the story.

Nonetheless, Kim and I keep working. We're convinced that a good story is a good story and somehow needs to be told. We're able to find examples of business owners already canceling their workers' insurance due to Obamacare. I go back to *Evening News* and tell them that the cancellations have already begun; we don't have to wait until 2014 to do the story. Still no interest. Fortunately, we're able to find a home for the report on *CBS This Morning* on November 26. And that's pretty much the last in my string of in-depth or investigative health-care stories to make it on TV in 2013. From then on, the broadcasts want only basic stories from me that mark time but don't uncover anything new.

As I've said, I'm never privy to exactly what turns the tide and halts a line of investigative reporting. Polls show unquestioningly that viewers remain keenly interested in all things HealthCare.gov. I do know from my sources that I'm not the only target of the incessant White House campaign of emails and phone calls. Obama officials are bearing down on many reporters and news organizations that have uncovered inconvenient facts. Appealing to the higher-ups, searching for sympathetic ideologies, trying to stop the negative coverage.

This sudden loss of interest also coincides with the administration calling in the special teams to handle Congress and the spin. It hires media relations specialist Jen Friedman, who worked on President Obama's reelection campaign as well as at a bevy of federal agencies. The administration also brings in Jennifer O'Connor, a former private practice attorney who once helped defend President Clinton in congressional investigations. More recently, she helped the Obama administration defend the IRS targeting of Tea Party groups seeking tax exemptions. These women are the equivalent of private PR crisis management flacks being brought in on your dime to manage the fallout. It's become so commonplace for the federal government to spend tax money on whatever resources it needs for its self-serving goals—no matter how supposedly tight the budget—the practice doesn't even raise eyebrows.

The CBS Washington bureau is still trying to pitch HealthCare.gov stories though the appetite in New York has faded. The bureau asks me to try to get access to the facilities where HealthCare.gov's miracle fixes are under way. But HHS won't let us in. So much for transparency.

For a story about how the repairs are progressing, I conduct a phone interview with John Engates, a technology expert with a company called Rackspace Hosting, a leading firm specializing in high-capacity e-commerce. Engates has been a vocal critic, calling the HealthCare.gov launch "one of the most spectacular public failures of any website ever." He's also attacked the lack of transparency.

But as we begin our interview, Engates sounds like a different man. He says the Obama folks have the best people making heroic efforts to fix the site. He says there are no politics involved and he couldn't be more impressed and confident.

It's so far out of line with what Engates has said in the recent past, I wonder what's changed, so I ask him. He tells me that a few days before our interview, he'd gotten an invite from the White House to attend a private briefing on HealthCare.gov. So he hopped on a plane from San Antonio to Washington for a special session held in the White House Situation Room. Other invited companies included IBM, Salesforce.com, and ExactTarget.com. Some of the White House heavy hitters on hand were Chief of Staff Denis McDonough, Chief Technology Officer Todd Park, Chief Information Officer Steven VanRoekel, and the official heading up the tech surge: Jeff Zients. It's the kind of access the media can only dream of. After the White House briefing, the group was shuttled to the Maryland operations headquarters of contractor QSSI, where the government's "war room" fix-it site is centered.

Engates tells me he has to be careful about what he reveals in our interview because the group was instructed not to share some aspects of what they observed, including specific website numbers and statistics displayed in the operations center.

The whole scenario is outrageous from a public access standpoint. There's no legitimate reason why the Obama administration should exclude the media, then grant handpicked corporate officials special access—and tell them not to share what they see with the public. The White House is wielding control over assets and information that rightfully belong to the people, and doling them out to a chosen few in private industry in hopes they'll become emissaries to advance the self-serving cause.

It seems to be working: Engates, the onetime critic, has turned positively bullish. I don't blame him; in fact, he gives a very informative, honest interview, which I use in several daily news stories on the status of HealthCare.gov. If the White House had invited me to a special briefing, I would have gone, too. But I never get those invites.

It's time to contact HHS again and ask when they'll allow our camera into the facilities. I point out in my email to Peters that it's inappropriate for the government to allow corporate executives admittance to public-funded facilities that have been denied the press. I get no response.

About this time, late November, other major news outlets that were pursuing the Obamacare story also seem to suddenly back off. The *Christian Science Monitor* notes the trend in an article published November 26, 2013: "Bit by bit, the media narrative around the travails of Obamacare and its main enrollment vehicle, HealthCare.gov, is starting to look up. Or to put it more precisely, it is no longer so crushingly negative . . . a competing story line is starting to emerge."

The *Monitor* theorizes that the new "wave of positive stories" may be the result of reporters getting tired of wall-to-wall negativity, seeking out "happy stories for a change of pace." But I see it as far less random. First of all, good reporters don't make story judgments based on whether they're "tired" of the direction of a story: they let the story dictate the coverage. If it's negative, it's negative. What I think is the bigger reason for the change of mood is also noted in the *Monitor* article: "The Obama administration has also ramped up its public relations efforts. . . ." And it's working.

| THE BIG "GET"

I'm now plugged in to a wide variety of well-informed sources. The news hasn't stopped happening just because the broadcasts aren't interested in what I have to report. I keep digging. I can publish on the CBS News website, which provides a golden opportunity to reach a large number of people and has a nearly insatiable appetite for diverse content. For the many outside influences that work so hard to keep certain stories off TV, their efforts backfire when I publish on the Web. Those versions are sometimes more widely circulated than the broadcast stories and can be more thorough since the length restrictions aren't as tight.

As 2013 draws to a close, the quintessential example of the political propaganda machine in action—and the media's susceptibility to it—rears its head.

For a couple of weeks, I'd gotten tips that Oversight Republicans were bringing in various HealthCare.gov officials for closed-door interviews. Secondhand accounts from my sources lead me to believe that news is being made, but I don't know the details. I work sources on the committee but come up empty.

"What did Tony Trenkle say?" I pinged my Hill contacts in an email, after learning that the newly retired CMS top technology executive had been there the day before.

No response.

I keep trying over the next few days. Nothing.

Then on Tuesday night, December 17, my home phone rings. The caller ID reads "unidentified." When I answer, it's one of my sources letting me know that CMS's lead cybersecurity official, Teresa Fryer, has just spent six or seven hours answering questions before Oversight and she dropped a couple of bombshells.

Wednesday morning, I'm up on the Hill to fill in the blanks. I ask for an on-camera interview with Oversight's chairman, Issa, and also with the lead Democrat on the Committee, Representative Elijah Cummings. The Democrats' spokeswoman, Hoffman, says Cummings isn't available so I also ask to speak to his deputy on the committee, Gerald Connolly, or any other Democrat who can talk about the issue. Since the House isn't in session, I've offered to go to Cummings or Connolly wherever they may be. Hoffman says that no Democrat can be available for an interview. Later, Democrats would falsely claim that I didn't give them the chance to weigh in.

In our interview, Issa tells me about one of Fryer's shockers: that prior to October 1, she wanted to reject HealthCare.gov's security certificate—the Authority to Operate—due to security risks but was overruled by her superiors.

"My recommendation was a denial of an ATO [Authority to Operate]," Fryer had told Democrats and Republicans in a recent closed-door interview. She said she gave the advice to her boss, CMS's chief information officer, Trenkle. The man who had just retired and wasn't talking publicly.

"I had discussions with him on this and told him that my evaluation of this was a high [security] risk," Fryer testified. She said she briefed HHS officials as well.

This *is* a bombshell. The Obama administration has expended a great deal of effort trying to craft the impression—sometimes under oath—that there were never any serious security concerns. But now we know that the top official over security at CMS believed things were so bad, the website shouldn't have been launched at all. And she can't be labeled as a politically motivated, disgruntled ex-employee. She's a current, sitting, senior manager.

By any neutral measure, this is an important advancement in the HealthCare.gov story. But with the light switch at CBS firmly in the "off" position, it will be next to impossible to get this kind of information on a broadcast.

So I'm in the familiar position of applying my efforts on two simultaneous fronts: first, reporting the story amid strong pushback from the administration. Second, trying to convince my New York superiors that this *is* a story.

I ask HHS and Oversight Democrats for comment on Fryer's testimony. They pretend this is the first they've heard of her negative security recommendation.

Peters from HHS: "[C]ould you all share with us exactly what it is that you would like for us to comment on? Do you have a transcript or other document that you have received?"

(Mine and Pump Strategy.)

Peters also makes a boldly false statement. She claims her agency doesn't know anything about Fryer's startling testimony because "we were not in [her] interview with Oversight."

The thing is, I know from my sources that HHS *was* in the interview, represented by Jennifer O'Connor, one of those special advisors HHS hired in late November. Oversight Committee Democrats were present for the Fryer interview as well. It's ridiculous for Peters to claim they're all in the dark.

"I'm told you did have staff in the interview," I tell Peters. "Jen O'Connor. Didn't you know that? She can tell you more than I can."

Peters acknowledges that O'Connor was present for the interview after all, but keeps her hard hat on and continues mining without missing a beat. It takes a certain kind of person to be untruthful and then display utter lack of contrition when caught.

"If there are specific comments Teresa made about this issue or documents that you have obtained, it would be helpful to see those so that we can make sure we're getting you the right information you are looking for," Peters emails. The persistence with which she's fishing leads me to believe that Fryer must have said something *else* damaging. Peters is trying to figure out if I know.

Later on the phone, Peters reverts to her claim that "we didn't have anyone in the Fryer interview." She must be reading to various media outlets from the same talking points and has forgotten that I know better. I remind her.

"Jen O'Connor works with you at HHS, right? I told you, she was there," I tell her.

"Yes," Peters relents.

She's still touchy over that recent story I'd done about Chao and the high-risk security findings.

"We want to help you be sure your story is accurate and fact-checked," Peters tells me, "so that you don't make any mistakes and can avoid a repeat of your last story."

The idea that I would rely on HHS to fact-check a story is ludicrous.

"There were no mistakes in the last story, we're very happy with it," I correct her.

"I'm sure you are," she shoots back.

Several hours after Kim and I first contacted Oversight Democrats, at 3:17 p.m., their spokeswoman Hoffman complains that I'm being unfair in expecting them to have any response to Fryer's testimony so quickly. And she's got her miner's hard hat on, too.

"We are working very hard to respond to this request with extremely short notice," Hoffman writes in an email. "As we discussed, it would be most helpful if you could provide information about the documents you obtained from the majority. Without this context, it is hard for us to provide a complete and thorough response to your inquiry. It is unfortunate when outlets report on excerpts selectively leaked from the majority without giving the minority access to the same information so we can provide a full response. This would also help ensure that your story is fully vetted, fact-checked, and balanced. Please let me know what additional information you can provide so that we can respond appropriately."

The tone deviates from Hoffman's usual informal, friendly style. I get the sense that she (or whoever wrote the email) is writing it to share with media surrogates who will assist in the post-story spin. It's incredibly disingenuous for her to claim the majority is leaking information "without giving the minority access to the same information." Democrats had the information before anybody: Fryer works for HHS, was debriefed by them before her interview with Oversight, and Democrats and HHS attended her interview.

Think about how twisted the spin is: The public officials who are withholding public information are claiming to be out of the loop on information that they've had longer than anybody. They're criticizing Republicans for "leaking" material that belongs to the public, which they, the Democrats, have misrepresented and withheld. The very public officials who have repeatedly provided untrue information are suggesting that I should rely on them to fact-check and vet my reports.

I reply.

"Sorry but I disagree that notice is 'extremely short' since your folks heard everything Fryer testified to in real time yesterday, the same time everybody else there did. In fact, I'm told the administration was well aware in advance as to the scope of what Fryer was going to say, so you guys have actually had more time than anybody else to think about all of this. I'd love to have any documents that you can offer that are relevant, but I don't have any to share with you at this time. Our inquiry is quite simple and I don't think there is really anything difficult or obtuse about it so we are still looking forward to your prompt response."

I run Fryer's impeaching testimony by an inside source who supports Obamacare and has been helpful in providing context on its flaws. This source tells me, "It's pretty damning when the top CMS IT security person strongly recommends that a project [HealthCare.gov] not be cleared to operate but then is overruled. Well done—it looks like you've got a scoop on your hands!"

Kim says surely the *Evening News* will find this story too big to pass up, even in the current discouraging climate. So we pitch it. But my Washington senior producer has already told us the broadcast isn't very "keen" on the story. And the New York group doesn't usually put stock in guidance from the reporter level—at least not from me.

Nonetheless, I argue to the managers that we, the media, didn't do a very good job looking into HealthCare.gov before the rollout and we have a responsibility to do a better job now. I say that we have a public duty to report the security vulnerabilities, especially on the eve of the deadline for a large number of Americans to sign up on the website. But I'm not changing their minds. This isn't about the worthiness of the story. Other forces are at play.

I'm not the only reporter who's meeting up with resistance from superiors on this story. I know from my sources that other national news reporters are on the case but also having trouble getting this same story past their editors.

Meanwhile, at 4:18 p.m. on Wednesday, HHS sends me a comment that doesn't directly address Fryer's testimony that she recommended HealthCare.gov not be allowed to launch due to security risks. Instead, HHS states that all the fears about security risks in the past never came to pass.

I'm about to find out that's yet another misrepresentation.

It turns out, Fryer had dropped a second bombshell when she testified to Oversight: two high-risk security findings surfaced on HealthCare.gov *after it went live October 1*. One had been flagged the day before Fryer spoke to Oversight. This must be what Hoffman and Peters were mining to see if I knew about.

I return to Peters with this new information and she reacts as though it's the first she's heard of it. I'm to believe that the most serious category of security issues was flagged inside HHS and that Fryer discussed it in a congressional interview at which a top HHS spinner was present—but that Peters, the HHS spokesman, knew nothing of it until I mentioned it just now.

About the same time, Oversight Democrats are also fishing to see if I've learned of this new revelation.

"Has Chairman Issa's office provided you with any specific info from the [Fryer] interview? We would like the opportunity to provide additional context," Hoffman emails.

Additional context? They haven't given any yet.

"Not disclosing sources," I tell Hoffman, "my information is that Fryer reported there have been at least two high [security risk] findings, one discovered in testing last week related to a November incident and another on Monday of this week. Your folks know of this."

I can almost hear Hoffman muttering, *Crap, she knows!*

It's closing in on 10 p.m. Thursday and Peters emails HHS's response to Fryer's testimony about the high-risk findings: one has been fixed and the other was a "false alarm." That may or may not be true. No proof is offered (though plenty should exist since the security process requires extensive documentation). Some in the media will accept these claims, as they do each new assertion the government rolls out, as if there's no history of misrepresentation. But without any documentation, it should rightfully be characterized as their side of the story and nothing more. I ask Peters whether there have been other high-risk findings besides the two that Fryer referenced. She won't answer.

All of this news is a game changer: The worst category of security risk is no longer just theoretical. It's actually surfaced and we're learning of it for the first time from a knowledgeable insider: Fryer. It contradicts Obama administration claims that there haven't been any real security issues, only unfounded fears whipped up by Republicans. I write up an informational summary for CBS. One executive recognizes the significance and responds, "Pretty damn good story, Sharyl."

In the end, though, no broadcast takes the story. So I publish it on CBSNews.com the next morning. ABC News and FOX have just published their own versions, also online. None of the big three networks finds room to mention these important findings on their evening broadcasts. In fact, it's as if they're going out of their way to avoid it, seeing as how it would have fit so naturally with news that they *do* air about President Obama holding his final news conference of the year—largely devoted to HealthCare.gov controversies.

But with the story widely circulating on the Web, it's time for the next phase of the administration's PR campaign. Representative Cummings and Oversight Democrats now issue their first comment on Fryer's testimony, after my story has published.

Predictably, once again, they personally attack Issa and, by implication, the news media.

(Controversialize.)

At almost eleven that night, Hoffman fires off an angry, accusatory email to me out of the blue.

"Why did you refuse to tell us that Chairman Issa provided you with [Fryer] transcript excerpts—was that a condition of his leak to you?"

The outrage seems conspicuously manufactured, written for her third-party audience, whoever it may be. Her question is loaded with incorrect assumptions, such as that "Issa provided [me] with transcript excerpts." And only those trying to hide public information would think of its release as a "leak," as if it's to be frowned upon and discouraged. A better question might be why Hoffman's team or the administration didn't release all of this information themselves, especially considering that it's covered under Freedom of Information Act requests I filed weeks ago.

More important, Hoffman doesn't seem to understand that I'm not obligated to report to her or anyone in the government. It's the other way around.

I reply, "I think you have it a bit backwards."

I know they're setting in motion their next step.

Some media outlets that were disinterested in the potential security threat to millions of Americans now eagerly comply with the Democrats' prompt to report about the reporting of the story.

A reporter from one Internet news organization calls the CBS press office. He says that Representative Cummings is saying that I didn't give him a fair chance to respond to my story and this reporter wonders if I have a comment. I flash off a quick background note to my press office that shows we asked Cummings and his staff and other Democrats on Oversight for on-camera interviews and comments over and over but none were provided prior to publication. One CBS manager comments to me, "[T]he only thing more ridiculous than Cummings's claim is that [another news organization] is calling our press office to ask about it."

Before long, a predictable string of "articles" begins to appear, all designed to controversialize the reporting and distract from the facts. A colleague sends me one such article published in the *Los Angeles Times*. The article is an opinion piece by a writer named Michael Hiltzik. It appears in the newspaper's business section and, surprisingly, is not labeled as an opinion piece.

Hiltzik echoes the Democrats' spin, complete with incorrect assumptions, misleading material, and fact errors. He also adheres to the strategy of trying to make the story be about Issa. Though the damaging testimony and documents actually originated within the Obama administration, Democrats portray it as having come from Issa and, therefore, not to be believed.

Hiltzik's obviously one-sided blog isn't likely to change any minds. These overt propaganda efforts, employed by both Democrats and Republicans at times, are simply preaching to the choir. Yet there must be some sort of cumulative advantage to getting the articles into the public domain or else they wouldn't bother. Maybe it's as simple as arranging to have these favorable blogs return prominently high in Internet searches to overshadow, counter, or confuse the real news.

It's easy to see why Democrats focus so much effort on controversializing Issa: it's because of the committee he leads. Oversight is among the most powerful and effective watchdogs in Congress. Whether it's led by Democrats or Republicans, it boasts some of the best staff on the Hill. In my experience, Oversight's seasoned investigators have been thorough, careful, and accurate in how they've portrayed information to me over the years. They dig into hot-button issues and aren't afraid to use subpoena power to get documents that might otherwise languish indefinitely at the other end of an unanswered Freedom of Information Act request.

So if the administration can convince the media and the public to dismiss everything from Oversight out of hand, because "it came from Issa," they'll have eliminated one of the few serious threats to their agenda. That's what they're trying for.

A choice example of the formidable threat Oversight poses is a letter that Issa dispatches to Secretary Sebelius on January 8, 2014. His investigators have compiled her allegedly false or misleading testimony.

First, on October 30, 2013, Sebelius told House Energy and Commerce that MITRE, the contractor hired to conduct security assessments, was performing "ongoing" tests for extra assurances. In fact, the committee says, MITRE's pre-launch security testing ended September 20, 2013.

Second, Sebelius testified that MITRE "did not raise flags about going ahead." But the committee points out that MITRE actually raised such serious issues that Fryer, CMS's top cybersecurity expert, didn't think the website should launch.

Third, Sebelius told Senate Finance on November 6, 2013, that "no one . . . suggested that the risks outweighed the importance of moving forward." Actually, Fryer says she did just that.

And fourth, Sebelius said MITRE "made recommendations to CMS, as is required" and did not suggest delaying the rollout. But MITRE told the committee that it was "not informed, nor asked, by CMS about a 'go-ahead for HealthCare.gov.'"

There are many more misrepresentations that could be added. HHS spokeswoman Peters falsely claiming that nobody from HHS was present for the congressional interview with Fryer. (A high-level HHS specialist was there.) Chao claiming he didn't brief anybody at the White House prior to the launch. (He'd spoken to the White House's Todd Park.) Administration officials insisting no enrollment figures existed. (They were collected from day one.) White House spokesman Carney promising worker insurance would be unaffected. (The administration's own calculus predicted 14 million workers would lose insurance.) CMS head Tavenner stating under oath that there were no volume issues revealed in testing prior to launch. (Her agency's internal tests showed the website repeatedly failed with just a few hundred users.)

In a different environment, all of these things might be exposed and examined and analyzed on the news. Public officials might be held accountable for mistakes and misstatements. They might be pressured to turn over public documents that they're hiding. We might learn more about the true reasons why things went wrong, how to fix them, and how to avoid the same mistakes next time. Maybe we'd be able to avoid future waste of tax dollars.

And in a neutral news environment, it might be time to ask whether Obamacare has, for all intents and purposes, collapsed. With the multiple delays, a poor risk pool, millions booted off their existing plans, employers canceling insurance, employees dropping out of the workforce—the Affordable Care Act is barely a shadow of its grand vision.

But, like I said, the news decision makers appear to have lost all interest in these sorts of things in late November.

So viewers don't hear much about it when, on January 23, 2014, the credit rating agency Moody's downgrades the outlook for health insurers from stable to negative, naming the Affordable Care Act's many problems as a significant factor. There's little more than a passing reference on February 10, 2014, when the administration announces yet another year's delay in implementation of rules for certain employers—until 2016. Most people don't hear meaningful debate over the president picking and choosing how to implement pieces of the law, a practice that some claim to be illegal. Most of the news media don't examine the trend of Democrats who are up for reelection in challenging races distancing themselves from the Affordable Care Act. There aren't prominent reports fleshing out the debate over whether delays in implementation should also be extended to individuals, not just businesses. There are no high-profile stories providing smart financial analyses with revised estimates of costs, including new taxes and fees, versus benefits. And the continuing difficulties with many Obamacare recipients failing to receive proof of their insurance, patients having to switch doctors, insurers failing to get paid, and other problems may as well be nonexistent.

Replacing what should be critical analysis is the media's tendency to adapt the government's propaganda, or at least allow it to sway us from conducting meaningful oversight. HHS holds conference calls during which officials take reporters' questions, but consistently give pat nonresponses to queries they don't wish to answer. We note this trend but don't launch objections: we just complain to each other and continue to take part in the dog and pony show, gaining no real information other than what they wish to spoon-feed us.

The White House holds daily press calls featuring success stories and asks Democrats in Congress to circulate success stories gathered by their offices as well as coalition groups. The administration makes use of opinion pieces, blogs, and social media. A favorite go-to remains the *Los Angeles Times*' Hiltzik, who continues to publish his opinion articles in the business section, so closely in synch with the White House's own messaging, so utterly in line with the administration's agenda, attacking its enemies, pushing its self-proclaimed achievements, they seem one and the same. There are new websites, a page on the Department of Health and Human Services website, Twitter accounts, and Facebook pages featuring "ACA Success Stories."

In mid-February 2014, the government releases new enrollment totals for January and the spin couldn't be more positive. Record enrollment! Three point three million! Goals met! Young, healthy desirables signing up in great waves! The rainbow has emerged after the storm. The gray, stormy skies are gone.

Of course, considering the track record of misinformation, on this story in particular, journalists should know they must treat the government's report like the press release that it is, and dig into the statistics with other experts to see if there are opposing viewpoints or alternate analyses.

Strangely, many reporters don't do this. They unquestioningly accept and report the government's spin, just as it's presented in its press release, as if it's undisputed fact.

But perhaps the greatest PR coup of all is that the administration's expert spinners successfully lead the media by the nose down the path of concluding there's no true controversy unless there's a paper trail that lays blame directly on the president's desk. Time and again, with each scandal and each new damaging fact, Democrats and the White House read from the script that says, *"there's no evidence President Obama knew"* or *"there's no evidence of direct White House involvement."* Anything short of a signed confession from the president himself is deemed a phony Republican scandal, and those who dare to ask questions are crazies, partisans, or conspiracy theorists. The press fails to independently step back and note that those implicated are Obama administration people, sometimes top handpicked officials. A headline that might read, "Administration officials hid HealthCare.gov's pitfalls . . ." instead might read, "No evidence Obama knew . . ."

Substitution Game: If past presidents had received similar treatment, the headline for Hurricane Katrina in 2005 might have read, "No evidence Bush had direct involvement in botched Katrina response" instead of "The botching of hurricane relief will affect Bush's legacy" (U.S. News and World Report)

Under President Obama, the press dutifully regurgitates the line "no evidence of White House involvement," ignoring the fact that if any proof exists, it would be difficult to come by under an administration that fails to properly respond to Freedom of Information document requests, routinely withholds documents from Congress, and claims executive privilege to keep documents secret.

Even accepting the most generous interpretation, many in the media fail to see news: the White House claims to be in the dark about massive mismanagement or wrongdoing by its own federal officials and agencies; about Obama's HHS secretary, Sebelius, overseeing the botched rollout of HealthCare.gov; about his energy secretary, Chu, overseeing billions in poor investments of green energy tax dollars; about the controversial surveillance of citizens and the press; about a massive cross-border gunwalking operation; about misuse of IRS authority; about an incorrect narrative on Benghazi; about Obama's State Department under Clinton denying security requests for Benghazi; about his director of national intelligence, Clapper, giving incorrect testimony to Congress; about his Justice Department under Attorney General Holder providing false information to Congress.

FEB. 13, 2014

CBS THIS MORNING

This morning, a milestone for the government health insurance marketplaces: they've finally met their monthly enrollment targets. The Obama administration reports 1.1 million people signed up for insurance in federal and state programs in January. Since they opened in October, nearly 3.3 million have signed up for coverage. There's also a surge in the number of young people enrolling, those 18–34 years old now make up 25% of the applicants.

It turns out there's much more to the story if one bothers to scratch beyond the surface. Out of curiosity, knowing there will be no interest in a broadcast report containing a critical analysis, I've nonetheless reached out to several experts who have proven to be uncannily accurate on this topic thus far. One of them is insurance industry representative Robert Laszewski of Health Policy and Strategy Associates. Another is an insider source who's a great barometer, beyond his verity, because he's a stalwart Obamacare supporter: he's not skewing his analyses to undercut the initiative. Both men provide nearly identical evaluations that are polar opposites of the government's.

"They made a big deal about the age results," says Laszewski. "But the greater challenge for them is the low number of people enrolling. There is no way you can get a good spread of risk with such a small percentage of the total eligible signing up."

The insider tells me that the bump of young enrollees in January to 27 percent is "progress," but added that government officials "neglect to point out that they need roughly forty percent to help achieve a balanced risk pool" necessary under a successful business model.

Both sources unequivocally state that, far from being an encouraging number, 3.3 million people is a small proportion of the population that "should be" interested in signing up. And that the true number is even lower because the government is counting 20 percent of enrollees who haven't paid, and because two-thirds of the enrollees were already insured prior to Obamacare so shouldn't be counted as previously uninsured.

"Looking at the total of 3.3 million, netting out the non-pays, and listening to the anecdotal carrier reports, it doesn't look like we have more than a fraction—certainly something less than ten percent—of the previously uninsured," said Laszewski.

To me, this is a headline—and an important one. I write up the story for the CBS News website.

Less than two months later, in April 2014, President Obama claims wild success with "marketplace" or "exchange" enrollment at 8 million customers, beyond all expectations. Most in the media accept the selectively released statistic without pressing for basic evidence to back it up. Having recently separated from CBS, I conduct an independent review using the government's own projections and statistics, industry surveys, and expert sources. Out of 38 million eligible Americans, only an estimated 3.4 million previously uninsured had been picked up through the insurance exchanges. One supporter involved in implementing Obamacare called the results extremely disappointing.

So many conflicting accounts. In so little time. But the biggest of all is owned by the president.

On December 12, 2013, the fact-check site PolitiFact.com dubs the president's pledge, "If you like your health care plan, you can keep it," the "2013 Lie of the Year."

CHAPTER 6

| I Spy |

The Government's Secrets

On January 8, 2013, I'm on my way to meet the contact who will be part of the process that gets my computer analyzed by a confidential source inside the government. I refer to my direct contact as "Number One." He's suggested a rendezvous at a McDonald's in Northern Virginia. When I enter with my laptop tucked under one arm, I scan the patrons and correctly guess which one is my guy. I slip into his booth and we shake hands across the table. No need for formal introductions. After a little small talk, he addresses the issue at hand. He's a matter-of-fact kind of guy.

"I'll tell you one thing. People would be shocked to know what this administration is doing in terms of spying on the American public." That's uncannily close to what Jeff had said to me just a few weeks before. And the two men don't know each other. But both are connected to government three-letter agencies.

Number One explains his arrangements to have my computer analyzed. What I'll receive is a verbal report. Because of who's helping me, I won't get an official written report. I understand the terms.

The next day, I'm working at my desk at CBS News when my mobile phone rings. It's Number One.

"I thought I'd give you an update," he says. "Our friend started looking at the product. He's not finished yet but it's proving very . . . interesting."

He stops.

"Did he find something?" I ask, filling the silence.

"Yes. It's positive."

Positive. For what? Positive that nothing is wrong? Positive for some sort of spyware?

"Really?" I say.

"Yeah," Number One continues. "I wouldn't have believed it. It's pretty shocking. We're all kind of in a state of shock right now. I don't want to say too much on the phone. In fact, I'd advise you to start using a burner phone. Do you know what that is?"

I do. The kind of phone that drug dealers and terrorists use so they can't easily be followed. He says I should use burner phones and switch them out frequently. At least every month. And don't use them from my house.

"I'll be able to give you more information tomorrow," he says.

We meet at the same place. We settle into a McDonald's booth and look around. For what, I don't know, but we look. Number One hands me my laptop and a piece of paper containing some typed notes. For both of us, our worldview has changed just a little.

"First just let me say again I'm shocked. Flabbergasted. All of us are. This is outrageous. Worse than anything Nixon ever did. I wouldn't have believed something like this could happen in the United States of America," says Number One.

He's impassioned. My attention level escalates. Just two days ago, I'd been fully prepared to be told there was nothing suspicious in my computer. Or maybe that all the evidence was gone. I might be told that the idea of the computer being tapped was the stuff of science fiction or an Orwellian novel. I never thought I'd hear what I was hearing.

Referring to the typed notes, Number One tells me that my computer was infiltrated by a sophisticated entity that used commercial, nonattributable spyware that's proprietary to a government agency: either the CIA, FBI, the Defense Intelligence Agency, or the National Security Agency (NSA). This particular intrusion came in silently attached to an otherwise innocuous email that I received and opened in February 2012. The intrusion was "redone" in July through a BGAN satellite terminal. I don't even know what a BGAN satellite terminal is, but I later look it up online and find this ad:

> BGAN Portable Satellite Internet & Phone. Connect a Laptop, Smartphone or Any Wireless Device to a satellite terminal for High-Speed Internet and phone from anywhere on the planet. Terminals are small enough to be carried inside of a laptop case, yet deliver broadband up to 492 Kbps. . . . BGAN is the hands down winner for carry portability, and ease of setup by anyone.

Number One continues.

The intrusion was "refreshed" another time using Wi-Fi at a Ritz Carlton hotel. The uninvited programs were running constantly on my laptop. They included a keystroke program that monitored everything I typed, visited online, and viewed on my screen. They accessed all of my email including my CBS work account. They obtained the passwords to my financial accounts and other applications, some of which are noted on the typewritten paper that I'm staring at. I'm told that I should assume my smartphones are also afflicted.

Continuing on, the intruders discovered my Skype account handle, stole the password, activated the audio, and made heavy use of it, presumably as a listening tool. As I understand it, the intrusion stopped abruptly about the time that I noted my computers quit turning on at night. Did the intruders know by reading my emails and listening to me on the phone in early December that I was on to them?

Did they remotely attempt to stop the programs at that time and cover their tracks, resulting in the end of the overnight computer activity?

Number One goes on to say that this was probably not a court-sanctioned action. He says the government's legal taps are usually of much shorter duration and they don't end abruptly as this one did. I'm also told flatly that my surveillance doesn't match up with a PATRIOT Act order. An insider checked for me. I have many questions, but Number One can't answer them. He's just the messenger.

There's one more finding. And it's more disturbing than everything else.

"Did you put any classified documents on your computer?" asks Number One.

"No," I say. "Why?"

"Three classified documents were on your computer. But here's the thing. They were buried deep in your operating system. In a place that, unless you're some kind of computer whiz specialist, you wouldn't even know exists."

"Well, I certainly didn't put anything there."

"Just making an educated guess, I'd say whoever got in your computer planted them."

That's worth pausing to let the chill run all the way up the back of my neck to the part of my brain that thinks, *Why? To frame me? A source?* My heart accelerates. I'm thinking it, but it's Number One who finally breaks the silence to say it.

"They probably planted them to be able to accuse you of having classified documents if they ever needed to do that at some point."

So a government-related entity has infiltrated my computer, email, and likely my smartphones, and that included illegally planting classified documents in a possible attempt to lay the groundwork to eventually entrap or frame me . . . or someone who talks to me? As it begins to sink in, I think of the whistleblowers and sources who have spoken to me over the past two years, often confidentially. By having well-placed sources help me discover this infiltration, did I just dodge a bullet? Did I get *them* before they got *me*?

Number One has firsthand experience in covert government surveillance. "Reporters used to be off-limits," he opines. "Even when we had a court order on a bad guy, if a reporter even lived anywhere in the vicinity, we stayed away. You just didn't go near journalists. It was sacrosanct. Obviously, that's changed."

I tell him about the extra fiber optics line on the back of my house.

"It's possible somebody was using that," he tells me. "But taps aren't usually done at people's homes anymore. It's all done through Verizon. They cooperate. There's no need to come to your house; we can get everything we want through the phone company."

This is months before Edward Snowden would reveal exactly that, building on revelations by *New York Times* reporter Risen and others who had written as far back as 2005 of phone companies assisting the government with surveillance.

I gather my laptop and notes, get a Coke to go, and know that the next step I need to take is notifying my supervisor at CBS News. The implications far surpass my own computer and personal life. The infiltration includes the CBS email system and the news division's proprietary software used in writing scripts and organizing the daily news broadcasts. The intruders could have accessed the entire CBS corporate system. This is huge. I can't reveal to CBS who's helping me or exactly how I know what I know, but they're aware that I have well-placed sources.

| NOTIFYING CBS

I walk straight into the CBS News Washington bureau and look for my bureau chief, Chris Isham. Isham is a longtime investigative reporter with plenty of knowledge about the way the government operates. He'll understand more than most the implications of what I'm about to tell him. He invites me into his office and closes the door. He sits on a short couch, and I plop into an adjacent chair with my notes and fill him in.

"I can't be the only one they're doing this to," I conclude.

"I know," he agrees. "You can't be."

But Isham doesn't want to sound the corporation's alarm bells yet. He explains that since my sources have to be protected, even from CBS, we will reach out to a trusted, private analysis firm and see if they can duplicate the findings of an intrusion on the CBS computer. If so, he says, we can then go to CBS News chairman Jeff Fager and CBS News president David Rhodes with the information.

But there's a challenge with this plan: I notice that that typewritten note from Number One says my computer is now "clean." Does that mean everything has been wiped from it?

I communicate with Number One to ask the question. The next day, he returns with an answer. The inside government analyst *did* wipe the computer.

"Why did he do that?" I ask Number One. I'm forever grateful for the help he's given. Without it I probably wouldn't even know today that I'd been the subject of a criminal intrusion. But why did he wipe the evidence?

"I don't know. I'm not sure in the beginning we really expected to find anything. And I guess we never talked about what the procedure would be if we did," says Number One.

It's true. In fact, I'm pretty sure none of us in the group actually expected any real evidence to be discovered. We never played out the scenario.

"Maybe he thought he was doing me a favor," I suggest. "Maybe he thought he was helping me by cleaning up my computer and getting it running smoothly again."

Cleaned up. Running smoothly, say the notes on the typewritten paper. Duplicating the evidence now will take a miracle.

| THE MCALLEN CASE

The MCALLEN Case begins on February 2, 2013.

We're expecting snow on a chilly Saturday in Northern Virginia. The doorbell rings and I greet the very businesslike Jerry Patel,* the private computer forensics analyst hired by Isham at CBS. Patel is doing CBS a favor by coming here. I haven't shared many details with him and I can tell at the outset he doesn't really expect to find anything significant. He thinks he's here to put my mind at ease. To assure me that the strange goings-on with my computers aren't the work of any intruder. Maybe just ordinary malware, a nagging virus, or a glitch.

I begin with niceties but none are necessary. Patel patiently tolerates the introduction before asking to be directed to the star of the show: my computers. I lead him upstairs into my bedroom and adjacent office. At night, this entire area becomes my workspace. My husband knows that when I'm on an important story, this is the business space until one or two in the morning. Forget about lights out.

Patel sits on the couch in my bedroom and unlocks a briefcase full of gear like a high-tech handyman. He tells me he's given this job a code name: The MCALLEN Case. I give a brief summary of what's been going on. Then he opens up the CBS News laptop and begins deconstructing the files. He transforms the user-friendly format of my Toshiba Windows into a baffling screen full of lines punctuated by brackets, forward slashes, and question marks. He looks in places that most of us have no idea exist in our computers. I'm practically breathing down his neck as I watch his fingers dance

---

* Not his real name.

along the keyboard and his eyes scan one line after another. As the hours pass and my mind gets accustomed to looking at the gibberish, it almost begins to make sense to me.

Other than a few "nonstandard" observations, the process is frankly pretty mundane. That is, until the date of December 9, 2012, surfaces. That was the time frame when I noticed that my computers had stopped freelancing on me.

"It looks like what we're seeing here is a log-in attempt at 4:20, approximately 4:20 and three seconds in the morning on December 9, 2012."

His voice has escalated from the soft monotone to somewhat expressive for the first time on the visit. I wasn't the one who attempted to log in at 4:20 in the morning. Patel spots another suspect message on December 12, 2012.

"What's unusual is audit policy changes."

He tells me that someone with administrative privileges, not me, has taken action in my computer. His voice becomes excited.

"Someone changed the audit policy at 8:48 in the morning . . . your computer rebooted at one o'clock in the morning. . . . So we'll go backwards. Here we go. December 11 we're back at the time in question. 4:05 [a.m.] . . . all right."

I don't know how to interpret what he's saying but I'm following along as he points to the lines on the screen.

"But you see . . ." he says, pointing to 4:05 a.m.

"There's nothing there . . ." I observe.

"Oh boy."

"What does that mean?"

"Ohhh boy. Look at the difference. December 10, 5:00:50 seconds. December 11th. Someone removed 24 hours."

He exhales, makes a whoosh noise, and summarizes.

"We have evidence that shows 24 hours, 23 hours of log messages have been removed. That's suspicious behavior."

Now he's breathing heavily. It alarms me because it alarms him and he's not easily alarmed. His voice becomes more formal and he launches into what sounds like a speech for posterity.

"In my professional opinion, someone has accessed this box. I'm going to be honest with you. I was hoping you weren't infected. But . . . I see evidence that shows a deliberate and skilled attempt to clean the log files of activity.

"Approximately 23 hours . . . 22 hours, 55 minutes of log messages have been removed. That is extremely nonstandard, especially considering the act of clearing a log is a log message in and of itself. So I am now going to concur with . . . I'm starting to concur with your suspicions."

His findings are lining up with what my earlier analysis found.

"Well, I suppose this visit wasn't for nothing then," he says. Deeper offsite analysis will be required.

It's dusk and the clouds are heavy with impending snow. Patel has been here six hours now and needs to head back to town to meet friends for dinner. Before he leaves, he wants to take a quick look at my personal Apple iMac desktop computer. Since his time is short, I ask him to go straight to December 9 on the iMac, too. If the intruders removed evidence of their presence from my laptop around that time, they might have tried to cover their tracks on the iMac desktop as well. Within a few minutes, it's confirmed.

"Oh shit!" The high-tech handyman is now fully animated. "Pardon my French but . . ."

"That's gone, too?" I say, looking over his shoulder.

"That's now a pattern. . . . We have a gap," Patel reports in the official posterity voice. "A second gap from December 8, 2012, 10:12:11 p.m. to December 9, 2012, 3:18:39 p.m. That's not normal. Someone did that to your computer. Two separate instances showing the same MO. That shows knowledge of the event logging and it shows skill. Somebody's deleting days of messages. . . . That shows skill."

He then searches through what he says is a key file.

"It should be bigger than that. It should be huge. Somebody deleted the file on December 11. It's not supposed to be like that. It's supposed to have lots of data in it and it doesn't."

"So what does that mean?" I ask.

"Someone was covering their tracks." Long exhale.

"So they would've done that remotely? 'Cause no one's been in the house."

"Yeah. We're examining the last log. And we have a deletion wtemp log that actually begins Saturday, December 11. Suggests the log was deleted on that day."

He proposes conducting further analysis at his office. But he tells me at the outset that he doesn't think he'll be able to attribute the intrusion to the guilty party. He can already see that from his cursory analysis. They're too sophisticated, he tells me. Too skilled. This is far beyond the abilities of even the best nongovernment hackers. They'll have covered their tracks.

It's snowing now. And dark. Patel remarks that sometimes his computer forensics job is a little dull. But the MCALLEN Case is not. He rushes off to meet his friends, leaving me and my compromised computers. I look out the window and watch his headlights track down my long driveway and down the road until they disappear. *What now?* As someone who's usually constantly online, I don't much feel like working on my computers tonight.

Two days later, Patel sends an email to Isham and copies me. I hear his voice in my mind as I read his words. "It is my professional opinion that a coordinated action (or series of actions) have taken place. I don't wish to go into details because the integrity of email is now in question. . . . It bothers me that I was not able to leave Sharyl with an increased sense of security Saturday evening, but hopefully we can all work together to remedy this ASAP."

It's February 4, 2013. Three and a half months before revelations about the Obama administration's seizure of AP phone records and those of the FOX News reporter. Almost exactly four months before the news that the NSA is secretly collecting Verizon phone records, as revealed by Edward Snowden.

THE DISRUPTIONS CONTINUE

When you challenge powerful institutions in the twenty-first century, you conduct your business with the notion ever present in the back of your mind that somebody's listening. Tapping your phone. Reading your computer files. Trying to learn what your sources are telling you. Finding a way to stop you. These thoughts float through your mind, escalating in direct proportion to the strength of the story and the power held by whomever it challenges. You think of it, but you don't really believe it's actually happening. You certainly don't think someone will turn up one day and hand you proof.

In fairness, I've begun telling my sensitive sources that our communications aren't secure. Funny thing is, none of them is surprised. They tell me they already assumed they were under government surveillance. But we do start crafting more secure ways to exchange information. For example, as I make contact with important confidential sources about the Benghazi attacks, I set up meetings on the phone but then later change the time and place in a way that can't be monitored. Of course, the intruders now know that I know. And I know that they know that I know. And so on. It's the loop of the paranoid wrapped in suspicion codified by truth.

CBS has remained strangely unfazed by the official news from Patel confirming what I'd told them: that an intruder has been in my computers and in the company's news and corporate system. I'd thought that the moment they got the corroboration, it would set off processes and inquiries. That corporate forensics experts would descend upon me and my house, looking to secure my personal and professional information, to protect my sources and look for the origin. That my colleagues would be officially notified so that they, too, could make their sources aware and a damage assessment could be made.

But none of these things happens.

CBS does ask Patel to conduct further investigation, but there seems to be no particular urgency, and he comes to the Washington bureau to pick up my laptop. We've kept it off the CBS system since the day Number One first gave me the news. I sign the chain-of-custody document and hand over the computer. I wonder if the intruders have already penetrated my newly issued CBS News laptop. When I earlier recounted to Number One how I heard the castle lock sound one night and assumed the intruder had been locked out of the CBS system, he practically chuckled, like a patient elder speaking to an ingénue.

"You may have heard that sound but I hate to disappoint you—we can cut through that firewall like butter. It's not an impediment."

Patel and his company are working for CBS. They're clearly tasked with protecting the network's security, not mine. But they do sit down with me and Isham and have a serious conversation to say that I should find ways to better protect my computer privacy. Aware of the persistent interruptions in my FiOS service, they tell me that I should have my Verizon FiOS box replaced again, and relocated inside the house.

"Insist on it," one of the experts tells me. "Don't take no for an answer. Don't let them leave the house until they replace it and move it."

Add to the glitches a new one: our Internet has begun disconnecting anytime a landline is in use. My kid's on her iPad, the phone rings, I answer it, and *blop*, she's bumped offline. I'm doing business on my Apple desktop, I pick up the phone to make a call, and *blop*, my Internet connection drops. You don't realize how often you use the phone and the Internet at the same time until you can't. So in early February 2013, a Verizon technician visits our home and two supervisors show up, too. A three-fer. The tech sits upstairs and works on my Apple desktop beside the router. The male supervisor comes, takes a look around, and leaves. The female supervisor chats up me and my husband downstairs in the kitchen. We mull over the familiar disturbances and I direct them to replace the whole outdoor box and move it inside. They tell me it's not necessary. I keep thinking of Patel saying, "Don't take no for an answer." So I tell the Verizon pair that I have a security expert who insists this step be taken. But they're formidable. It's not necessary, they say. They know their business. As adamant as I am about moving the box, they're just as adamant about not doing so. If I'm concerned about security, they say, there are lots of private consultants whom I can hire to help me. The tech gives me a name and number for one of them. He says there are many folks in Northern Virginia who need those special types of services. When the Verizon pair departs, our Internet is working, but the other same old problems persist.

I've been an Apple user since my first personal computer purchase circa 1989. My Macintosh, my Quadra, my Color Classic, my Performa, my iMac. As far as I know, I've never had viruses or major malfunctions with my Apples. I replace them not because they break but because they eventually run out of memory or I want the next generation. But now, my Apple iMac desktop begins a new behavior I've never before observed: it winds itself into a fever. The fan starts churning and the pitch gets higher and becomes so loud, it sounds as if it's going to explode. We shut it down and restart it but it happens again. On the third day of this, my daughter runs from the computer down to the kitchen.

"It's burning up!" she tells me.

I rush to the iMac to find it frozen, whining in its pre-explosion-sounding state, and it won't let me shut it down. This time there's a pungent smell of burning electronics. I reach underneath the desk and unplug it: that's all she wrote. The iMac is deceased. R.I.P., faithful Apple, you were so young.

My husband and I are weighing whether and how to file a criminal complaint over the intrusion. A crime has been committed. Someone has, in essence, illegally entered my property and violated the privacy of my entire family. They've stolen my property by rifling through my work and removing data. They've placed classified materials on my computer for motives that can't be considered anything but nefarious. But when the culprit is believed to be connected to the government, to whom, exactly, does one go to complain? Can you really turn to the Justice Department's FBI when the Justice Department might be part of the plot? I consult some trusted advisors and decide to file a complaint with the Department of Justice inspector general.

Every federal agency has its own inspector general designed to serve as an independent watchdog. The way I figure it, the best-case scenario is that the IG is honest and conducts a real investigation. Worst-case scenario: nothing comes of it, but at least the inquiry puts operative insiders on official alert: *your actions are known and being probed*. The idea is to try to create an environment that makes their deception and cover-up that much more difficult. So on April 3, 2013, I file the complaint. It's six weeks before the government snooping scandals would be revealed.

In a way, I'm at the center of the ultimate story. As disturbing as it is, I also find it intriguing. A widening circle of sources and contacts is interested, too. Some of them want to help me. They clue me into the many possibilities that exist. There are a thousand ways to spy on a private citizen. When we meet, before they speak to me, they put away their smartphones and tell me to lose mine, too. They don't want to talk in my house. I lose count of how many of them tell me that the government—or anyone with skill—can remotely turn on my smartphones and listen to me. Not just when I'm using the phone, but even when I think it's powered down. As long as the battery's in it, they can activate the microphone to hear what I'm doing and to whom I'm speaking. And when they're doing this, the phone doesn't appear to be on at all. Other sources tell me that sophisticated intruders have the capability to suck information out of my smartphones and computers, or for that matter put stuff in them, without even physically connecting to them. The devices simply have to be in proximity to the perpetrator's smartphone or device. Just innocently put one on a table next to another and *Floop!* it's compromised. *How many times have I set my BlackBerry or iPhone near a colleague's, a stranger's, or a business associate's?* And pretty much all of my self-appointed advisors tell me to use burner phones, which I am. They suggest I should have an acquaintance who's not closely connected to me purchase the device and buy the minutes. Switch it out a lot. One intelligence source advises me to remove the phone battery before I cross the threshold into my driveway. Don't put the battery in or use the phone while in my house.

Two acquaintances with knowledge of government surveillance and spy methods insist on sweeping my house and vehicle for bugs and signs of intrusions. They don't know each other and each uses different methods. They're not official, professional sweeps, just what can be done with devices like simple signal detectors and a FLIR thermal imaging device. They feel that the government has overstepped its bounds by spying on me, and helping me makes them feel like they're doing something about it. I appreciate their consideration, but I don't think they'll find anything.

"What's the point?" I ask.

"You never know, you might be surprised at what turns up. And it's no trouble to look," says one.

Between the two of them, they check the walls, the telephones. Lamps, bookshelves. They climb into the attic, where the Verizon man once lurked. They disassemble my electric power strips, examine the alarm system, and sweep the inside and outside of my car. Nothing.

The truth is, I've given up on the idea of privacy for the moment. Those who possess the skills to do what they've already done can pretty easily penetrate most any computer or device, most anytime, most anyplace. One source explains to me that Microsoft works on coding with the government so that anti-malware programs view the government's spyware as something friendly that belongs in the Microsoft environment. *I belong here*, the intruder tells the virus scanner. *Move along, nothing to see, you amateurs.* I can switch out phones, put a Band-Aid over the camera in my computer, and run debugging programs all day long. For those who have the toys and technology, defeating my defenses is child's play.

On May 6, 2013, I make contact with an excellent source who has crucial information: the name of the person responsible for my computer intrusions. He provides me the name and I recognize it. I'm not surprised. It strikes me as desperate and cowardly that those responsible would resort to these tactics. That's all I can say about that for now.

The inspector general's office checks in and gives me a bit of information. It's the same thing Number One told me in January: there's no PATRIOT Act order on me. The IG official also says the FBI denies having anything to do with my situation. Naturally, I'm dubious. I wonder who at the FBI was asked, what words they used in their denial, and was any of this put in writing. I suggest to the IG official that he might not be getting the whole story. He wants to know if my sources will speak with his office. I approach Number One.

"Frankly, I'm not comfortable," he tells me. "The IG works for the people who did this to you."

Inspectors general are supposed to be independent watchdogs of their agencies, and the Justice Department IG has a good reputation. But there can be an element of political influence even in some of the best IG offices. Number One's been around the block. He doesn't trust the IG. He says I shouldn't, either.

It's with great interest that I retrospectively view an interesting publication on WikiLeaks to which a contact directs my attention. On February 27, 2012, WikiLeaks began publishing five million emails purported to be from the Texas-headquartered "global intelligence" company Stratfor. One document of particular interest is dated September 2010 and is titled, "Obama Leak Investigations."

"Brennan is behind the witch hunts of investigative journalists learning information from inside the beltway sources," it says. "There is a specific tasker from the [White House] to go after anyone printing materials negative to the Obama agenda (oh my). Even the FBI is shocked."

All of this tees up the global news that's about to break revealing the Obama administration's surveillance of reporters—and the general public.

Obama Leak Investigations (internal use only—pls do not forward)

Released on 2012-09-10 00:00 GMT
Email-ID: 1210665
Date: 2010-09-21 21:38:37
From: burton@stratfor.com
To: secure@stratfor.com
Brennan is behind the witch hunts of investigative journalists learning information from inside the beltway sources.

Note—There is specific tasker from the WH to go after anyone printing materials negative to the Obama agenda (oh my.) Even the FBI is shocked. The Wonder Boys must be in meltdown mode. . . .

OBAMA'S "WAR ON LEAKS"

Four months after Number One first identified my computer intrusions, I'm watching the news. It's May 13, 2013, and there's a breaking story that sets off a pang of familiarity. I instinctively feel that it's related to my own situation. It's not so much that the details are the same—they're not. But there's something about the story line: a U.S. government entity secretly, audaciously, reaching into the private communications of news reporters.

The news is that the Justice Department had seized the records of twenty phone lines used by employees of the news organization Associated Press. AP says the records are from personal home and cell phone numbers belonging to editors and reporters, office numbers of various AP bureaus, and AP phones used in the press quarters in the House of Representatives, where members of the media have office space. It's unheard-of. Why did the government take this drastic measure? To try to catch and prosecute the government source who provided information for a 2012 AP story about a foiled underwear bomb plot. The Justice Department had issued the subpoenas to telephone companies but granted itself an exception to its own normal practice in deciding not to provide advance notice of its intentions to AP. Advance notice would have given AP the chance to challenge the move in court. Only now, months after the fact, is the Justice Department disclosing its controversial subpoenas to the news outlet's managers. Incensed AP officials publicly attack the action as a "massive and unprecedented intrusion by the Department of Justice into the news-gathering activities of the Associated Press."

It's perhaps the first time the Obama administration feels the sting of meaningful criticism from such a wide-ranging group of news media. They're calling it Obama's War on Leaks. On May 14, 2013, a coalition of more than fifty news organizations, including ABC, CNN, NPR, the *New York Times*, the *Washington Post*, and the Reporters Committee for Freedom of the Press writes a strongly worded letter of objection to Holder. It reads in part:

> The nation's news media were stunned to learn yesterday of the Department of Justice's broad subpoena of telephone records belonging to The Associated Press. In the thirty years since the Department issued guidelines governing its subpoena practice as it relates to phone records from journalists, none of us can remember an instance where such an overreaching dragnet for newsgathering materials was deployed by the Department, particularly without notice to the affected reporters or an opportunity to seek judicial review. The scope of this action calls into question the very integrity of Department of Justice policies toward the press and its ability to balance, on its own, its police powers against the First Amendment rights of the news media and the public's interest in reporting on all manner of government conduct, including matters touching on national security which lie at the heart of this case.

The Justice Department responds to the growing privacy concerns by the media with a statement saying that it "takes seriously the First Amendment right to freedom of the press" and that Holder "understands the concerns that have been raised by the media and has initiated a reevaluation of existing Department policies and procedures."

How does this story fit into my circumstances? It's a puzzle I'm trying to sort out but a lot of the pieces are missing.

The AP story turns out to be the first in a rapid-fire succession of strange-but-true revelations about the government's aggressive actions against news reporters. Less than a week later, on Sunday, May 19, 2013, comes word that the Obama administration has targeted another national news journalist: FOX News reporter James Rosen. Again, it's supposedly part of a government leak investigation, this one into a State Department contractor who was later indicted. Attorney General Holder himself had approved the search warrant for Rosen's Gmail account.

It's so Orwellian for the government to aim its investigative resources and prosecutorial tools at reporters who are doing their legal job. Is this all part of a broad, secretive program to target the Obama administration's reportorial enemies? Am I on the list, too?

It's becoming clear that the administration is going after journalists and sources whom it views as the most harmful to its own self-interests. I think about when I was covering *Fast and Furious* and how the story reached all the way into the White House, prompting the president to declare executive privilege to keep from releasing documents to Congress. The government surely wanted to know what I knew and who was talking to me. Perhaps they felt they could justify monitoring me as another in this series of "leak investigations." My *Fast and Furious* coverage bled over into the Benghazi period. The Obama administration was just as frantic over my reporting on that topic. Just as desperate to learn who was talking to me and what I was learning from them.

With the discovery about the intrusions on AP and FOX reporters, a new public sentiment seems to be building: ordinary people are frightened by and outraged over the perceived assault on journalists and their sources.

Just days into news of these controversies, I'm doing a round of radio interviews centered on my current Benghazi reporting. I'm on the air with Philadelphia radio talk show host Chris Stigall of WPHT 1210 AM when he segues to the subject of the government intrusions on reporters. I haven't publicly discussed my own situation, which predates the public revelations about AP and FOX. But Stigall pops an unexpected question:

"Do you know if your phone was tapped or your emails watched or seized while you were having conversations with unnamed sources on Benghazi, Sharyl?"

Does he know? I hadn't given any thought as to what I might say about my own computers. I answer the question on the spot without opening the door too wide.

"I'm not ready to fully speak publicly about some things that have affected me because I'm trying to be methodical and careful about what I say. But there has been an issue in my house, and there's been an issue with my computers that's gone on for quite a long time that we're looking into."

Stigall seems as surprised by my answer as I was by the question. For several minutes, he continues to press for more information and I give limited responses. I bring the interview to a close by saying, "There's definitely been an intrusion into my computer system. I really can't say more than that right now."

I wouldn't have predicted the avalanche of interest that this brief radio interview would generate. Within minutes, word of my computer intrusions is being circulated on Internet blogs and is being tweeted about on Twitter. I know nothing of the chatter until I get a call from the CBS News press office. Inquiries are pouring in. It's not long before friends and family email to tell me that bloggers are speculating that the White House is bugging me. Or that I've mistaken a common computer virus or automatic Windows updates for something nefarious. Or that I'm being hacked by an old boyfriend. It's funny to hear some work so hard to discredit so much with so few facts.

I haven't named the Justice Department as a culprit or suspect. But considering the AP and FOX News incidents, it's only natural that someone else in the media would ask the Justice Department to comment on the Attkisson case.

In response, the agency issues this statement: "To our knowledge, the Justice Department has never 'compromised' Ms. Attkisson's computers, or otherwise sought any information from or concerning any telephone, computer, or other media device she may own or use."

As someone who's now an old hand at the way the administration parses words, my brain automatically shifts into read-between-the-lines mode.

To our knowledge . . . says the Justice Department's quasi-denial. Okay, that's a qualifier. Leaves open a little room. And who is "our" referring to in "To our knowledge"? Does it mean the guy who wrote the statement and another who pressed the SEND button? The whole press office? The entire Justice Department? Did officials there really, in the blink of an eye, conduct an investigation and question 113,543 Justice Department employees? That's impressive! I'm still waiting for answers to Freedom of Information Act requests I filed with them years ago, but they're able to provide this semi-definitive statement within minutes of the question being posed.

Oddly enough, most of my colleagues have been avoiding the whole topic of my computer intrusions. It seems they don't want to think about it or talk about it or know about it. As if it's somehow contagious. I haven't offered up much information, but several of them are aware that the CBS analyst has confirmed my intrusion. Yet the natural curiosity you might expect from fellow journalists, the outcry, seems strangely absent. If the shoe were on the other foot, I'd be outraged that anyone had illegally entered the CBS computer system. If I were them I'd want to find out as much as possible to see if the same thing might be happening to me, potentially compromising my story information and sources. I'd wonder if the infiltrators had peered in my home computer, too, and if they'd rifled through my private files.

The new revelations about AP and FOX seem to trigger the first spark of interest from some colleagues.

"Is this what's happening to you?" one of them dares to ask. Another ventures a little deeper.

"How does it make you feel to know the administration is going after you like that?"

I think for a moment.

"Effective."

They don't want to linger on the topic. They broach it, ask a question, make a joke, and move on. Like a butterfly lighting for a moment and then, thinking better of it, fluttering off.

| SNOWDEN AND CLAPPER: HARD TRUTHS

It's hard to imagine there are more shoes to drop. But the next one is a bona fide rubber-soled size 14 extra wide. So large and damaging, it stands to undermine the credibility of the nation's entire intelligence infrastructure.

On Wednesday, June 5, 2013, the *Washington Post* and the *Guardian* begin exposés that vault an unknown National Security Agency (NSA) contract employee named Edward Snowden into cult status as an American Patriot, Public Enemy #1, or both, depending on your viewpoint. Snowden's information reveals a shocking government effort to watch over, or spy on, its own citizens—depending on your viewpoint.

Snowden reveals how the NSA has obtained direct access to the systems of all the trusted Internet giants that Americans commonly use, such as Google, Apple, and Facebook, as part of a program called Prism. Through Prism, government officials can collect the search histories, emails, file transfers, and live chats of ordinary, law-abiding citizens. The depth and breadth of the surveillance is mindboggling. The implied privacy violations and government overreach confound normal alliances. Some Democrats strongly question the initiatives. Many Republicans defend it.

Drip, drip becomes gush, gush, gush as a rolling wave of Snowden revelations washes up one sensitive and embarrassing government secret after another. Like the government's controversial April 2013 order from the clandestine Foreign Intelligence Surveillance Act (FISA) court. The order compelled Verizon to provide the NSA, on an ongoing basis, all of its call detail records, or "telephony meta-data." Not only for calls that go abroad, but also for ones that take place wholly within the United States, including local telephone calls. The initiative is supposedly to protect us from foreign terrorist threats. But casting the net so widely—even applying to next-door neighbors calling one another here in the U.S.A.—arouses shock and outrage. The authority was first granted in 2001 under the PATRIOT Act. As Congress debated renewal of the act in 2011, two Democrats, Senator Ron Wyden of Oregon and Mark Udall of Colorado, foreshadowed the controversy to come. Both members of the Intelligence Committee, which oversees the intelligence community, the senators were privy to the surreptitious ways in which the government was granting itself and expanding authority, and pushing the bounds of the definition of "metadata"—which refers to impersonal data about data—to include more information, and compiling it in such a way that it can reveal personal details that were intended to be protected.

"I want to deliver a warning," Wyden stated during the 2011 congressional debate over renewal of the PATRIOT Act. "When the American people find out how their government has secretly interpreted the PATRIOT Act, they will be stunned and they will be angry."

Wyden's words sound much like those of my sources the previous fall.

The average American would be shocked at the extent to which this administration is spying on its own private citizens.

Patel continues his examination of my computers but it seems to stall and languish. Weeks. Months. CBS managers are conspicuously silent on the issue of a possible connection between what's happened to me and what we're learning about the government's overreach through the cases of AP, FOX, and Snowden. As if it hasn't occurred to them. As if they're not even a little outraged—or at least curious. In fact, they seem extremely uncomfortable with the fact that I've discovered unauthorized trespassers in my computers. I can't explain it, but I'm now getting a vibe from CBS as if *I'm* the one who's done something wrong for learning that my computers were infiltrated.

The strange vibe persists when I seek out an update on Patel's computer forensics work. I find myself suddenly cut out of the loop. The computer firm had been communicating directly with me. But now, they won't readily respond to phone calls and emails. It's as if they've been instructed to slice me out of the communications channel. As I continue to press to find out what has become of the investigation, I eventually learn secondhand that Patel provided CBS a near-final draft report on May 9, but CBS hasn't provided me with a copy or even told me that the report has been sent. I can't explain why, other than intuition, but I get the eerie feeling that CBS wants to downplay what's happened—maybe even try to advance a narrative that there was no computer intrusion. Why am I not in the loop on the findings of incidents that happened to me in my home?

To me, the pieces are starting to fit together. My case and that of AP and FOX are enough to suggest that the government had a coordinated effort at least by 2012, and probably beginning earlier, to target the leakers and reporters who were perceived as making the administration's life difficult. Snowden's revelations tie it all together.

If CBS is blind to the connection, it's nonetheless occurred to some members of Congress and their staff. A number of them in the House and Senate approach me and ask if they can help me in the effort to hold the perpetrators in my case accountable. For the moment, I'm looking for answers in a way that keeps the conversation out of the spotlight.

CBS finally agrees to provide me a copy of Patel's draft report. I've had further conversations that lead me to conclude my company may try to spin my computer intrusions as something dubious and indefinite. I'm given additional pause for thought when I learn that some CBS managers are quietly implying to selected colleagues, who are happy to spread it around, that the computer intrusions might be a figment of my "paranoid" imagination. I can't figure out why they would say such a thing when their own analyst had long ago confirmed the intrusions verbally and in writing, in no uncertain terms. Why would some in my own company now attempt to discredit the computer issue and their own forensic expert? Weren't they as alarmed as I was to learn that unauthorized parties were in the CBS system?

As if enough weren't going on, this all was happening against the backdrop of my trying to separate myself from CBS contractually for reasons discussed elsewhere in this book—an effort that would end with my agreeing to remain on staff for about another year. But the discussions caused a great deal of stress and tension between me and some of my bosses.

Even more disturbing, word came to me that a CBS manager had convened a private meeting with a colleague asking him to turn over the name(s) of the inside confidential source(s) who had first helped me identify the computer intrusions back in January. The colleague didn't have that information.

Weird.

Although I've pretty much been frozen out of the investigation into my own computer intrusions at this point, I don't give up until I finally reach Patel personally on the phone and ask him what's going on. He says he's preparing his final report. I tell him that I'm getting the feeling that some at CBS might try to bury the computer intrusion.

"That's impossible," he tells me. "They can't deny it happened. The facts are clear."

While preparing his final report for CBS on June 10, 2013, Patel makes an additional breakthrough and sends a direct message that will make it impossible for anyone to legitimately soft-pedal my computer intrusions. He writes an email to CBS managers marked "URGENT" and states that his analysis using a special investigative tool has revealed definitive evidence of one or more invaders attempting to remotely run commands on my computer. Additionally, he explicitly makes clear there's proof that the entity deliberately removed evidence of its handiwork, tried to cover up its tracks during that mid-December time frame in which I had noticed the frenetic nights of computer activity had slipped into quiet slumber. The infiltrator ran commands that nobody should have run. It collected my passwords and contacts with a special program. It securely erased entries and histories of certain commands. Other clues left behind: the cyber-spies changed the internal clock of my work laptop not once, not twice, but 1,358 times, possibly in an attempt to disrupt any temporal analysis we might try to do. If this had been a legal tap, they wouldn't have needed to tamper with the evidence.

Everything Patel has found serves to confirm my January source and analysis. Patel tells me that only a few entities possess these highly specialized skills. One of them is the U.S. government. I already know this from Number One. But now CBS knows it, too. And it will all be in his final report to the network.

On June 15, 2013, Isham telephones me after work and asks me to meet him the next morning in his Washington office. When I arrive, I enter his office to discover not only Isham but also CBS News president David Rhodes from New York. Isham closes the door and I sit. Rhodes and Isham take turns telling me Patel has completed his final forensics report more than four months after he began investigating. They say the report confirms the computer intrusions in some detail. I've been living with the knowledge for five months, but getting CBS management officially on the same page is a positive step. Their mood is markedly different than in the past few weeks. They're smiling and appear happy. They tell me this is all good news in the sense that they now have solid, documentary evidence from their own independent expert. They say they're "a thousand percent" behind me in all matters of support and in pursuing the perpetrator(s). I don't know what seems to have turned them around, but they say that they also think we should begin covering this as the news story that it is. They hand me a piece of paper containing a brief statement that's been prepared for public release as soon as our meeting ends:

> A cyber security firm hired by CBS News has determined through forensic analysis that Sharyl Attkisson's computer was accessed by an unauthorized, external, unknown party on multiple occasions late in 2012. Evidence suggests this party performed all access remotely using Attkisson's accounts. While no malicious code was found, forensic analysis revealed an intruder had executed commands that appeared to involve search and exfiltration of data. This party also used sophisticated methods to remove all possible indications of unauthorized activity, and alter system times to cause further confusion. CBS News is taking steps to identify the responsible party and their method of access.

The next morning, *CBS This Morning* briefly interviews me about the case. It's generating a great deal of interest and requests for interviews from other news media. The only non-CBS entity that the company wishes me to speak with is Bill O'Reilly from *The O'Reilly Factor* on FOX News. I fly to New York and appear on his evening program.

Meanwhile, during this very same time period, Senator Wyden stokes the embers of another controversy that would keep the Obama administration set back on its heels. He accuses Director of National Intelligence James Clapper of not giving a "straight answer" to the Senate Intelligence Committee three months before.

"Does the NSA collect any type of data at all on millions or hundreds of millions of Americans?" Wyden had asked Clapper at the March 12, 2013, hearing.

"No, sir," Clapper replies, quickly shaking his head and pressing the fingers of his right hand against his forehead, almost shielding his eyes from making direct contact as he looks down, up, down, up, down, all inside of about two seconds.

"It does not?" Wyden repeats, eyebrows raised.

"Not wittingly." Clapper continues shaking his head and begins stroking his forehead with the four fingers. "There are cases where they could inadvertently, perhaps, collect—but not wittingly." Clapper looks up and down fifteen times, by my count, in the span of that brief answer.

Call it a mistake, a misunderstanding, or a lie—depending on your viewpoint—but Clapper's testimony was wrong. The whole world now knows what Senator Wyden, with his access to classified information knew, when he posed the question: NSA programs collect data belonging to hundreds of millions of Americans from U.S. phone call records, online communications, and Internet companies.

Now Wyden wants public hearings "to address the recent disclosures" and says "the American people have the right to expect straight answers from the intelligence leadership to the questions asked by their representatives."

You might think everyone would agree that giving bad information to Congress, under oath, is improper.

But this is Washington.

Clapper's defenders say that Wyden "sandbagged" him. That by asking a loaded question at a public hearing, Wyden forced Clapper to either tell the truth, thus divulging top-secret information, or tell a lie.

The sandbag argument doesn't stand up, factually. Wyden says he sent the question to Clapper's office a day in advance of the hearing so that he'd be prepared for it. In any event, Clapper should have been able to produce a better and honest answer. In 2006, then–attorney general Alberto Gonzales apparently did when asked a similar question at a Senate Judiciary Committee hearing. Rather than mislead or divulge secrets, Gonzales found a third option. He told Congress: "The programs and activities you ask about, to the extent that they exist, would be highly classified."

As damage control for Clapper's misstep, the Obama administration mounts an outreach effort on Capitol Hill. Clapper is now sent to defend the very programs he swore didn't exist. Senators get three classified briefings in a week's time. NSA director Keith Alexander joins Clapper's PR campaign to exalt the controversial intelligence-gathering methods. They explain, behind closed congressional doors, that they've thwarted dozens of attack plots and saved the lives of countless Americans. (This is a claim that would later be roundly debunked by an independent committee investigating the policy.) America should be grateful, not critical. Perhaps in those private briefings, the senators urge Clapper to clear the air with a formal, public apology. Whatever the genesis, he writes a letter on June 21, 2013, to Senate Intelligence Committee chairman Democrat Dianne Feinstein admitting that his March testimony was "clearly erroneous." He indicates that he had misunderstood Wyden's question. That seems to differ with his earlier June 9 interview with NBC News, in which he'd said that he'd given "the least untruthful" answer that he could give.

Wyden isn't moved by the apology. A week later, on June 28, 2013, he leads a group of twenty-six senators in asking Clapper to publicly provide information on the "duration and scope" of the intelligence collecting as well as examples of how it's provided unique intelligence "if such examples exist." Twenty-one Democrats, four Republicans, and an Independent sign the letter.

During this time, I hear and read a lot of opinions from colleagues, viewers, friends, and strangers about the government's secret collection of data. Many of them say they don't mind if the government collects their information.

"They're welcome to look at anything I have," says one acquaintance. "I'm not breaking any laws."

Part of that sentiment may come from the fact that we long ago began trusting nearly every aspect of our private lives to credit card companies, banks, electronic mail, and Internet connections. Despite the dire warnings we hear every day about identity theft and other serious threats, such problems account for a relatively small proportion of the number of transactions we conduct. Every day, without giving it a second thought, we expose ourselves to dozens of opportunities for our personal information to be compromised, but for the most part we suffer few serious consequences. Also, many Americans have come to accept the idea that for the government to help keep us safe in a post-9/11 reality, it must be able to use diverse tools and methods, even if that means sacrificing some measure of our privacy and liberty. On top of that, the social media culture has dramatically faded privacy boundaries. We post everything from the embarrassingly inappropriate to the intensely private. Some view privacy as having become an old-fashioned, overrated notion.

By implication, the people who are happy to trust their personal communications to the government are conferring trust upon whoever and whatever the government may become in the future. What's more, they fully trust each and every person who may gain access to the information. These people don't foresee a time when there may be facets of the government that aren't benevolent. They don't envision the possibility of dishonest players in the mix. To them, the motivations of the government and all those who are in it will always and forevermore be good: their government would never break the law, violate ethics, or exploit private information for inappropriate use.

I'm not quite there.

History and experience lead me to be more circumspect. There are thousands of examples over the decades, but one need look no further than *Fast and Furious* to find government misconduct, bad actors, and false information all wrapped up in one. Or consider the 2013 IRS scandal in which the government got caught targeting nonprofit groups for political reasons after insisting it would never do such a thing.

Even if we could assume 100 percent altruistic motives on the part of the government now and forevermore, there are still serious questions to consider. Wyden is getting at the heart of them with his inquiries. I'll illustrate them with an analogy.

What if your local police were to claim that they can prevent crime in the community if they mount twenty-four-hour surveillance cameras on every public street corner? You might say okay. What if they say they can prevent more crime if they monitor every resident's emails and phone calls? That's a little tougher. You might have some questions. How much crime would be prevented? Where's the proof? Have the police tried less intrusive methods? What independent body will monitor for abuse? Okay, now let's ratchet it up another notch. What if the police decide, in secret, that they can theoretically prevent one murder a year if they mount hidden surveillance cameras inside every room inside every family's private home? Shouldn't anyone who's innocent of breaking the law be willing to sacrifice his family's privacy to save a human life?

(Why the pregnant pause?)

Apply the analogy to today's ethical and privacy questions.

How many terrorist acts would have to be thwarted to justify what level of intrusion in our privacy or on our civil liberties? The calculus is entirely theoretical since there are no accurate predictive models. Nobody can say for sure how many supposedly prevented plots would have been carried out or how many lives would have been lost but for the privacy invasion. Is bulk collection of data solely to credit in examples of foiled terrorist acts? Were less broad, less intrusive methods tried and proven ineffective before each more intrusive effort was launched? If so, are the more intrusive methods providing measurably better results? What independent controls and audits are in place to guarantee protection of private information from abuse by those with political or criminal motivations? Can the public trust the government officials who want to use the secret techniques to provide accurate and honest assessments of these questions—even when the same officials have provided false information in the past? Should the public be excluded from policy debates about these issues?

A real-world example provides additional reasons to question the merit of mass data collection.

On March 4, 2011, U.S. officials were alerted to Tamerlan Tsarnaev, the future Boston Marathon bomber. The tip didn't come from NSA collection of metadata, the tracing of cell phone calls, or the tracking of Internet activity: it came from Russia, which sent a notice to the U.S. Embassy in Moscow requesting the FBI look into Tsarnaev, who was living in America. The FBI later said it did all it could to investigate and even interviewed Tsarnaev but found nothing suspicious. Six months later, in

September 2011, Russia sent another alert about Tsarnaev, this time to the CIA. But like the FBI, the CIA also found nothing of concern. Off the official radar, Tsarnaev went on to murder three people and injure an estimated 264 in the April 15, 2013, bombing attack at the Boston Marathon. He was killed in a shootout with the police. His brother is awaiting trial.

In the end, U.S. officials pretty much blamed the Russians in public news reports. They said the Russians should have provided more explicit detail about why they'd been so suspicious of Tsarnaev back in 2011. It's an embarrassing admission: our best U.S. intelligence officials were handed a future terrorist but couldn't detect the threat because, they say, Russia should have helped us more?

Is it reasonable to believe this same U.S. intelligence structure has the skill, then, to cull through hundreds of millions of phone call records for subtle leads and then connect the dots to terrorist plots? Or is the government simply expanding its own bureaucracy: building an unwieldy, expensive database ripe for misuse that will require an increasing army of manpower to maintain, store, and guard it?

Answers aren't easy. Like a lot of people, I place great value on the intelligence community's role in protecting the public. Many skilled and devoted agents and officers often do a tremendous job. But I believe it's possible to give the public a role in the discussion in a way that doesn't divulge crucial secrets to the enemy.

As a footnote to the Tsarnaev story, I can't help but think about how the government found no cause to monitor this future terrorist at the very same time it aggressively targeted leakers as well as American journalists who had committed no crimes.

| THE TURNAROUND

Now mired in the bad press about Clapper, AP, FOX, and Snowden, the Obama administration is working overtime to try to turn it all around—not the government's behavior, mind you, just the public's perception of it. That translates into tightening the noose around government secrets and those who hold them.

One of my sources is called into a group meeting at a government agency.

"If you speak to reporters, we'll fuck you up, put you in a box," they're told.

The message: don't view the current whistleblower environment as an opportunity to join in on revealing the federal government's possible misdeeds. Federal supervisors circulate internal emails reminding the line staff and field guys, in so many words, that this administration has prosecuted more leakers than all previous administrations combined.

If there's one thing I've learned through years of dealing with federal whistleblowers, it's that they're terrified of losing their jobs and eventual retirements. I guess most people would be. But federal workers have pretty sweet retirement deals and the threat of that evaporating usually convinces them to keep their mouths shut about suspected ethical and even criminal violations by their bosses and agencies. It's effective. ("We'll fuck you up," is pretty effective, too.)

On June 21, 2013, the Justice Department unseals a criminal complaint charging Snowden under the Espionage Act.

The Big Chill is on.

Many sources, including congressmen, become more wary of communicating the ordinary way. One evening, I'm talking with a member of Congress on my regular mobile phone about a somewhat sensitive news matter. He's avoiding giving straight answers. I keep pressing. Finally, sounding exasperated, he blurts out, "Sharyl, your phone's bugged!" I can't argue the point. We decide to meet in person and work out alternate ways to communicate. It's the new reality in a society where journalists and politicians suspect their government is listening in.

Beyond its move to privately contain and even threaten some federal employees, the Obama administration must also try to recapture the hearts and minds of the public and the press. How? One strategy is to convince the public to view Snowden as the villain. This might not fly if too many people decide he's a hero. But if enough people buy the argument that he put American lives at risk, it just might turn things around for the Obama White House.

Thus begins *Operation Where's Waldo*. Only it's *Where's Snowden*. Attention is diverted from the questions that Senator Wyden and Snowden have raised. It turns away from Obama's War on Leaks. It's redirected from the targeting of journalists. Instead, we're consumed by the imponderable question of Snowden's whereabouts. *What country is he in? What plane is he boarding next? Is it the 2:30 p.m. nonstop to Moscow? Or the 4:45 p.m. to Cuba? Who will grant him asylum?*

Where's Snowden dominates the White House briefings and the news headlines.

Before long, the quest branches out into a full-blown news media obsession with all things Snowden. Everything except the editorial content of what he revealed. *How many documents did he get? How did he get access? Who passed his background checks? Did he graduate from high school? And what about rumors of a questionable discharge from the army?* Looking into Snowden's background is certainly a legitimate and reasonable area of inquiry. But it seems as though disproportionate media attention is being devoted to dissecting his character rather than also looking into the merits of the issues he raised.

"How much did Snowden steal?" screams a July 18, 2013, subheading on a news wire service. Unidentified sources are quoted in the article as saying Snowden took "tens of thousands" of documents. Nowhere does the article represent Snowden's side of the story or that of those who view him as a whistleblower.

If Snowden leaks, it's a crime. But if the administration leaks to implicate Snowden, it's a virtue? In other words, government leaks are okay as long as the leaks flow in the right direction.

Snowden's story isn't black-and-white. He may have indeed violated national security rules and hurt the country. At the same time, he may have believed himself a patriot and also done an important service in exposing potentially improper and overreaching behavior by the U.S. government. The scenarios aren't mutually exclusive. Surely Snowden doesn't see himself as a traitor. To date, there's no evidence that he peddled information to enemies of the United States or anyone else. There's no evidence that he stole the information for personal financial gain. Quite the opposite: he gave it to the public, free of charge, at great personal peril, as if he has incredible conviction and belief in the importance of what he's revealing.

"Even if you're not doing anything wrong you're being watched and recorded," Snowden said in an interview with the *Guardian*. "The public needs to decide whether these programs or policies are right or wrong." Snowden has given up a comfortable life in Hawaii and a six-figure salary. "I'm willing to sacrifice all of that because I can't in good conscience allow the U.S. government to destroy privacy, Internet freedom and basic liberties for people around the world with this massive surveillance machine they're secretly building."

Many in Congress assist the administration's diversionary plan. They don't treat Snowden's revelations as deserving of scrutiny. Instead, it's *how did a guy like Snowden get his hands on all those secrets?* Senator Feinstein announces a proposed legislative fix to prevent contractors like Snowden from handling highly classified technical data.

Meantime, no sanctions are proposed against Clapper for his misleading testimony. And nobody seems to think it's odd that he's trusted to spearhead efforts to address concerns over the very programs about which he misled Congress. The AP reports that Clapper's new plans include "a sweeping system of electronic monitoring that would tap into government, financial and other databases to scan the behavior of many of the 5 million federal employees with secret clearances, current and former officials." Nobody seems to notice that, if anything, the administration is ramping up, not tamping down, its controversial War on Leaks.

Allowing Clapper and other government officials to be in charge of solving their own surveillance controversies is like inviting the fox to guard the henhouse. Except the fox is also getting the keys to the henhouse and the recipe for chicken fricassee.

In a fictitious world, one can imagine a meeting in which any member of Congress calling for Clapper's head gets a closed-door visit from Clapper or his team. They slide a file bearing the name of the member of Congress or someone close to him across the desk, J. Edgar Hoover–style. The file contains materials surreptitiously gathered under the auspices of a government leak investigation or surveillance program. The member of Congress opens the file. Perhaps his eyes flicker. Maybe his face becomes white. The materials are very . . . *personal*. The imaginary Clapper rubs his forehead with his four fingers. No words are spoken because none are necessary. The file is closed and Clapper drags it back across the desk, never to be spoken of again. Unless necessary. Suddenly the member of Congress is no longer out for Clapper's head.

Or here's another fictitious premise. CIA director Petraeus deviates from the Obama administration's official line on Benghazi. Somewhere in a private room, a small group of government operatives culls through data to find out who Petraeus has been emailing and calling. Any skeletons in that closet? A review of his file reveals some unseemly contacts with his former biographer. That information could come in very handy.

Now, I remind you that those are wholly fanciful scenarios. The stuff of imagination. The government would never misuse its authority or information, right? Still, the fact that these notions can be conjured up, even if chimerical, illustrates why it's so important to have public discussion and oversight.

| OTHER REPORTERS WEIGH IN

In late June 2013, I'm flying back from the Investigative Reporters and Editors conference in San Antonio, Texas, and am seated next to another journalist: Len Downie. Downie is former executive editor of the *Washington Post* and had spoken at the conference on the very topic at hand.

"The Obama administration's War on Leaks is by far the most aggressive that I've seen since the Nixon administration, and I go back that far," Downie told the audience of investigative journalists.

As we strike up a chat shoulder to shoulder on the plane, I bring up the subject of Snowden. I ask Downie if it doesn't seem as though more attention should be focused on the content of Snowden's claims instead of where he's hiding or whether he graduated from high school. Downie agrees.

Four months later, Downie would publish a definitive report for the Committee to Protect Journalists. It establishes the Obama administration as the news media's top choice for Least Transparent American Presidency in Modern Times. When you think of all the transparency promises, it's stunning to read the actual experiences of national news reporters, not those working at conservative outlets but journalists from the *New York Times* and the *Washington Post*.

David Sanger, chief Washington correspondent of the *Times*, says, "This is the most closed, control freak administration I've ever covered."

Times public editor Margaret Sullivan: "It's turning out to be the administration of unprecedented secrecy and unprecedented attacks on a free press."

Financial Times correspondent Richard McGregor: "Covering this White House is pretty miserable in terms of getting anything of substance to report on in what should be a much more open system."

ABC News White House correspondent Ann Compton: "He's the least transparent of the seven presidents I've covered in terms of how he does his daily business."

Josh Gerstein of *Politico*: "If the story is basically one that they don't want to come out, they won't even give you the basic facts."

Washington correspondent Josh Meyer: "There is across-the-board hostility to the media. . . . They don't return repeated phone calls and e-mails. They feel entitled to and expect supportive media coverage."

Post managing editor Kevin Merida describes what he sees as the White House's hypersensitivity, saying that officials often call reporters and editors to complain about something on Twitter or a headline on a website.

I have a slightly different interpretation of the administration's sensitivities. It's not that they're really so sensitive. They're simply executing a well-thought-out strategy to harass reporters and editors at the slightest air of negativity so as to impact the next news decisions. To provide so much unpleasant static and interference that we may subconsciously alter the way we report stories. To consume so much of our time explaining and justifying what we've reported, that we begin to self-censor in the future. They accuse us of "piling on," when all we're doing is accurately covering their actions and the outcome of their decisions. But what human being doesn't instinctively learn to avoid negative, unpleasant feedback?

Let's not use that phrase in our story. Yes, it's accurate, but the White House will go nuts over it. Maybe if we soften it a little, we can avoid some headaches. We don't want to appear to be—piling on.

What we don't seem to realize is that our never-ending pursuit to avoid the static is a fool's errand. Their relentless objections are not because they want accurate reporting; their goal is to spin and stop negative reporting. When we allow them to wrap us up in their game, it furthers their propaganda goals. We risk inadvertently giving them inappropriate influence over our reporting, of becoming their tool rather than their watchdog.

On July 8, 2014, the Society of Professional Journalists directs a letter to President Obama objecting to what it calls the "politically driven suppression of news and information about federal agencies." The esteemed group of journalists uses strongly worded phrases to make its point.

"We consider these restrictions a form of censorship."

"The problem is getting worse throughout the nation."

"It has not always been this way."

I'm all too familiar with the pre-story stonewall. The post-story harassment. The ignored requests for interviews and public information. But the Obama administration has aggressively employed the additional PR strategy: controversializing potentially damaging stories, reporters, and opponents to undermine them. It can be a highly effective tactic—unless the public learns to recognize it. Just how does one take a fact-based, solid story with sourced opinions and turn it into a controversy to therefore be questioned by an unsuspecting public? By putting into motion a well-oiled machine that launches post-story complaint calls and emails; comments to other reporters (often not for attribution); bloggers who circulate manufactured outrage and counterspin; and personal attacks against the journalist. Pretty soon, the administration has controversialized an entire line of reporting. Not because it *is* controversial, but because their machine has made it appear to be. They can point to blogs and articles that say so. Even Wikipedia says so, so it must be true!

Journalist Michael Hastings once discussed this phenomenon.

Hastings had authored the award-winning *Rolling Stone* profile of General Stanley McChrystal that led to McChrystal's resignation. He spoke of the "insidious response . . . when you piss off the powerful. They come after your career; they try to come after your credibility. They do cocktail party whisper campaigns. They try to make you 'controversial.' Sadly, the Powers That Be are often aided by other journalists."

| THE CBS CONNECTION

The Justice Department inspector general is looking into my computer intrusions and asks to see the CBS-commissioned report from Patel. The head of the IG forensics unit suggests that if we hand over my computers, his experts can conduct an independent analysis and possibly find more information, perhaps even the proof as to who's responsible. The IG has its own technical staff and lab that are separate and apart from the FBI's analysts. But CBS declines. One CBS official points out, as had Number One, that the IG works for the same agency that we believe is responsible.

"Do you really trust the IG?" the CBS official asks me. "Why should CBS trust our computers to the same agency that could be implicated?"

I explain my rationale. Worst-case scenario: the IG comes up with nothing more than we already know. Best-case scenario: he finds more. Who better than the government's own technicians to dig into a government intrusion? But the bigger hurdle to the concept of handing over the CBS computer is that news organizations vehemently protect their independence and resist attempts by law enforcement to obtain company property. Granted, this situation is a bit different: the law enforcement body isn't reaching into the news organization uninvited. Instead, a crime has been committed and the IG is asking for the computer and report to act in my interests. Nonetheless, policy is policy, there are legal implications, and CBS decides that the IG can't have the CBS laptop computer or Patel's report.

If no law enforcement or investigative body can have access to my CBS computer, then in some respects I'm the victim of a crime that can't be thoroughly investigated. At least not in the ordinary way. I can't expect the FBI to investigate impartially if some of its people are involved in the crime. In fact, I can't expect anyone to investigate if CBS won't let them analyze the computer. And the main concern of CBS News is the integrity of its professional network systems rather than my individual circumstances. The corporation hasn't demonstrated any interest in getting to the bottom of the crime committed against me and my family, and potentially my sources. The news division hasn't expressed even a modicum of concern for my potentially compromised and chilled sources or its own compromised newsroom operations.

It didn't make sense that the moment I reported the intrusion, no alarm bells were sounded at the highest levels of the CBS corporation. I imagined there would be technology security experts who would ask a lot of questions, visit my house, and devise ways to make me feel more secure and to ensure that all of CBS's sources and materials are protected. I thought they'd want to examine my supposedly compromised smartphones. But nobody did.

In fact, CBS has specialists tasked with doing this very sort of work, but I only learn of them when a colleague asks me what work the "special team" is doing on my case.

"What special team?" I ask.

"The guys headed up by Joel Molinoff," says my colleague. "Haven't they been working on your case?"

"Never heard of them."

My colleague is surprised. He goes on to explain that Molinoff is CBS's chief information security officer. He's held seminars with *60 Minutes* staff on cybersecurity issues such as protecting their information abroad. He's a wealth of information and a great resource on computer security. But in all these months, he's yet to reach out to me.

"He's a former NSA guy," adds my colleague. "I'll find his extension and send it to you."

A former NSA guy?

I do a quick Internet search. It turns out that Molinoff came to CBS after having just served in Obama's White House as the assistant director of the President's Intelligence Advisory Board. Prior to that, says his bio, he was an executive at the NSA.

Why wouldn't a guy with that kind of background be keenly interested and involved in investigating my computer intrusions?

Not long after I learn that there's a former NSA guy at the helm of CBS information security, he sends a company-wide memo that seems to refer to my situation without mentioning me. The memo on June 7, 2013, explains what should be done if someone suspects a security breach of their CBS computers. Once the incident is reported, says the memo, there will be a response team that will take steps to resolve the issue.

Since the memo is clear that the victim has a duty to report, and since Molinoff has never acknowledged my incident nor has he contacted me, I send him an email asking whether he's briefed up on my computer intrusions. I offer to answer any questions he may have. He doesn't reply. A week later, I follow up. This time, I get a perfunctory response from Molinoff saying that he and his team are aware of the situation and take any breach "very, very seriously." He asks no questions and to this day no CBS security officials have attempted to ask me the details of what happened.

| SPY CLASS 101

As the story of the government's overreach expands and word gets around about the investigation into my computers, sources step forward to privately offer me moral support, information, and assistance. They fill my head with stories about the government's secret capabilities and how they could be misused by those with malicious motives.

For example, one of them tells me about a covert skill the U.S. government is actively perfecting: the ability to remotely control vehicles. There are several ways to do it. The former U.S. national coordinator for security, infrastructure protection, and counterterrorism Richard Clarke discussed the technology in a June 2013 interview with the *Huffington Post*. He said that intelligence agencies know how to remotely seize control of a car through a "car cyber attack."

"It's relatively easy to hack your way into the control system of a car, and to do such things as cause acceleration when the driver doesn't want acceleration, to throw on the brakes when the driver doesn't want the brakes on, to launch an air bag," Clarke tells the online blog. "You can do some really highly destructive things now, through hacking a car, and it's not that hard."

In this particular interview, Clarke is responding to questions about the fatal single-car crash of reporter Michael Hastings as he was said to be researching a story related to the scandal that forced the resignation of CIA director Petraeus in 2012. Shortly before Hastings's death, he reportedly said he thought the FBI was investigating him, which the FBI denied. Officials who investigated the car crash say no foul play was suspected and Clarke doesn't dispute that. But Clarke says, hypothetically, "If there were a cyber attack on the car—and I'm not saying there was—I think whoever did it would probably get away with it."

Clarke's assessment of the available technology is based in part on a 2011 report by university computer scientists. It states that computer hackers can gain remote unauthorized access to vehicles much like a computer, controlling the engine and other basic functions. Apparently, the car hacking can be accomplished using cellular connections and Bluetooth wireless technology. Hackers can take control, track, and even listen in without having any direct physical access to the vehicle, according to one of the lead researchers, Stefan Savage of the University of California, San Diego.

My source tells me something about a related technology he says the government is developing. Covert operators can substitute the stock electronic control units in vehicles for special replacements: one to control the car's transmission and another that controls the engine. A remote controller can then slow, stop, or speed up the car and make it impossible for the driver to do much about it. The government developers, working in secret with black budgets that don't appear on any ledger, are having a little trouble keeping the demo units from overheating. They're expediting the troubleshooting and sparing no expense. Money is no object. There's an endless source of tax dollars for this project.

The source shows up at my house one wintry evening and wants to check out my car for anything suspicious. He says that I've upset so many people at high levels that anything is possible, even the idea that somebody has tampered with my vehicle. I appreciate the thought but tell him it's unnecessary. He insists and my husband says to go ahead and let him look. It concerns me that somebody with links to covert agencies actually thinks that a government operative might be capable of sabotaging my car. The source and my husband spend forty-five minutes shivering in the garage, flashlight in hand, rooting around under the hood and in the front seat of my car, and find nothing.

As a matter of protecting my own interests, I've begun working with a small group of people who aren't connected to CBS. This includes an attorney, another independent computer forensics expert, and several sources.

In July 2013, I'm preparing to leave the country on vacation. It'll feel good to get away from everything. But before I go, an acquaintance contacts an intermediary and asks me to call. It's been more than a year since we last spoke.

"Can we meet me at your house—tonight?" Terry* asks. He doesn't want to say much on the phone.

"Sure," I reply.

"Can you meet me in the driveway? And . . ." He hesitates. "Can you leave your phone inside the house?" Terry is a very polite guy. By the tone of the brief conversation, I already know he's going to talk to me about my computer incidents.

I finish my tae kwon do workout and get home just in time for the driveway rendezvous. I sit on the brick stoop in front of my house and wait, still damp with martial arts sweat. It's humid and warm and starting to get dark. Terry pulls into the driveway, hops out, and joins me on the stoop. He's carrying a Baggie and a folder.

"I know what's been happening to you," he says with genuine concern. "If there's anything I can do to help, I want to."

Terry, like so many in this region, has connections to the three-letter agencies. He tells me in quiet tones that he's angry at the thought of the government conducting covert surveillance on law-abiding private citizens and journalists.

"I've spent my whole career developing and using techniques that are meant to be used on terrorists and bad guys. Not people like you."

He opens the Baggie and shows me an array of bugging devices of different sizes and shapes. He pulls them out one at a time and explains how each one could be disguised to fit into a different host. I don't think anyone is using bugs in my house. But I remind myself that not long ago, I didn't think anybody would break into my computers. In any event, Terry is giving me a crash course: Spy Class 101.

He looks around. Up the driveway. Both sides and across the street. "Let's take a walk."

Terry tells me of a conversation he'd had with my husband back

---

* Not his real name.

in 2011. He'd noticed a white utility truck parked up the street by a pond.

"I didn't like that. I didn't like it at all," he tells me now, shaking his head. "I talked to your husband about it at the time. He'd already noticed the truck, too.

"I didn't like it because I recognized the type of truck and the type of antennae it had. And if you look"—he points up the street—"there's a direct line of sight from where it was parked to your house." My husband, who once worked in law enforcement intelligence, had on several occasions in the past couple of years mentioned the presence of nondescript utility trucks parked in our neighborhood—trucks that were working on no known utility projects. Neighbors noticed, too. Ours is a small community filled with people who pay attention to such things. Some of them worked for the three-letter agencies.

For more than an hour, Terry tells me fantastical stories of incredible covert capabilities the government has. I think about James Bond getting briefings on secret gadgets from Q Division. Terry says there's a way to shoot an arrow from a distance into the outside of a building and have it penetrate through the outer wall, just far enough to stop short of the drywall, where it plants a listening device. Or the government may find out you're attending a professional conference and plant spyware on every CD to be given out at the event, in hopes that you'll take one and insert it into your computer. Or they find out when you're taking your car in to be serviced and arrange to install transmitters in your taillights.

"That's sort of like the antennae. Then an audio receptor can be placed inside your car. That way they know where you are and when you're coming home."

Terry tells me about the government's secretive departments of Flaps & Seals. They specialize in—well—flaps and seals. For example, they intercept something you've ordered in the mail, and open the "flaps" and break the "seals" to outfit the product with a bug or malware. Then they reseal the flaps and seals so expertly that you can't tell anyone has been in the package. When it arrives at your house, you install the software or attach the device to your computer and *voilà*! You've bugged yourself. Simple and clever.

Terry tells me that the government's technical surveillance tools are limitless. Wide domestic use of drones has opened a whole new world of possibilities. A small drone with a camera can easily hover quietly above my house for forty-five minutes while it uploads data or downloads software.

"And then there are lightbulbs," Terry says. "Your audio can be monitored through lightbulbs. Lamps. Clock radios. Outdoor lights."

The lightbulbs have ears?

"How can a lightbulb emit a signal?" I ask. "If it's transmitting, can that be detected?"

"It doesn't use a transmitter," Terry explains. "It operates off the electrical current in your house. It's called electric current technology."

That blows my mind.

"The names of the people who are executing surveillance on you won't be found in a criminal database," Terry tells me. "More likely they're in Scattered Castles."

He explains that Scattered Castles is a database used across all components of the intelligence community that verifies personnel security access to Sensitive Compartmented Information and other caveated programs.

This is all fascinating but a little academic. And in a way, some of it sounds so 1990s. From what I've learned, it seems the government and its operatives don't need to go to these extraordinary lengths to track and monitor people. We're all so wired through the Internet and our smartphones: that's all they really need. No reason to plant a bug or follow people around on foot. That's expensive, time-consuming, and potentially traceable. Accessing communications through the major telecommunications companies or Internet providers and search engines—that's free, easy, and undetectable. Piece of cake.

It's dark now. Terry darts a glance up and down my neighborhood streets for the tenth time and redirects our walk back to the stoop. "I'll do anything I can to help."

| JUSTICE DEPARTMENT ON THE HOT SEAT

Senator Tom Coburn, a Republican from Oklahoma, is hopping mad over the government's antics in targeting news reporters. In July 2013, he poses a lengthy list of questions to Attorney General Holder at the Justice Department. Some of them have to do with my case. The questions are carefully crafted to cover a number of scenarios.

1. During your tenure as attorney general, has any employee, contractor or other representative of your Department secretly, without notice to the subject, obtained information regarding the communication of any journalist, including Ms. Attkisson?

2. During your tenure as attorney general, has any employee, contractor or other representative of your Department obtained access to any computer used by a journalist or news organization, including Ms. Attkisson and CBS News, without the knowledge of the journalist or organization?

3. During your tenure as attorney general, has any employee, contractor or other representative of your Department attempted to remove, exfiltrate or otherwise transfer data to or from any computer used by a journalist or news organization, including Ms. Attkisson and CBS News, without the knowledge of the journalist or organization?

Though the letter should have been promptly addressed, five months would pass before the Justice Department would provide a response. And in the response, which follows, none of the relevant questions were answered:

"Your letter asks whether the Department is responsible for incidents in 2012 in which the computer of Sharyl Attkisson, a CBS reporter, was allegedly hacked by an unauthorized party. The Department is not. It also does not appear that CBS or Ms. Attkisson followed up with the Federal Bureau of Investigation for assistance with these incidents," writes the Justice Department to Coburn.

Instead of answering the questions at hand, the administration had posed an entirely different question and chosen to answer that one. Senator Coburn's letter hadn't referred to "hacks," it didn't narrow its questions to 2012, didn't ask whether the Justice Department was "responsible," and didn't isolate its questions to the Justice Department alone. I conclude there's a reason they stuck to posing and denying a very narrow set of circumstances, using such specific language, rather than simply answering the questions Coburn asked.

I find irony in the fact that, in its brief response, the Justice Department implies I should have approached the FBI for "assistance." Especially since I now have learned that, months ago, the FBI opened a computer intrusion case with me listed as the "victim" but, oddly enough, never bothered to reach out to me. How often does the FBI start a case without notifying, or trying to collect basic information from, the supposed victim? It doesn't seem as if they're trying very hard to help me get to the bottom of it.

I see Coburn on Capitol Hill and he tells me that my case may be the worst, most outrageous violation of public trust he's ever seen in all his years in office.

"And it's not because it's *you*," he adds. He wants me to know that he's judged the gravity of the situation based not on how I might have been personally or even professionally affected. It's about the broad implications for government, the press, and society.

"I know," I say.

On February 18, 2014, Coburn issues a follow-up letter to the Justice Department pointing out that none of his questions from the previous July had been answered in its December response.

"The [Justice] Department's restatement of my questions reflected neither the intent of the original questions, or the spirit of the inquiry at hand," Coburn wrote. He then asked Holder to re-review the original questions and provide numbered responses.

Five months later, more than a year after the original congressional query was posed, the Justice Department had still provided no further response.

| AUDACITY

In September 2013, Ambassador Thomas Pickering agrees to do a sit-down interview with me about his work heading up the State Department Accountability Review Board's (ARB) controversial Benghazi report. The ARB is under fire for possible conflicts of interest and for its decision not to interview relevant officials, including then–secretary of state Hillary Clinton.

The White House is already panicky over my reporting on the ARB controversies, some of which are raised in a Republican congressional report in advance of a hearing. On September 18, 2013, White House officials deploy the usual tactics. Direct contact with CBS officials. Multipronged approach.

On this occasion, the White House dispatches separate emails to different CBS officials an hour apart. Each email is signed by a different White House official, as if each one had written the email himself. But the text is nearly identical. Clearly they've held their regular spin meeting (on the taxpayer's dime), coordinated their pushback plan, and distributed the wording each spinner would use in his email to various CBS officials and probably others in the media.

First, an email from White House spokesman Carney to Bureau Chief Isham. Carney begins by referring to a prior email he'd already apparently sent to CBS managers complaining about my Benghazi reporting earlier in the week:

> Hey Chris—not sure if you saw my email marveling at Sharyl A's exclusive preview of a Darrell Issa press release. It got me wondering whether she, or CBS, might be interested in giving equal weight to a Benghazi story based on some hard facts. Since CBS has been relentless in promoting the idea that there's a scandal and cover-up, I think overlooking the exonerating material after months of heavy coverage of political accusations does a disservice to everybody.

An hour later, White House spinmeister Eric Shultz tries our White House correspondent Major Garrett with this similarly worded email:

> Hello sir . . . Yes, I am actually pitching you a Benghazi story and I think this is fairly important. Usually this stuff gets lost in between Hill and WH beats—want to be sure this doesn't this time. CBS has been relentless on this so I want to make sure you guys don't overlooking [sic] the exonerating material.

Carney continues to Isham:

> Because we know if it was the reverse—we'd be deluged in coverage. So only seems fair to report on the exculpatory material. Three

different themes we noticed below (with page number cites!) . . . let
me know if we can otherwise be helpful.
—Jay

And Schultz to Garrett:

And we know if it was the reverse—we'd be deluged in coverage. So
only seems fair to report on the exculpatory material. Three different
themes we noticed below (with page number cites!) . . . let me know if
we can otherwise be helpful.
—Eric

Both emails include identical spin referring to "Republican conspiracy theories" and quotes that dispel the theories. The material
isn't exculpatory at all in terms of anything that I've reported, but the
White House must be sending versions of these emails to media representatives all over Washington and New York in hopes that media
surrogates and bloggers will adopt the spin and treat it as if it's factually setting the record straight.

That very night, with Schultz, Carney, and company freshly
steaming over my Benghazi reporting, I'm home doing final research
and crafting questions for the next day's interview with Pickering.
Suddenly data in my computer file begins wiping at hyperspeed before my very eyes. Deleted line by line in a split second: it's gone,
gone, gone.

I press the mouse pad and keyboard to try to stop it, but I have no
control. The only time I've seen anything like this is in those movies
where the protagonist desperately tries to copy crucial files faster than
the antagonist can remotely wipe them.

I press down on the mouse pad of my MacBook Air and it pauses.
I let up and the warp-speed deletions resume. Interesting. I have to

either sit here stuck with my thumb on the mouse pad or lift it and watch my work disappear. The whole file would be erased in a matter of seconds. My iPhone is sitting on the bed next to me and I grab it with my right hand while using the thumb of my left hand to keep the mouse pad depressed and the action paused. Hit the video camera function, record, and lift my thumb off the mouse pad long enough to capture a few seconds of the action on video. Don't want to let it erase too much. While still holding down the mouse pad with my thumb, I use my index finger to try to work the cursor up to the file button, hoping to save and close the file. But the drop-down menu is disabled. Eventually, I find that all I have the ability to do is close out the file. As soon as it shuts, another file that's still open begins slow deletions as if the backspace button is being held down. But I'm not touching the keys. I close that file, too, and disconnect the computer from my FiOS Wi-Fi, which stops the weird behavior.

The next day, I show the video recording of the deletions to two experienced computer experts who are familiar with my case. They both agree that it shows someone remotely accessing my computer. Somebody who apparently wanted me to know it.

"I wouldn't have believed it if I didn't see it with my own eyes," says one of the technicians. "They're fucking with you. There's no other purpose. They want you to know they're still there."

"I've never seen anything like it," says the other. "I'd have to agree they're trying to send you a message. They're saying, 'We're still watching. See what we can do to you.'"

It takes audacity. To be so bold after all the public scandals, long after they know I discovered their presence in my private and work computers. It reminds me of an impetuous child sticking out his tongue while standing behind his mother's skirt. It's the mission of cowards. Of people who have little confidence in their own abilities and believe their only hope at maintaining control is to intimidate and steal and suppress information. What power that they have isn't earned; it's what they're able to grab for a short time while they have access to all the toys. We only have ourselves to blame. They wouldn't be able to do this unless we—the public, Congress, and the news media—allowed it. But we do and they know they can act with impunity.

| THE YEAR OF MASS SURVEILLANCE EXPOSED

In October 2013, one of my sources who currently works in the government says that his federal bosses have pulled his phone records to see if he's talking out of school. Not because he's leaked classified information or done anything wrong. Quite the contrary: he knows of others in his agency who have committed ethical and possibly legal violations. So they're snooping into his phone records. How does he know? They told him so. They *want* him to know. That way, maybe he'll keep his mouth shut. After reviewing his calls, including some to an official on Capitol Hill, they approach him and say, "You're talking to *them*?"

My name and number aren't in the records that they checked. The source and I have figured out an alternate way to communicate. But the government monitoring of its employees, citizens, and news media—to protect its own political interests, not to protect us from terrorists—is becoming a fact of life. If nobody stands up to stop it, we'll all have to just get used to being watched by our government.

As 2013, the year of mass-surveillance-secrets-exposed, draws to a close, we're not finished learning about the government's reach into our private lives. In an article in the *Washington Post* on December 4, Snowden's documents reveal the NSA is collecting nearly five billion records a day on cell phone locations around the world, "enabling the agency to track the movements of individuals—and map their relationships—in ways that would have been previously unimaginable." According to an NSA official quoted in the article, the agency is "tapping into the cables that connect mobile networks globally." Even when you're not using your phone, it's broadcasting its location. "The government is tracking people from afar into confidential business meetings or personal visits to medical facilities, hotel rooms, private homes and other traditionally protected spaces," reports the *Post*. Other highlights include the fact that this particular NSA database is more than twice the size of the text content of the Library of Congress print collection, and that there's so much material the NSA has had trouble ingesting, processing, and storing it.

Though this is as big as any Snowden revelation so far, the reaction from most of the public, the press, and Congress seems a bit bored. These complex surveillance systems have been difficult to explain, digest, and comprehend. If you ask most ordinary Americans, they might be able to tell you the government has gotten caught invading the public's privacy, but they probably couldn't tell you much more than that. Some of us in the media haven't done an adequate job explaining all of this in a clear and accurate fashion.

Also, there have been so many staggering revelations in a short period of time, people have become desensitized. We've suffered through all the stages: outrage, denial, rejection. I wonder if the public has reached a complacent sort of acceptance.

| THE JUSTICE DEPARTMENT IG

When the two agents from the Department of Justice Inspector General's office pull into my driveway, on January 15, 2014, I try to size them up. White guys, nice looking, early forties, impeccable dark suits, colorful ties. No rumpled collars here. One of them, Digital Forensics and Technology Investigations Unit Director Keith Bonanno, comes from a buttoned-down bureaucratic background. The other, Special Agent Harry Lidsky, looks more like a cop or spook.

They're here to pick up my personal Apple iMac desktop computer for a forensics analysis. It's been one year since Number One first confirmed the intrusion on my CBS laptop. The IG can't have my work laptop since that belongs to CBS. But the iMac is all mine and there may be evidence on it, too. I've decided to let them examine it.

I'm taking a chance entrusting my computer to a team that's connected to the agency that may hold responsibility for my intrusions. But it's okay. My personal forensics team is conducting its own analysis. I continue to believe that the worst-case scenario is the IG finds nothing. Best case? Maybe they turn up something we don't yet have.

Bonanno drags in a rolling briefcase and the two men step into my living room. I have a little help to size them up: my husband, who's the most accurate profiler I know, and a friend who's taken an interest in the case.

Bonanno and Lidsky also want to look at my Verizon box where the mysterious, dangling cable was found and removed before it disappeared a little more than a year ago. The three of us take the two of them outside to the Verizon box and Bonanno takes pictures while they ask what the cable looked like and how it came to disappear. I explain that after the Verizon man removed it, I asked him to leave it, but it was gone when I later went back to retrieve it.

"I have photographs of it," I tell the agents.

We go inside and I show them the pictures of the cable. They say they've never seen anything like that.

We make small talk. Before the IG, Bonanno says he worked at the Department of Transportation. Lidsky's former DEA and CIA. When he mentions the CIA, my friend says, "There are a lot of us ex-agency around . . ." alluding to his own status as a one-time CIA officer.

"What did you do there—if you can tell me?" asks Lidsky.

"Intelligence," answers my friend.

So they've got one and we've got one, I think, referring to the CIA backgrounds.

After conducting a brief interview, Bonanno and Lidsky have me sign a piece of paper authorizing them to take my iMac. Then, they pack up their gear and my computer, and head out.

| LESSONS LEARNED

On November 20, 2013, I re-interview *Fast and Furious* whistleblower John Dodson. Pretty soon it'll be three years since he first came forward and exposed the government's gunwalking secrets on the *CBS Evening News*. He's written a new book about the whole experience (*The Unarmed Truth*, published by a division of CBS partner Simon & Schuster). There are still many unanswered questions. During our interview, Dodson reflects on his own situation and how it applies to the scandals that have happened since.

He sees Benghazi, the IRS targeting of conservative groups, and the government spying stories as variations on the same theme.

"It's so reminiscent of everything that happened in *Fast and Furious*," Dodson tells me. "It's the same thing repeating itself over and over again. You know I refer to it as the self-licking ice-cream cone of the federal government. It's there to simply enjoy itself while the rest of us have to pay for it."

ATF originally tries to block the book's publication, saying it will hurt morale and damage ATF's working relationships with the DEA and the FBI. When the American Civil Liberties Union and Senator Grassley stand up for Dodson's right to publish, ATF relents and clears the book for publication.

I contact ATF for comment on the Dodson book, and spokeswoman Ginger Colbrun, who succeeded the *Fast and Furious* era's Scot Thomasson, reacts frostily. It's the Tuesday before Thanksgiving.

"How are you?" I'm attempting to start off with a moment of small talk. "Do you have to work the holiday?" I ask, referring to the holiday the day after tomorrow.

"I answered the phone, didn't I?" Colbrun snaps back. Not a very professional response from a publicly paid PR official working on behalf of the public. Okay, this isn't going to be friendly. Maybe not even courteous. She's following in Thomasson's footsteps.

Colbrun says the agency has no interest in doing an interview about Dodson. Her tone indicates ATF still views Dodson as the enemy rather than a whistleblower who helped halt a misguided and harmful policy. No matter what mea culpa government officials have made for the benefit of the public or Congress, their basic attitudes haven't changed. In a less political world, Dodson might be rewarded for his honesty. Instead, he's odd man out. Colbrun conveys no sense of gratitude to or pride in Dodson. No sense of embarrassment over the government lies told to me, Congress, and the public along the way. No sense of regret for lives lost. They're just mad at Dodson for telling the truth. Mad at me for reporting it.

Interestingly, the Justice Department has barred Dodson from accepting payment for his book, claiming it would violate ethics rules. Dodson states, "I do find it hard to reconcile how the very same agencies who thought of, approved, and employed the strategies used in *Fast and Furious* only to later attempt to cover it up by lying to Congress and the American people, ignoring the rule of law, withholding documents, and smearing whistleblowers, now asserts themselves to be the sole authorities who preside over this or any other 'ethical inquiry.' The conflict is obvious."

Today, Dodson wants to stand as an example to others who see wrongdoing: you can step forward and expose it.

"[My story] shows that they can't totally take away your empowerment. You can make a difference," Dodson tells me in an interview. "And there's a lot of people out there that were in my position, that know things that are going on in the NSA, in the State Department, in the CIA or IRS. . . . It is their greatest fear, as a government, that we ever realize how much of that power *we* actually have. And what *they* have is, you know, given to them by us."

All I know is that, so far, the main impact of the exposure of the government's dirty little surveillance secrets is that the government has doubled down on leakers and whistleblowers. A chilling effect has been administered with surgical precision on anyone who might have thought about stepping forward.

It's July 2014 and one member of my team, Don Allison of Kore-Logic, has been working on my computer puzzles for more than a year. I've come to understand why he came so highly recommended. The work has been difficult and tedious. But there's no great hurry. Patience must be exercised. His task has been to unmask some of the most sophisticated computer intrusion efforts in existence. And he's gathering clues and intel. Revealing new information, even now, about the surveillance of both my work and personal computers by an outside presence.

Regarding my work laptop, Don tells me that his analysis shows CBS had the means and opportunity through corporate software to perform its own inside, complete remote acquisition and forensic analysis of the laptop as well as other platforms on their network as soon as I first informed them of the intrusion. If they did so, they didn't tell me about it. Don can see that one party looking through my laptop showed particular interest in my Benghazi reporting work, opening and reading a key file.

Don is also able to provide the best forensics detail yet of my personal desktop iMac. It reveals a sophisticated set of intrusions that were at least as invasive as the ones into my work laptop. The interlopers were able to co-opt my iMac and operate it remotely, as if they were sitting in front of it. They used a program to control parameters that allow for complete remote graphical access as one of the authorized users of the system.

The unauthorized presence had complete control.

It had access to emails, personal files, Internet browsing, passwords, execution of programs, financial records, and photographs of not just me but of my family members as well.

The illegal infiltration included the ability to capture passwords and account information for my extended computing footprint as well, such as my external accounts with Hotmail, Facebook, Twitter, online banking credentials, and CBS corporate systems.

The invaders were able to access anything connected to my computer systems and they used their technology and expertise to comb through the photo records on my BlackBerry, specifically snooping through materials I had photographed regarding my *Fast and Furious* research.

While a great deal of data has been expertly wiped in an attempt to cover-up the deed, Don is able to find remnants of what was once there. There's crucial evidence of a government computer connection to my computer. A sort of backdoor link that leads to an ISP address for a government computer that can't be accessed by the general public on the Web. It's an undeniable link to the U.S. government. Don says the importance of this link can't be overstated.

"Let me put it this way," he tells me. "This ISP address is better evidence of the government being in your computer than the government had when it accused China of hacking into computers in the U.S."

"The greatest fear that I have regarding the outcome for America of these disclosures is that nothing will change."

—Edward Snowden to the *Guardian*, June 2013

| The "Sharyl Attkisson Problem" |

Look at the right hand so you don't see what the left hand is doing.

Distract from the real issues. That's what the story line advanced about my departure from CBS News was designed to do.

Anonymous sources at the network falsely claim in media reports that I specifically cited "liberal bias" in my resignation to CBS management. The fabricated quote is picked up and passed along like urban lore until it becomes widely accepted as fact. It's too scrumptious to resist. For many liberals, it continues a convenient narrative that attempts to undermine my independent reporting. For many conservatives, it makes me the ultimate insider giving up the family secrets.

Once I left, some of my former colleagues gleefully advanced the assumption that, naturally, I had already cut a deal with FOX News. That would put a delicious period at the end of their delectably false thesis: that all the fuss was caused by my irrational devotion to right-wing stories.

After a few weeks, during which I got outside the beltway and dealt with my father's terminal illness, I agreed to a fraction of media requests I received to talk about journalism or my ongoing coverage of news stories. I consented to appear on FOX, CNN, MSNBC, NPR, ABC, Al Jazeera, C-SPAN, RealClearPolitics, Sinclair Media, and Reason, to name a few. But the propagandists frantically publicized the FOX events, excluding the others. Their storyline was that the FOX appearances proved I'm conservative.

They're nothing if not inconsistent.

They didn't similarly cast my appearance on MSNBC as proof that I'm liberal. They don't argue that well-known liberal commentators Juan Williams, James Carville, Mara Liasson, Marc Lamont, or Bill Richardson are conservative because they showed up on FOX. Same with dozens of journalists from various news outlets who discuss their stories on FOX News, such as ABC political director Rick Klein and former *New York Times* reporter Judith Miller.

Continuing in the same vein, though I contributed reporting to a variety of outlets, the same propagandists selectively publicized my work for the conservative *Daily Signal* without noting that the subject matter, an allegedly unethical federal study on premature babies, had great appeal to liberal interests, quoted a Democratic congresswoman, and largely pulled on research from the liberal-leaning watchdog group Public Citizen.

As with the news stories and images they manipulate, these expert spinners craft their preconceived narratives in isolation from the facts. Much like the news managers who order up stories and prewrite them regardless of the fact-finding in the field, the propagandists wait to fill in the blanks, selecting those they can twist and shape to their liking, discarding the inconvenient facts that fight the chosen narrative.

Periodically, a few friends and colleagues send me copies of blogs and articles filled with misrepresentations so wild and provably false, they advise me to step up and correct them. One article called me "admittedly conservative," as if I had identified myself as such. A second used shamefully inaccurate figures to try to contradict and controversialize my recent definitive report on the status of HealthCare.gov, though my reporting relied almost entirely on the government's own statistics and sources. And a third made the slanderous, false claim that my Benghazi reporting had been discredited and retracted by CBS. There wasn't even a grain of truth hidden in that statement.

Why don't I jump into the fray in each instance? There's little point in trying to get the truth across to those who are on a mission that doesn't involve the truth. It would only feed them. It's a bit like tossing scraps to hungry puppies from the dinner table in hopes that will keep them quiet. It just encourages their bad habits.

One media writer came up with the brilliant implication that maybe my decision to leave CBS was a well-thought-out career path on my part—"cry bias" to get a lot of attention and money.

Points for creativity but a big deduction for lack of accuracy.

The truth is, I never explicitly raised concerns about bias during my separation discussions with management. Not in 2013, when I first proposed leaving ahead of my contract, and not in March 2014, when I finally did. It doesn't mean there weren't issues. Most everyone I rubbed shoulders with inside CBS, including management, had privately verbalized worries about the strong-arm tactics of the current New York *Evening News* managers and some on other broadcasts, often—in our view—forcing their proclivities, sometimes ultraliberal, sometimes otherwise biased, into story decisions and scripts like never before.

Before I asked to leave, a number of well-regarded veteran correspondents had already gone to the top to complain about various aspects of the *CBS Evening News with Scott Pelley*. And more than one found themselves so disgusted with the state of the *Evening News* under Pelley and his executive producer Shevlin that they sought to negotiate contracts under which they wouldn't have to appear on the broadcast.

You know there's a problem when reporters are trying to stay off your flagship news program rather than get on it.

But for me, there were additional concerns and challenges. More on those in a moment.

Some of the managed response to my departure tended to prove a thesis of this book. The liberal opinion blog Media Matters revived its trademark propaganda campaign to smear me and my reporting.

Predictable.

Most people in the country have never heard of these inside-the-beltway blogs and battles. But it's common knowledge among those whom Media Matters has attempted to disparage that the left-wing blog is little more than a paid surrogate for Democratic interests, including Hillary Clinton, the Obama administration, and those close to them, at times in direct consultation with Obama officials.

Together, these interests employ a range of bully tactics and strategies to systematically attack journalists and undermine reporting that they view to be effective and, therefore, damaging. The content of what they write is so riddled with silliness and fact errors, it's not taken seriously by any informed neutral party. Their audience is a small but influential group of news media and politicos. If they can just get a bit of their propaganda to cross over and be discussed in a forum that resembles what Americans consider the real news media, then they've earned their money. Sometimes, it works. They strategically exploit partnerships, such as the liberal blog Talking Points Memo, which report on and codify each other's false claims in an effort to build the perception that there's a groundswell of grassroots sentiment on their side.

But it's astroturf all the way.

Perhaps my CBS departure set off panic in their ranks. Maybe they sensed that with no fearful news executives in my chain of command to intimidate, with no ideologues at a network attempting to filter my output, with no corporate master, some of my reporting could prove more dangerous than ever to their interests.

They have every right to advance their cause in any legal way they see fit. But as journalists, it's our job not to allow them to improperly influence our reporting. For me, that's easy. It's only when one is encumbered by corporate tethers or ideological managers that it can become difficult.

Naturally, interests like Media Matters aren't paid by their ideological donors to bark at parked cars. When they target me, it means I'm on to something. Usually, something big. The more apoplectic and accusatory they become, the closer I know that I am to reaching truth.

> **EXHIBIT A**   Three major topics of my reporting that prompted the most vitriolic response by some on the left are *Fast and Furious*, the green energy debacle, and Benghazi. Each was singled out for national excellence as judged by independent peer journalists and news management professionals; each was nominated for or received Emmy and Edward R. Murrow awards. It becomes clear that the volume with which these special interests squawk is directly proportional to the significance and credibility of the story and reporter they seek to discredit.

Therefore, treating a group like Media Matters as if it's a serious arbiter of good journalism is akin to letting a defendant evaluate the prosecutor who put him in jail. It defies logic. We're left to wonder why so many in the media routinely do this. A number of media critics ask me if I'm concerned about Media Matters–type criticism, as if I should be moved by it.

Aren't you playing into their hands by appearing on conservative news outlets? they ask.

I mentally play the Substitution Game: These same critics don't ask similar questions about my many appearances with other outlets, including liberal-leaning ones. In fact, they ignore those entirely. Additionally, I don't see them treating seriously the opinions of right-wing media watchdogs. They aren't seeking balance by treating the conservative equivalents with the same deference.

So some in the media choose to ask the jailed convict what he thinks of the prosecutor. Various reporters and bloggers embrace the charged rhetoric of Media Matters as if it were an esteemed journalism organization providing neutral observations. They use the partisan blog as a primary source for their background research on me in much the same way that I might rely on THOMAS, The House [of Representatives] Open Multimedia Access System at the Library of Congress, to research the *Congressional Record*; or the Lexis database to research legal cases.

Media Matters has called your reporting shoddy and inaccurate, say these reporters, as if it's an accusation to be considered seriously.

If they were to think it out, they might realize how absurd it is to ask why I'm not trying to please special interests like Media Matters (or its right-wing counterparts), or whether I'm upset by their attacks. It's as if these reporters are suggesting I should bend to propaganda rather than independently pursue the facts wherever they lead. If I were to decide my actions based on avoiding attacks by special interests, I'd be doing stories on the weather and features on animals.

One day in April 2014, Media Matters somehow obtained my private contact information, and began calling and emailing to get me to respond to their criticisms. Within minutes, the liberal Talking Points Memo blog, which had also, coincidentally, somehow, obtained my private phone number and email address at the exact same time, began calling to ask what I thought of Media Matters asking me to respond to their criticisms. Within minutes of that, a *Washington Post* media gossip blogger began calling and emailing for my response to the calls by Media Matters and Talking Points Memo for me to respond to their criticisms. You begin to see how it works. A paid propaganda blog and its helpers work together to gin up a big controversy that's actually the brainchild of a very small, special interest.

If I were still at CBS, they'd all be calling the network's press office, trying to create the impression that there's a giant grassroots movement against me. Exerting pressure. Making the PR officials at CBS uncomfortable. Causing them to notify management. Creating a hassle. It's part of the plan: to controversialize me not only with the public but also at my job.

Now that I've left that job, their tactics are largely neutered. I have no boss for them to call. And I see right through them. But my colleagues left behind are still subject to the propagandist ploys.

In May 2014, the *Huffington Post* was somehow convinced to report on Media Matters' letter to CBS News demanding that the network reinvestigate a Benghazi report done by a *60 Minutes* correspondent. Substitution Game: Right-wing media watchdogs such as Accuracy in Media have launched complaints about the networks for years but there aren't many news outlets reporting their complaints as news.

Politico picks up the *Huffington Post* report, furthering a nonstory, but at least that article includes appropriate skepticism. It notes that Media Matters' founder is a "Hillary Clinton attack dog" and head of American Bridge Political Action Committee, "which has devoted itself to Hillary Clinton's election in 2016." It also states, "In the past year, [Media Matters' founder] has served as Clinton's public advocate against the media, combating NBC, CNN, the *New York Times* and *60 Minutes* wherever and whenever there is even a whiff of anti-Clinton sentiment."

Back to the efforts to controversialize me; whether it's silly allegations by Media Matters or misreporting by other outlets regarding my departure from CBS, I can't help but think of how easy it would have been, at any time, for media reporters to simply seek the facts themselves and divine some firsthand truth based on evidence rather than parroting what they read on blogs. But, as I've said, some reporters have come to value what they hear others report or say on the Web far more than fact-based, original research. Especially if it's what they want to hear.

"People hear what they want to hear. They see what they want to see."

So, as partisan interests slander my stories as "shoddy," it goes unmentioned that that very reporting received national investigative Emmy Awards for the past two years straight. (The "shoddier" my reporting got, the more awarded it became.) Likewise, as critics hawk the claim that my reporting is inherently, *gasp*, conservative, few bother to conduct a superficial search that would reveal a balance in my news repertoire that de facto disproves allegations of an ideological bent. Here are just a few examples for the record.

I hit the George W. Bush administration on its secrecy and lack of Freedom of Information Act responses as hard as I pursued the Obama administration on related topics. I aired dozens of reports on the many controversies surrounding Bush's Food and Drug Administration, Bush administration mismanagement at the National Laboratories, alleged fraud and abuse by federal war contractors such as Halliburton, and a hard-hitting series examining the Bush Treasury Department's bait and switch on the Troubled Asset Relief Program bank bailout. That effort received the 2009 Emmy Award for investigative reporting.

I did dozens more reports on congressional shenanigans, including Republican Richard Shelby's controversial hold on Obama nominees, Republicans who call themselves fiscal conservatives but embrace pricey pet projects, and questionable earmarks supported by Republicans Jerry Lewis, Virginia Foxx, Ted Stevens, and Don Young. And there was my undercover investigation into fund-raising by Republican freshmen, which received the 2013 Emmy for investigative reporting.

Perhaps the strongest, but now-forgotten, liberal endorsement of my work comes from MSNBC host Rachel Maddow. She built a seven-minute-long segment based entirely on my investigation into Republican congressman Steve Buyer's suspicious charity. The liberal Talking Points Memo complimented the same report. This is, of course, before it became a chief critic of mine. Substitution Game: When left-wingers praised my work, it didn't seem to ruffle any feathers among my colleagues at CBS. But when conservatives expressed support for my stories, some insiders viewed me as the enemy. *She's not one of us. Or else she wouldn't be pursuing stories like that.*

So the theory apparently goes something like this: I was a fair reporter when I examined the Bush-era controversies. But when I started digging into Obama administration problems, I was suddenly a fanatic bent on destroying the president and all good things liberal.

Not even the Obama folks believe that.

But successfully deploying that story line was part of a primary strategy: fight indisputable, damaging facts by controversializing the reporter and politicizing the subject matter. Harassment. Intimidation. Obstruction. And the Obama administration had many willing advocates and believers to help, both outside and inside CBS.

Why is it that the targets of legitimate questions or criticism seek to stop the reporting altogether rather than simply provide their side of the story and address any problems? Clearly, they're afraid that their side of the story isn't convincing and that the problems aren't easily fixed. The Obama administration needn't be concerned with the opinions of ultraliberals who will usually forgive and defend the president no matter the transgression. Nor need they bother with ultraconservatives who will usually side against the president regardless. It's those crucial Americans in the middle who are of interest. The ones who can sway opinions—and elections. They must not hear about, lest they come to believe, the administration's self-imposed controversies. With this administration, any facts that aren't considered positive—any reporting that doesn't toe the party line—must be labeled as crazy. The stuff of conspiracy theories. Like Vincent Foster suicide rumors or aliens at Area 51. The public must be convinced that any and all scandals surrounding the Obama administration are "phony" or "bogus." All critics are "nutty." The alternative could prove disastrous.

Obama officials clearly viewed me as a wild card. In the past, I had done stories that happened to please them. But they later came to see me as unaccepting of spin. Someone who makes independent checks. Unmoved by peer pressure. Uniquely motivated to get at hidden facts. Not intimidated by threats of my access being limited. (*What access?*) Not even influenced by my own managers' disapproval.

While reporting a story in 2012, I was working to get an interview with a political figure. I told his spokesman that his boss might not like the story but that he'd get a fair shot in an interview. The spokesman said, "I know. I've asked around. I know you're fair. And I know you can't be bought."

Can't be bought?

In nearly thirty years of journalism, nobody else had been so blatant. It made me wonder. *Are some reporters really "bought"?* I began asking my friends who are journalists what they thought. Most of them speculated that yes, absolutely, reporters are bought, but not with cash. They're bought with implied promises such as "if you don't use this negative information today, I'll funnel a bigger story your way tomorrow." Or "if you back off, there might be a nice, high-paying job waiting for you outside of journalism down the road."

I think more reporters are lured by the path of least resistance than by bribery. We've watched many of our talented peers give up trying to get original, meaningful stories on the air. Why battle the organized interests who mercilessly disparage the stories—and you? Why fight your own managers who discourage rather than value the digging and tenacity? Why put yourself through having to answer late-night phone calls, legal threats, and angry emails as some of the broadcast managers cower rather than support you?

On the other hand, the "day-of-air" reports, weather and transportation stories, features about animals, stories that everybody else is covering on a given day—*those* sail onto the news. Today a television journalist can earn a healthy six-figure salary barely lifting a finger and the news supervisors are happier than if they'd gotten an exclusive investigation. It's Alice in Wonderland and everybody sits at the table, smiles, and drinks hot tea as if the Hatter isn't Mad.

I received more kudos from the *CBS Evening News* managers for doing a thirty-second live shot that contained virtually no insight after the August 2011 East Coast earthquake than for investigations that my producer, Kim, and I sweated over for months, night and day. In fact, most often in the last couple of years those investigations were met by important people within the news division with a silence that signaled disapproval. And the propaganda whispers about me being a conservative grew to a loud roar.

Judging by the response I received after concluding my CBS News career, most people out there in the so-called real world who care at all about the drama didn't fall for the creative story line. A friend forwarded me an online opinion piece in *Commentary* that reflected on my job change. The magazine describes itself as "neoconservative Jewish." The article was memorable for its clear expression of how propagandists today don't seek simply to influence the debate; they wish to censor contrary facts and opinions.

Speaking of the president's supporters on Benghazi, the commentary states, "They aren't interested in winning a debate. They want to silence opposing views." The article also provides the astute observation that some who work in the news "are so biased that they actually think critical reporting about a liberal President they personally support is somehow wrong and those who pursue such stories are worthy of suspicion rather than praise."

| NEW ERA

As in most any news organization, there were editorial and story challenges over the years. But, over time, with the help of my producers and support from key executives along the way, I was generally able to successfully navigate the challenges and establish a meaningful career and a strong record of reporting at CBS. For about seventeen years.

There was a sudden and insurmountable change when the *CBS Evening News with Scott Pelley* era began in May 2011. Many of us inside the company would later come to often speak to the irony that the broadcast, desperate to develop a reputation for original and investigative reporting, was in fact moving ever further from both.

Strangely enough, Pelley and his executive producer Shevlin showered verbal and written compliments on the first investigative story and script that I offered the new broadcast. It was an exclusive, nonpolitical report about alleged travel industry deception involving a powerful group of influential people. Pelley and Shevlin called the story incredibly compelling and said that it was the sort of reporting that made them proud. I'd already gotten the seal of approval from our CBS lawyers. The story was scheduled to air.

From there, it all went downhill.

A few days later, I learned that the story was pulled off the schedule. Postponed. I had no idea what discussions had transpired. At first, it seemed Pelley just wanted to put his own style and spin on my work. That was unusual for an anchor at CBS. Dan Rather, Bob Schieffer, and Katie Couric had big-picture ideas and editorial input on stories but had never rewritten my scripts.

I acquiesced to Pelley's oppressive editing, the countless style changes and revisions. I felt a pit in my stomach as I agreed to alterations that softened the facts and made the story convoluted and difficult to follow. But I needed to understand and adjust to Pelley's style so that we could work together successfully. As the process dragged on for weeks, it became clear that I was on a fool's errand. The revision process never ended. Were they scared of going after the powerful entities in the story? Were they feeling heat from the entities' strong pushback? They didn't say. All I know is, the story would never air on Pelley's broadcast. The report that he had so effusively complimented was permanently sidelined.

This soon became a distinguishable pattern. Profuse compliments were often proven hollow. In fact, some of us in the field remarked that it seemed like the more the New York fishbowl claimed to "love" a story, the greater the odds it would never air. They rarely *said* the story wasn't going to air. They just let it sit around and "loved it" until it began to stink like old fish.

At first, many of us held out hope that there was a way to overcome these new challenges. Getting stories on television, especially ones that address controversies and that challenge the powers that be, is rarely a cakewalk. It requires winning the confidence of managers who must have confidence in themselves.

But there would be no movement. With few exceptions, the writing was on the wall. A number of us sharing the same observations and experiences engaged in countless conversations speculating as to why the Pelley-Shevlin regime was so hostile to original and investigative reporting.

This new environment belied what the new CBS News CEO, Jeff Fager, had told me. In July 2011, just a few months into Pelley's leadership, I told Fager that I was inexplicably meeting with roadblocks in getting any investigative stories on the *Evening News*. He asked me to fly to New York to talk about it before I went off for summer vacation. During our meeting, Fager was supportive and encouraging. He assured me that, under his vision, the *Evening News with Scott Pelley* would benefit nobody's reporting more than mine. He envisioned my brand of reporting as the mainstay and mission of the new, hard news newscast. Considering Fager's expressed vision, which I shared, it was particularly ironic that the Pelley broadcast ended up being the death knell for that type of journalism. At least when it came from me.

The universe of what they desired narrowed to a paper-thin slice that was inversely proportional to the expanding universe of what was censored or deemed undesirable. Several New York broadcast managers displayed an overtly visceral rejection of stories that they perceived as negative toward the Obama administration, which eventually equated to nearly any story that critically examined any facet of government or its functions.

There were exceptions. If a story reached such critical mass that many other news outlets were pursuing it, or if the *New York Times* covered it, our folks might jump on board and air some reports on that topic, too. But in general, the environment for my brand of reporting was poisonous.

Meanwhile, the New York–based investigative unit led by the award-winning team of correspondent Armen Keteyian and senior producer Keith Summa was following a similar trajectory. Their original investigations—once a valued staple of the *Evening News*—were now generally unwelcome. Instead, the *Evening News* largely relegated the accomplished producers to chasing an endless stream of rumors and leads on breaking stories copied from other outlets.

In part because of this issue, Summa asked CBS News management to remove the investigative unit from the *Evening News* budget, in hopes that the investigative team would be free to make original contributions to other broadcasts. To our amazement, *Evening News* agreed to let go of the New York investigative unit without a fuss. No broadcast that valued investigative reporting at all would dream of doing that. We didn't know why they felt this way, but it confirmed my inferences: they simply had no serious appetite for true, investigative reporting. *Don't let the screen door hit you on the way out.*

Unfortunately, with Summa, Keteyian, and their team freed up to offer stories to other broadcasts, the overall decline in the environment for investigative reporting continued. Keteyian, the New York unit's only on-air correspondent, left and wasn't replaced. Now there was a New York investigative team with no investigative correspondent. And nobody seemed to care. In 2012, senior producer Summa departed as well, and went on to become vice president of news partnerships at Univision, where he helps oversee many investigations.

The decimation of the CBS investigative infrastructure didn't make sense.

Together, Kim and I (and other Washington-based producers who assisted) and the New York–based investigative unit had helped forge a formidable reputation on behalf of CBS News. The decision to cut things off at the knees had to involve other factors besides journalism and viewer interest. We felt like we went from batting a thousand to zero practically overnight.

I'd never been better sourced and better positioned to break interesting stories. But never were the prospects for getting them on TV so grim. Kim and I began drowning in our endless sea of story pitches that would never be answered by New York or, if occasionally accepted, would never air. There were the ideological obstacles in New York. There was our belief that some of the broadcast managers were fearful of hard-hitting investigative reporting. There was their tendency to want to avoid most anything that hadn't already been published elsewhere first. It was a perfect storm of often competing and contradictory factors that resulted in that narrowing, paper-thin slice of what they desired.

We tried to adjust by offering noninvestigative but still original, interesting stories. Stories that happened to appeal to liberal interests, conservative interests, all interests, or apolitical interests.

Consumer mortgage scams, food safety, failed green energy investments, labor union complaints against corporations, use of tax havens, whistleblowers, environmental damage, a major military scandal, a national monument controversy, government surveillance, drug cartels, medical costs, taxpayer waste, a dozen sequestration stories (pro and con), an unethical federal medical study, the hookah trend, consumer fraud, medical fraud, the IRS targeting of conservatives.

Thanks, thanks . . . but no thanks.

Kim and I tracked down Nakoula Basseley Nakoula in jail, the Egyptian filmmaker whom Hillary Clinton and other Obama officials incorrectly blamed for inciting the September 11, 2012, Benghazi attacks with his YouTube video. We knew that whatever he had to say, his story would be of great interest to many. Though we were not permitted to interview him in jail, we worked to persuade him to do an exclusive on-camera interview with CBS News immediately upon his release from a halfway house in California. It took some convincing, as Nakoula told me that he and his family had received death threats.

Nakoula agreed to let us and our camera meet him in the car that he'd arranged to transport him to a secret safe house upon his release. Just a few years back, a story like that would have led the *CBS Evening News*. Kim and I were excited at the prospect. But in the current CBS climate, I could no longer make final arrangements for such a shoot unless I had the advance commitment from a broadcast to air the story. In fact, in the current CBS climate, it just might be that nobody would want what could prove to be a high-interest gangbuster. The only way to ensure a taker would be if I could get CBS News president David Rhodes behind the effort. So I told him about the opportunity for the exclusive. He was unenthusiastic.

"That's kind of old news, isn't it?" he told me.

My heart sank. How could the impending release from jail of the YouTube filmmaker, the only person really held accountable in the entire Benghazi debacle, who had never done an on-camera interview, who was in essence running for his life, be old news? It hadn't even happened yet. Many would surely find his story, whatever it may be, of interest. But clearly it would never air on CBS.

I broke the news to Kim, who was distressed. After spending all that time and effort convincing Nakoula to do an interview, and knowing how interesting the interview would be, we canceled on him.

We tried "selling" our stories to other broadcasts such as *CBS This Morning*, *CBS Sunday Morning*, and the *CBS Weekend News*. Occasionally, it worked. But the sales job grew more difficult as that universe narrowed, too.

For example, *CBS This Morning* enthusiastically accepted our original pitch about a school lunch fraud investigation. It was perfect for the morning show audience: popular, national school lunch food distributors were under criminal investigation for selling crappy, unhealthy products to schools in exchange for illegal kickbacks. We had exclusive information, an exclusive interview with a prosecutor on the case, and an exclusive interview with an inside whistleblower.

After traveling to several states to conduct the interviews, a senior producer on the broadcast began pushing us. The show was excited about the story and wanted to schedule it to air as quickly as possible.

How fast can you write the script? asked the senior producer. *Can we edit on Friday?*

I rushed to write the story, but before I could send the script to anybody to review, the whole vibe suddenly changed. The urgency cooled. They were no longer anxious to see the script. They changed their mind on scheduling a day to edit.

Kim and I had no idea why the light switch went off. We had grown accustomed to trying to predict objections from broadcast producers based on their political leanings, but we couldn't figure out what they saw as a political angle to this story.

Out of curiosity, I searched news topics on the Web using the term *school lunches*. A lot of stories turned up about First Lady Michelle Obama's initiative to make school lunches healthier.

Do they think this story will somehow negatively reflect on Mrs. Obama's efforts? we wondered. Several CBS colleagues pointed out that *CBS This Morning* cohost Gayle King is good friends with Mrs. Obama. Did she put the kibosh on the story?

They'll change their mind when they read the script, I think. It doesn't criticize Mrs. Obama and the information is just too interesting to pass up.

But after reading a first draft, the senior producers on the story said the subject matter just wasn't right for them. Wasn't interesting to their audience, after all.

Kim and I were befuddled. I had been discussing the story with acquaintances for weeks—often a good way to gauge reaction to a topic—and received 100 percent enthusiastic responses, especially from the very sort of women targeted by the morning broadcasts. Everyone seemed interested in learning about the little-known processes behind delivering mass quantities of food to schoolchildren, and how that system could be rife with fraud.

What was weird about the wholesale rejection of the script was the fact that they didn't want a rewrite. They were uncharateristically quick to accept the loss of the thousands of dollars they'd spent on the shoot. They didn't want to see a cut of the piece (I assured them they would find the interviews strong and compelling). They just didn't want the story. It was a complete 180 from just a few days before.

Among other disappointments was the almost wholesale rejection of the once-popular line of "follow the money" type stories I'd been assigned to do for years involving waste, fraud, and abuse of tax dollars. Almost every day, Kim and I were coming across new ideas for these important stories. They had become more relevant than ever with Congress unable to agree on a budget and spending more than it takes in, the debt growing ever larger, and sequestration looming. But there was near zero interest under the Pelley-Shevlin regime. During this time frame, New York producers initiated subtle edits that didn't make sense to me substantively but, in retrospect, might be explained from an ideological standpoint. For example, when I wrote about misuse or waste of "tax dollars," as I'd done for years, they began changing the phrase to "federal money." When it became a pattern, I wondered if they didn't want viewers reminded that it's their hard-earned tax dollars being wasted.

In 2013, Kim and I tried convincing the *Weekend News* executive producer that it would be in the interest of our viewers and the network to air our brand of taxpayer watchdog stories. We started small with a simple story that we figured even skittish broadcast producers could feel comfortable with: a hearing on waste within the federal Department of Housing and Urban Development. It was especially "safe" because it was the government itself, HUD's inspector general, who had unearthed the problems, so the facts were pretty well established: billions of dollars in wasteful and abusive spending. The IG had presented his findings in a public hearing—so there were no pesky, original investigative facts to worry the broadcast. Even so, I had the script approved by the CBS legal team. It should be perfect.

But when it came time for our script to be reviewed by the executive producer in New York, she was out of the office and handed the task off to her number two. Kim and I immediately sensed trouble. This particular senior producer was commonly referred to as Shevlin's ideological clone. The two had worked together on *Weekend News* for years prior to Shevlin's promotion to *Evening News* as Pelley's executive producer. This *Weekend News* senior, we predicted, wouldn't like a story that exposed waste by the federal government.

And so, what should have been a quick and simple process devolved into what we came to refer to as "death by a thousand cuts." After the senior read through the script, he reacted as if the story had disparaged his best friend. As if his best friend were *Mr. Federal Government*.

"Well, this is all the states' fault! It's the states' fault," he sputtered, recasting blame for the waste and abuse that the HUD inspector general had flagged. Viewing the story through his own political prism, he defended the federal government by claiming the fault rested with the states that receive the federal HUD dollars. "*They* should be tracking the money!"

"We can add your thought about how the states are to blame," I offered in the spirit of compromise. "I can look for a sound bite from the inspector general [at the hearing] where he refers to something like that."

But he wanted more changes. And he conveyed them in the pattern of questioning that I had come to recognize so well in the last couple of years. *It means they just don't like the subject matter.* Nonetheless, I tried to answer all the questions and revise the script to his satisfaction.

Among the changes:

REMOVED   the mention that the IG had found $3.5 billion of HUD fraud or waste in a single year.

DELETED   the visual and compelling example of the historic Hotel Sterling in Wilkes-Barre, Pennsylvania, that was set to get a facelift with $6 million in tax dollars from HUD. But, as we wrote, most of the money was improperly used to demolish the building. With the hotel destroyed, none of the 175 promised jobs were created.

DELETED   an example of a fraud case that we had written in the story.

CHANGED   the inspector general's sound bite.

CHANGED   a sound bite in which the interviewee was critical of the waste and replaced it with one that was less pointed and less interesting.

REWROTE   the example of misused HUD money in Louisiana (and changed the sound bite that referred to that).

All of those alterations in a story that ran under two minutes. I needn't have bothered to do the legwork and write it in the first place. In the end, it was reshaped by a New York producer, who hadn't done the firsthand research.

When the story aired, it was a shadow of its former self. And the last edit, removing a demonstrative example of waste from the final story, was made without anybody checking with me or Kim. We felt it was highly unusual and improper to make such a substantive editorial change without consulting us.

I can't help but think that viewers walk away from a story like that entirely confused. What was the point? In its final form, it seemed as if there were really no cause for major concern. It was a bland non-story that revealed little of interest.

We found no sense in complaining. This was the new reality.

It was the last attempt we made to get a government waste story on CBS News.

So what *did* the *Evening News* want from us during this time? A spot news story on the regional earthquake. A feature about renovation of the National Cathedral after the earthquake. A feature about renovation of the Washington Monument after the earthquake. A feature about damage to the Capitol Building after the earthquake.

Meanwhile, the whisper campaign continued. If I offered a story on pretty much any legitimate controversy involving government, instead of being considered a good journalistic watchdog, I was anti-Obama. If I offered a story on alleged corporate misdeeds, instead of being seen as a reporter holding powers accountable, I was a troublemaker. If I wrote a normal follow-up on national controversies with unanswered questions, instead of being viewed as a classically trained journalist, I was considered obsessed.

None of this was said to me directly. It was passed around by certain managers and colleagues to undermine my reporting and justify their own misguided decisions to censor it.

If I were still thirty years old, I might be convinced that they were right about all of it. That I really had, quite suddenly, without explanation, become the purveyor of all bad story ideas. I might adapt to the new reality by agreeing to do the stories they want, shaped in advance according to their personal views. Happily copy stories from the competition. Forget about developing my own sources and leads. Devote my time to chasing down and confirming rumors from tweets, blogs, and other reporters' leads.

But, at this stage in my career, I knew better.

| WORRIED ABOUT THE WRONG THINGS

At this stage, I also knew better than to be party to journalism that I viewed as wrong. Over the years, when I raised concerns with the CBS ethics czar or expressed disquietude to my superiors, I always did so in the best interests of CBS News, which I considered my home. But my actions weren't always viewed as being conscientious. As I've explained, the network culture has an inclination—as do many corporate and government cultures—to worry about the wrong things and not worry about the right things. To label the one who's raising concerns as a troublemaker rather than view him as someone working to protect the company.

I'd seen that sort of marginalization used againt whistleblower Special Agent John Dodson in *Fast and Furious*. Against whistleblowers inside the FDA, the National Zoo, the American Red Cross, the U.S. Agency for International Development, Firestone, Enron, the National Institutes of Health, the State Department, the military, Los Alamos National Laboratory—so many over the years. Some of those whistleblowers saved human lives. Few, if any, were offered anything other than retaliation and ridicule at the hands of their employers. There are no rainbows for those who risk their careers to stand up for what they think is right. There's usually only a stormy aftermath filled with heartache that never ends.

I'd been at CBS a decade earlier, in September 2004, during Rathergate, when we'd worried about the wrong things.

Prior to the airing of Dan Rather's infamous story on *60 Minutes II*, a CBS senior producer hustled me into his office and said he had documents that *60 Minutes II* was billing as the "smoking gun" against President George W. Bush regarding his Vietnam-era National Guard service: military letters dated 1973. The senior said he was sharing them with me because if Rather's soon-to-air story made a "big splash" on *60 Minutes II* and merited a follow-up the next day on the *CBS Evening News*, I would be the correspondent assigned to do it.

He handed me the military letters. After reviewing them for no more than thirty seconds, I questioned their authenticity.

"Where's the source?" I asked, referring to the signatory.

"He's dead," answered the senior. "His widow apparently found the letters in storage in the attic."

"So did *60* get them—from the widow?"

"No. Rather's producer got them from a group of Republicans in

Texas," he answered. (Note: the CBS investigation into Rathergate later showed this to be untrue.)

I handed the papers back to him. He looked at me quizzically.

"I sure hope they have a lot more evidence than this," I said. "I assume that they do."

"What are you talking about?" asked the senior.

"These look like they were typed by my daughter on a computer yesterday," I answered. (My daughter was nine at the time.)

I knew very well what a typed letter from the era should have looked like. In 1973, I was a devoted student of a secretarial typing class at Brookside Junior High School in Sarasota, Florida. We used top-quality, modern IBM Selectrics—and even they weren't good enough to type with the uniformity of these obviously computer-generated documents. Heck, in the 1990s, some military bases I visited on assignment were still using old manual typewriters whose finished product was instantly recognizable by its rustic nature. Uneven lines. Corrected mistakes impossible to hide. Varied darkness and clarity of the individual letters, depending on the strength with which the user pounded the key. Even the electrics of the era had distinguishable, trademark irregularities.

Whoever had peddled these documents as genuine had to be a child of the computer age, otherwise they'd understand how unconvincing they looked. And whoever believed them had to be ignorant or blinded by their desire to push the story.

In the embarrassing aftermath of Rathergate, with the documents ultimately exposed as fakes, my colleagues and I suffered the fallout. We lived through the incredibly painful process of watching some insiders who knew the documents were bogus defend them anyway. They were banking on Rather surviving the scandal and were betting that when the dust cleared, Rather would take down anyone not on his side.

Prior to an *Evening News* conference call one morning, I advised my senior producer to strongly push our New York superiors to bring in an independent entity to oversee any news coverage we attempted to do on Rathergate as it unfolded. My rationale was that we shouldn't risk digging ourselves into a deeper hole by dabbling in conflicts of interest and covering our own story unfettered. The senior said it was a good idea, but, as far as I know, he didn't pass along the suggestion.

One day, the senior approached me to say that I would have to cover that day's Rathergate story.

"I can't do that," I told him.

"Well, you may have to. You're the only choice today." The regular reporter who'd been covering the story was off.

I doubted that I'd be given the independence to address questions about Rather's actions—in a story that Rather would be approving, to air on Rather's broadcast.

A couple of hours later, I found my senior producer in front of our M Street offices on a break.

"I can't do the story," I told him again.

"Why not?"

"Because I saw the documents ahead of time and I told you what I thought about them. My contract states that I'll uphold certain ethical standards. I can't report a story that says something that I know to be false."

He was quiet.

"And if you make me," I continued, "I'll have to call to my lawyer."

Nobody ever again suggested I report on Rathergate.

As predicted, CBS was later criticized for attempting to cover our own story when we, ourselves, were at the center of the probe. In my view, it was another example of the company being worried about the wrong things and not worried about the right things.

Such was the case once again in 2013 after *60 Minutes* apologized for what it said was a "deeply flawed" story on Benghazi, as reported by another correspondent, who relied upon a later-discredited witness. This new scandal led managers, already skittish about original and investigative reporting, to embark on illogical overreactions. *CBS This Morning* had asked me to report on the new book, written by *Fast and Furious* whistleblower John Dodson. There would be nothing legally precarious about this feature, but I had my script approved by the CBS legal department anyway, because I knew how fearful the broadcast producers were. The supervising producer approved the script as well.

Still, that wasn't enough.

"They also want John Miller to approve your script," the supervising producer informed me, referring to a fellow CBS News correspondent who had well-placed sources at the FBI, where he used to work. The backstory is that some inside the network believed if *60 Minutes* had asked Miller to check out its Benghazi source for their story, his FBI contacts would have waved him off and that CBS scandal would've been avoided.

Whatever the truth of that matter, it was silly to try to thrust Miller into the script approval chain on my story. A generous, smart, and well-connected colleague to be sure, he was nonetheless no better suited to "approve" my stories than I was to approve his. And he certainly wasn't better sourced on *Fast and Furious*.

In the end, I got word that Miller "approved" my script. To this day I have no idea what that approval could have possibly added or entailed.

While they were busy heaping unnecessary worry on my feature story, there were very real issues they should have been paying attention to.

But, by this time, I'd long since made up my mind that I would leave CBS at the end of my contract in December 2014, if not sooner. And the event that sealed that decision for me was related to Benghazi.

| BENGHAZIGATE

I should have known something was up when I received an unsolicited phone call from a White House official a few days before the second debate between President Obama and Republican nominee Mitt Romney on October 16, 2012.

The president was coming off a tough loss in the first debate, after which uncommitted voters, by a 46 percent to 22 percent margin, said Romney won; and 56 percent had an improved opinion of the Republican candidate.

The White House official and I chatted casually about unrelated topics and then he introduced a non sequitur: "The president called Benghazi a 'terrorist attack' the day after in the Rose Garden," he told me.

At the time, I hadn't given any thought to whether the president had or hadn't termed the Benghazi assaults "terrorism." The debate on that point hadn't widely emerged and I was still focused on the State Department's denial of security requests from Americans in Libya prior to the attacks.

Since I really didn't know what the president had said in the Rose Garden the day after, I didn't offer a comment to the White House official on the other end of the phone. He repeated himself as if to elicit some sort of reaction.

"He *did* call it a terrorist attack. In the Rose Garden. On September twelfth."

I had no idea that the question of how the administration portrayed the attacks—and whether it was covering up the terrorist ties—would emerge as a touchstone leading up to the election. But the White House already seemed to know.

A couple of days later, I'm watching the Obama-Romney debate at home on television as moderator Candy Crowley of CNN asks a Benghazi-related question. My ears perk up when the president replies using very similar language to that of the White House official on the phone.

> **OBAMA** The day after the attack, Governor, I stood in the Rose Garden and I told the American people and the world that we are going to find out exactly what happened. That this was an act of terror and I also said that we're going to hunt down those who committed this crime.

I now feel as though the White House official had been trying to prep me to accept the president's debate claim that he'd called the Benghazi assaults an "act of terror" on September 12.

The Benghazi question and the president's response are all Romney needs to try to seize control of the debate and score big points. He accuses the president of downplaying terrorist ties to protect his campaign claim that al-Qaeda was on the run.

> **ROMNEY** I—I think [it's] interesting the president just said something which—which is that on the day after the attack he went into the Rose Garden and said that this was an act of terror.
> **OBAMA** That's what I said.
> **ROMNEY** You said in the Rose Garden the day after the attack, it was an act of terror? It was not a spontaneous demonstration, is that what you're saying?
> **OBAMA** Please proceed, Governor. . . .

ROMNEY   I want to make sure we get that for the record because it took the president fourteen days before he called the
attack in Benghazi an act of terror.

OBAMA   Get the transcript.

The exchange feels strangely awkward. Romney seems genuinely
bewildered and President Obama seems oddly anxious to move on.
Then, the moderator, Crowley, comes to the president's rescue.

CROWLEY   It—it—it—he did in fact, sir. So let me—let me
call it an act of terror. . . .

OBAMA   Can you say that a little louder, Candy?

CROWLEY   He—he did call it an act of terror.

Crowley is quick with her take. It makes me wonder if she, too, had
gotten that call from a White House official in advance, telling her that
the president had immediately labeled Benghazi a terrorist act.

Why is this point so important to the Obama administration?

The next day, I look for a transcript of the president's Rose Garden
statement to see if I can figure out the puzzle.

When I locate and review the remarks that the president made in
the Rose Garden on September 12, 2012, I find that he did *not* say
Benghazi was "an act of terror," as he'd claimed in the debate. In fact,
at each point in his speech when he could have raised the specter of
"terrorism" or "terrorists," he'd chosen a synonym (examples of this
from his speech are bolded):

THE PRESIDENT   Good morning. . . . Yesterday, four of these
extraordinary Americans were killed in **an attack** on our diplomatic post in Benghazi. Among those killed was our Ambassador, Chris Stevens, as well as Foreign Service Officer Sean

Smith. . . . The United States condemns in the strongest terms this **outrageous and shocking attack**. . . . And make no mistake, we will work with the Libyan government to bring to justice **the killers who attacked** our people. Since our founding, the United States has been a nation that respects all faiths. We reject all efforts to denigrate the religious beliefs of others. But there is absolutely no justification to this type of **senseless violence**. None. The world must stand together to unequivocally reject these **brutal acts**. Already, many Libyans have joined us in doing so, and **this attack** will not break the bonds between the United States and Libya. Libyan security personnel fought back against **the attackers** alongside Americans. . . .

Nope, no mention of terrorism there.

Where the president may be granted some wiggle room, though there's no doubt he overstated it in the debate, is when his speech segued to the fact that the attacks happened on the anniversary of the 2001 terrorist attacks at the World Trade Center in New York and the Pentagon in Washington. That's when he used the word *terror*. But not referring directly to Benghazi.

THE PRESIDENT   Of course, yesterday was already a painful day for our nation as we marked the solemn memory of the 9/11 attacks. We mourned with the families who were lost on that day. I visited the graves of troops who made the ultimate sacrifice in Iraq and Afghanistan at the hallowed grounds of Arlington Cemetery, and had the opportunity to say thank you and visit some of our wounded warriors at Walter Reed. And then last night, we learned the news of **this attack** in Benghazi. As Americans, let us never, ever forget that our freedom is only sustained because there are people who are willing to fight for it, to stand up for it, and in some cases, lay down their lives for it. Our country is only as strong as the character of our people and the service of those both civilian and military who represent us around the globe. **No acts of terror will ever shake the resolve of this great nation, alter that character, or eclipse the light of the values that we stand for.** Today we mourn four more Americans who represent the very best of the United States of America. We will not waver in our commitment to see that justice is done for **this terrible act**. And make no mistake, justice will be done. But we also know that the lives these Americans led stand in stark contrast to those of their **attackers**. . . .

One might be able to believe that the administration's wholesale avoidance of the term *terrorism* in direct reference to Benghazi is an accident of wording. Except that the same accident happened in those early days when White House spokesman Carney briefed reporters, when Secretary of State Clinton spoke at the return of the victims' bodies, and when U.S. ambassador Rice appeared on Sunday talk shows. Except that the references to terrorism and al-Qaeda were purposefully removed from the talking points used to relate details to the public. In fact, one would have to go out of his way to use so many synonyms for the attackers and *not* say the actual word *terrorist*.

Taken together, it's difficult to believe the wording is anything other than a purposeful strategy. The main unanswered questions: Who spearheaded the strategy? Why? And in what form was it transmitted to all the officials who got on board with it?

So what does all this have to do with my own situation at CBS?

In an unexpected way, it came to expose the extraordinary lengths to which some of my colleagues would go to misrepresent and slant the facts when they had explicit evidence to the contrary, which they kept hidden. It was enough to irreparably destroy any confidence in and respect I might have had for those at the network who were involved.

In the Benghazi chapter of this book, I referred to the fact that *60 Minutes* correspondent Steve Kroft happened to have an unrelated interview scheduled with President Obama the day after the Benghazi attacks.

However, the contents of his crucial interview, as it related to Benghazi, were largely kept under wraps at the time. The interview was only pulled out of the archives more than five weeks later when *CBS Evening News* managers wished to cherry-pick an excerpt and dictate its use out of context in a way that supported President Obama's version of events.

It's October 19, 2012, three days after that fateful Obama-Romney debate and less than three weeks before the election. Obama had managed to turn around Romney's advantage. The president had held his own in the debate. Maybe even thrown Romney back on his heels with his Benghazi answer, insisting he'd immediately labled the attacks "terrorism." After being smacked down by Crowley, Romney would hesitate to raise the specter of Benghazi again during the rest of the campaign.

But still simmering in the background is the building flap over whether the Obama administration had tried to hide the Benghazi attacks' terrorist ties. The *CBS Evening News* wants the controversy addressed and, preferably, put to rest. The New York producers commission a story on the topic from a fellow CBS Washington correspondent.

Midday, I'm in the Washington newsroom when I overhear our senior producer relay strict instructions from New York. The instructions say that the other correspondent's story must include a specific, never-before-aired sound bite from President Obama's September 12

60 Minutes interview with Kroft. I'm busy working on my own story that day, but it's news to me that *60 Minutes* had spoken to the president about Benghazi weeks before. New York also dictates the precise wording that the other correspondent should use to introduce the chosen Obama sound bite. It appears to be an attempt to make the president's case for him—that he *had* called the Benghazi attacks "terrorism."

The resulting *Evening News* script reads as follows:

> It had been about 14 hours since the attack, and the President said he did not believe it was due simply to mob violence. "You're right that this is not a situation that was exactly the same as what happened in Egypt," Obama said, referring to protests sparked by an anti-Islam film. "And my suspicion is that there are folks involved in this who were looking to target Americans from the start." Shortly after that, Obama stepped into the Rose Garden and spoke of the killing of four Americans as if it were a terrorist attack. "No act of terror will ever shake the resolve of this great nation," Obama said in his Rose Garden remarks.

I mentally note that my own interpretation of the president's Rose Garden remarks isn't quite the same.

Meanwhile, in subsequent days, my producers and I break several more important stories on Benghazi as documents and witnesses chip away at the Obama administration's narrative.

On October 24, 2012, I exclusively obtain the email alerts issued by the State Department to the White House Situation Room and government and intelligence agencies as the attacks unfolded on September 11. One of the initial alerts stated what the Obama administration kept hidden from the public: that the Islamic militant group Ansar al-Sharia had claimed responsibility for the attacks. As evidence mounts, none of it supports the Obama administration's narrative about a spontaneous protest.

As I'm writing my script for the *Evening News*, the hotline from the New York fishbowl sounds in the Washington newsroom. New York is instructing me to insert the same Obama *60 Minutes* sound bite in my story that they'd told the other correspondent to use a few days before.

"It has to be used, and you have to use that same wording to introduce it: Obama 'said he did not believe it was simply due to mob violence,'" my senior producer tells me in the voice that conveys to me there's no arguing the point and don't-ask-why-because-he-doesn't-know-the-answer. Their minds are made up.

So for the second time in five days, New York has us insert the same line and Obama sound bite in an *Evening News* story to imply that the president had called Benghazi a terrorist attack the next day. It seems as though they're putting a lot of effort into trying to defend the president on this point.

It's not long after that story when the proverbial light switch on the Benghazi story turns off at CBS. The broadcast has gone from asking me to aggressively pursue all leads, to demurring when I begin to turn up more facts that show important inconsistencies in the administration's accounts. The election is drawing near. Witnesses and documents are raising more legitimate questions by the day. But I feel that familiar Big Chill.

Leave it alone.

Troublemaker.

Pretty soon, the only sure outlet for new developments is CBSNews.com. As with *Fast and Furious*, the public is thirsty for developments on the Benghazi story and the Web postings draw a great deal of traffic. Clearly, viewers are interested. But the broadcast producers are not.

It's not until the weekend before the November presidential election that I learn something that would shake any remaining faith I had in the New York fishbowl.

It's Friday afternoon. A colleague calls.

"You know that interview *60 Minutes* did with Obama in the Rose Garden on September twelfth?" the colleague says.

"Yes," I answer. "Why?"

"I just got a transcript. Of the entire interview."

"From who?

"I can't say. But *holy shit*."

"What's it say?" I ask.

"*Holy shit*."

The colleague proceeds to read to me from the transcript. It's undeniably clear to both of us. We instantly know that the interview that had been kept under such a tight wrap for nearly eight weeks is explosive.

The very first comment Kroft made, and the president's response, proved that Romney had been correct all along:

KROFT Mr. President, this morning you went out of your way to avoid the use of the word *terrorism* in connection with the Libya attack.
OBAMA Right.

Kroft's take on the president's wording and intent was the same as mine had been and, according to the president himself, at the time, our take was correct. All the synonyms used by Obama, Clinton, White House spokesman Carney, and Ambassador Rice *were* intentional. They "went out of [their] way to avoid the use of the word *terrorism*."

Then Kroft asked a question that offered the president the opportunity to clarify or at least hint at the behind-the-scenes conclusions already formed by nearly everyone on the inside: that the attacks were the work of terrorists. But the president balked.

KROFT   Do you believe that this was a terrorist attack?
OBAMA   Well, it's too early to know exactly how this came about, what group was involved, but obviously it was an attack on Americans.

Kroft had asked the question point blank. Though the president has told the world that he unequivocally called it a terrorist attack that very day, and though the media has largely sided with his interpretation, his own hidden interview with CBS belied the claim.

My thought turns to the selectively chosen Obama sound bite the *Evening News* had directed me to use a week before. To put it mildly: it was misleading.

This was a really bad thing.

Besides the implications for the story itself, I couldn't get past the fact that upper-level journalists at CBS had been a party to misleading the public. *Why wouldn't they have immediately released the operative sound bite after Romney raised the issue in the debate? It would have been a great moment for CBS. The kind of break that news organizations hope for. We had our hands on original material that no other news outlet had that would shed light on an important controversy. But we hid it.*

Now, eight years after Rathergate, I feared that we'd once again mischaracterized facts in advance of a presidential election to hurt a Republican. We not only had stood by silently as the media largely sided against Romney, but we'd also taken an active part in steering them in that direction.

Still on the phone with my colleague, we both knew what had to be done but I said it out loud.

"This has to be published," I said. "Before the election."

"I know," agreed my colleague.

What's really going to bake your noodle later on is—*How did the White House know CBS wouldn't use the part of the* 60 Minutes *Obama interview that disproved the president's debate claim?*

Thus began a frenetic forty-eight hours of activity inside CBS News during which a small group of us made individual contact with news executives and explained what we thought needed to happen.

I told the executives I spoke with that withholding the operative sound bite and information was extremely unethical and dishonest. I argued that we had no choice but to publish it quickly, prior to the election. It was up to them to decide the format, but it had to be published.

It was all going to come out one way or another. There were *60 Minutes* staffers who had been talking about it, wondering why the *Evening News* had avoided using the operative part of the Obama interview. And now, at the eleventh hour, the chatter had grown so strong that a transcript had been leaked to some of us outside *60 Minutes*. Like chewing on a gristly piece of bad meat, it was only going to get bigger. It was only a matter of time before people outside of CBS found out.

If we published quickly and took our lumps, at least we would have done so before the election. If we didn't publish, and outsiders found out later—and they would—it would be said that we engaged in a cover-up to try to affect the outcome of the election.

In no instance did any executive express disagreement to me or to others in our small group. In fact, they enthusiastically agreed. There had been a grave and purposeful error. We had to fix it. And so, the Sunday night before the election, nearly eight weeks after the Obama interview had taken place, the network posted it on CBSNews.com as part of a comprehensive Benghazi timeline that I and several colleagues had built.

I exhaled for the first time in two days.

I paused and thought back to the actual transcript I'd seen of the entire Kroft interview with Obama. *60 Minutes* had emailed it to the *Evening News* fishbowl in New York the very day it took place. Anchor and Managing Editor Pelley. Executive Producer Shevlin. They had to have known. They were emailed the full transcript on day one. They must have known after the Romney debate and when they dictated use of the misleading sound bites in October.

"Look, we fucked up," CBS News president Rhodes would tell me in our continuing discussions. "But what matters is that as soon as it was brought to my attention I took steps to correct it. And if there are [congressional] hearings, that's what I'll testify to, because it's the truth."

There were no hearings.

A few Republican members of Congress who were paying closer attention than others contacted CBS News executives with their concerns about the belated posting of the president's Benghazi interview. But by and large, the whole episode was mostly forgotten, eclipsed by the actual election, after which attentions were focused elsewhere.

I was relieved that the material was published before the election. But I felt the internal follow-up was crucial. There had been a serious breach of ethics that could have done irreparable harm to the news division, had it not been caught and remedied. Those responsible for the lapse have no business working in a news division. People like that can bring down a news operation by caring more about their own selfish motives than the good of the network and its duty to the public. If there ever were to be an outside inquiry, as there was after Rathergate, we would need to demonstrate that we'd taken all the appropriate steps. That we'd learned from our past mistakes. That meant there should be an internal ethics investigation holding accountable whoever was responsible.

But that was not to be.

A few weeks later, I met with David Rhodes during one of his regular visits to Washington. I asked for an update on the internal investigation. For me, there was no point in pulling punches. Speaking of the *Evening News* managers who I felt had been a party to covering up the Obama bite, I said, "They're dishonest, they're unethical, and they're not very smart. I don't trust them, I don't respect them, and I can't work for them."

David assured me that a full investigation was under way. Or was going to be conducted in the future. I wasn't entirely sure. It was a bit vague.

"Will the rest of us get to know the results?" I asked. Twice.

I wondered realistically what could be done. Pretty much the whole New York fishbowl was potentially implicated in the ethics breach. How could CBS really punish them all? And would the network risk taking action that could draw attention to something that had gone relatively unnoticed by the public?

David assured me that, yes, we would all know the results of the investigation when it was finished.

That was the last I ever heard of it.

| CONTROVERSIALIZING IN ACTION

It's spring of 2013 and, disillusioned about the network's handling of the Benghazi story, I nonetheless continue to turn up new information and offer stories. My sources and information on Benghazi are bearing serious fruit but, more often than not, it tends to die on the vine now. The partisan propaganda campaign to portray Benghazi as an Area 51–type conspiracy theory, a Republican-manufactured phony scandal, has successfully taken root with receptive audience members inside and outside CBS. Many other media outlets that had once enthusiastically covered the story have, like CBS, backed off.

I'm taking a day off on Friday, May 10, when Bureau Chief Isham contacts me and asks me to check out a story that's just been broken by ABC's Jonathan Karl about the Benghazi talking points.

For months, the Obama administration had refused to publicly release crucial emails showing the genesis of the controversial and misleading talking points that excluded mention of terrorism. But the administration had made some of the emails available to members of Congress and their staff on an extremely restricted basis: the documents had to be viewed in a special room during certain hours in the presence of one or more administration officials. Members of Congress and their staff were not allowed to remove the documents from the room. They were not allowed to make copies. All they could do was make handwritten notes about them.

Karl's news is big. He reports that ABC has "reviewed" "White House emails" and obtained "12 different versions of the talking points." They reveal for the first time that, from start to finish, the content of the talking points was transformed from revealing that terrorism and al-Qaeda were responsible, and that the CIA had issued prior warnings of an attack on the Benghazi compound, to a scrubbed version that removed all traces of terror references. This is the very thing that inside sources had suggested, but the administration had denied.

Isham wants to know if I can get the emails, too. I make some calls and pretty quickly discover that I can't get the actual emails. But I can find out what they said from a reliable source who reviewed them. I report back to Isham.

"I can't find anybody who has the administration's emails. The administration turned them over to Congress with a bunch of restrictions. But I *can* get a read on them from a good source who reviewed the emails and took handwritten notes," I tell Isham.

The source reads to me directly from notes and repeats the caveat that there may be paraphrasing because of the unusual arrangement whereby access was limited and they weren't allowed to photocopy the emails.

After the briefing, I compare my notes to Karl's emails and they match up very closely. Not exactly, which could be expected due to the paraphrasing, but the meaning is the same.

The series of Obama administration revisions chronicled in the emails is astonishing. The White House had spent months hiding the information in them, insisting it didn't know who was responsible for developing the talking points and refusing to release the drafts to members of Congress who requested them. Under any neutral assessment, Karl's break is the big story of the day.

I write up a comprehensive note summarizing the various drafts of the Obama administration talking points emails and I forward it to my Washington managers and our Capitol Hill staff. Then I brief them in a conference call. I make it crystal clear both in my note and on the telephone that neither I nor my source have the emails in hand since the administration had not allowed them to be physically turned over to Congress. For that reason, I reiterate, my source's notes are paraphrases, but can be trusted as accurate representations.

My Washington managers forward my email note to the substitute White House correspondent on duty and the *Evening News* fishbowl in New York. They send back a message for me to not bother to come into work. They'll have the White House correspondent use my notes to do the story.

Yeah, we're in that phase, I think.

Isham tells me to go ahead and post a write-up on CBSNews.com to match Karl's reporting. The very first line of my article contains the same disclosure I'd made to my managers:

NOTE　*Emails were provided by the Administration to certain

Congressional Committees for limited review. The Committees
were not permitted to copy the emails, so they made handwritten
notes. Therefore, parts of the quoted emails may be paraphrased.

The cleansing of the talking points is such a damning development in the Benghazi saga, the Obama propaganda forces focus their
full attention to trying to discredit it. Their crisis response is primarily directed at controversializing Karl, who broke the story.

STEP ONE   The White House releases the talking point emails—
the ones it had withheld all this time—and shows wording
that differs slightly from the quotes Karl had provided.

STEP TWO   The White House falsely claims the discrepancies
are significant, and then uses them to discredit Karl and
controversialize the whole damaging story.

STEP THREE   Assistance comes from the administration's surrogate bloggers on the Web who claim the unnamed source
of the email leaks lied by saying he had the emails in hand—
though the source had done no such thing. They accuse the
source of "doctoring" quotes. Again, utterly false. But pretty
soon, legitimate news organizations take the baton and per-
petuate the idea that the whole talking-point-email-fuss is a
Republican-created-scandal.

It's a familiar syndrome: the same news outlets that ignore a genuine controversy when it emerges are all too eager to jump in and pick
up the story if it means discrediting it . . . or if it means reporting on
the administration's defense.

In fact, the differences between Karl's presented quotes and the
actual emails were without distinction. Both demonstrated that the
Obama administration had seriously misled Congress and the public.

But all of that is lost in the furor whipped up by left-wing bloggers with help from the mainstream press.

I feel sorry for Karl. He doesn't have a chance against the White House spin machine, its surrogates on the Web, and a complicit news media on Obama's side.

A few days later, I inadvertently get wrapped up in the controversy. It starts with a text message from a colleague.

"Did you see what they did to your story?" the colleague asks.

"What are you talking about?" I reply.

"I'll call you."

On the phone, the colleague explains that the *Evening News* had required our White House correspondent to do a one-sided story discrediting Karl's reporting on the talking point emails and, by proxy, discrediting my own reporting on the same subject, as well as my source.

I was told that there were heated internal arguments over this particular *Evening News* story. That nobody in the Washington bureau thought it should air. Not the correspondent, not the producer, not the senior producer, not the bureau chief. But New York was hellbent. I was told that Pelley and his producers rewrote the entire script to their liking, "top to bottom."

So *CBS Evening News* anchor Scott Pelley introduces the resulting report, referring to the content of the White House emails "leaked to reporters last week." (That would include me.)

"It turns out some of the quotes in those emails were wrong," Pelley says. For reasons unknown, he ignores the fact that I had reported the "quotes" provided to me as paraphrases—they weren't "wrong" at all.

The correspondent's report then continues the fallacy by comparing supposed "quotes that had been provided by Republicans" (which are actually paraphrases supplied by a source) to the emails the White House later released, as if some sort of subterfuge has been unearthed.

But the differences are without distinction: a review of the emails proves that the original paraphrased quotes from a source the week before were entirely accurate in spirit, context, and meaning.

Tonight's CBS story is, in my view, inaccurate, misleading, and unfair. It may as well have been written by the White House. On top of that, it mentions the White House's Ben Rhodes as author of some of the talking points drafts in question, but fails to disclose that he's the brother of CBS News president David Rhodes.

I'm genuinely stunned that this story about my reporting and my source aired on my network with nobody picking up the telephone and speaking to me to get the facts. It's contrary to the most basic practices in journalism. Whoever wrote the story appeared to make no effort to seek the facts beyond the White House spin. I could have immediately told them that what they were about to report was wrong.

Although my source isn't named in the disparaging *CBS Evening News* story, I worry about potential liability. Not only have the facts been misrepresented, but the report, in essence, labeled my source a liar. I feel pretty certain that nobody had run this script by the CBS legal department. They never would have allowed it to air.

The White House and outlets such as *Mother Jones* seize upon this new *CBS Evening News* report as an admission that my report, and Karl's, had been wrong. That the GOP had "doctored" quotes, though my source had doctored nothing.

Several CBS colleagues encourage me not to let this inaccuracy go unanswered.

"[CBS is] selling you down the river," says one. "They'll gladly sacrifice your reputation to save their own. If you don't stand up for yourself, nobody will."

I email key CBS News executives, noting that my original article contained the explicit disclosure that the email quotes were paraphrased from handwritten notes, just as my source had explained. I point out that the content of the paraphrases and the emails match up perfectly. I reiterate that everyone who received my story note, including the New York fishbowl, knew this and so shouldn't have pursued a story that falsely implied quotes were doctored or a source had lied.

Next, I go to view the original article I'd written for the Web. As I click on the page, I quickly scroll up and down—something is missing. Somebody has edited out the key explanation I'd included at the top of the article about the paraphrased quotes. It's gone.

Who edited out the caveat—and why?

Within a matter of hours, I solve the mystery. An editor for CBSNews.com had made an innocent error. He had removed the disclosure paragraph because he simply didn't feel it was necessary.

The big question is: How to fix the whole mess? We need to add back the disclosure paragraph as I originally wrote it and include an explanation as to how it got inadvertently edited out. That way people would know that our source hadn't lied, and that my reporting had been accurate.

But that simple fix is met with resistance from management.

"If we amend the story, it will just draw attention to the [incorrect] *Evening News* story [the other correspondent had aired]," one New York manager tells me.

I decide to consult some trusted advisors within CBS Corporation. They agree I need to push the point both for the sake of accuracy and my reputation. They come up with this suggestion: if my managers won't agree to restore my Web story to the way I'd written it, then I should ask that it be removed from the website entirely.

I contact the relevant New York executive and ask that he facilitate getting my Web article reinstated to its initial version. He puts me off saying he's too busy to focus on it. But for me, the whole thing has already been drawn out too long and the propagandists are making serious hay out of the affair. I tell the executive that if he doesn't have time to address my concerns, I plan to consult our CBS lawyers.

"No, Sharyl," comes his quick reply. I've gotten his attention.

In the end, CBS management agreed to make the fix to my Web article.

Understandably, the whole Washington inner circle that watches these things seemed confused by the shenanigans surrounding the talking points emails, the spin, and the CBS News stories. So much so that a *Washington Post* fact-checker ultimately dissected the matter. He, too, was befuddled by the most recent *Evening News* story that seemed to contradict my reporting. But he was able to get a grasp on the facts. He noted that the paraphrases of the White House emails reported by me and Karl were identical in meaning to the actual quotes, though the White House spin claimed otherwise. He correctly reported that I had clearly disclosed that the material used in my Web article was paraphrased. He even pointed out that Ben Rhodes is David Rhodes's brother. As a result, he gave the White House three out of four "Pinocchios," meaning he found "significant fact errors and/or contradictions" in its claim that "GOP operatives deliberately tried to 'smear the president' with false, doctored emails."

"Indeed, Republicans would have been foolish to seriously doctor emails that the White House at any moment could have released (and eventually did)," noted the *Post*.

All of these unnecessary internal battles, largely prompted by propagandists, consume time and energy, and they take their toll. They steal efforts away from real newsgathering. They divert attention from important stories. And they result in convincing management more than ever that it's easier just to avoid these types of stories entirely. As intended.

Of course, to this day, the propagandists who manufactured the false tale about the "doctored" emails continue to promulgate the narrative. Yet another effort to controversialize the factual reporting on Benghazi. That's just what they do.

| THE DREAMLINER NIGHTMARE

It was early 2013 when the network assigned me to cover transportation issues. The beat had been passed around among a number of correspondents in recent years, kind of like Hot Potato, and the *Evening News* fishbowl was looking for a Washington correspondent to pick it up. Maybe they were happy to divert my attention from the watchdog stories I had been focused on. I told Bureau Chief Isham I didn't really want the assignment, but I'd take it and give it my all.

There was plenty to keep me busy. The current broadcasts *loved* anything that could go wrong on an airplane. A chute deploys midflight? That's a national story! A passenger stands up and shouts something crazy? That's a national story! A suspicious character passes through security at LAX? That's a national story! A jet slides off the runway? That's a national story!

They also loved industry and government press releases on aggressive driving efforts, cell phones on planes, lasers pointed at planes, drunk driving studies, distracted driving statistics, and crash safety tests. Safe stories fed to us by the powers that be. Stories that everyone covers.

My idea was to dig a little deeper on these stories and produce something more original. And one of the meaty transportation stories that merited further investigation was the Boeing Dreamliner.

The giant Boeing 787 Dreamliner was the first commercial jet to rely so heavily on lithium-ion battery technology, which saved money by making the plane lighter and burn less fuel. The downside is that lithium-ion batteries occasionally happen to burst into flames. There was a fire in January 2013 on a Japan Airlines Dreamliner parked at Boston Logan International Airport. Another battery incident less than two weeks later in Japan on All Nippon Airways. Soon Dreamliners were grounded worldwide.

Kim and I were all over the story and the broadcasts seemed pleased. At first. Like a lot of stories, they loved it before they hated it.

As we continued our daily news coverage, CBSNews.com asked me to look into the case of a Dreamliner whistleblower who had told his story to a few news organizations but had largely gone unnoticed.

His name is Michael Leon and, in 2006, he was a senior engineering technician at Securaplane, in Tucson, Arizona, working on the Dreamliner's prototype battery chargers. The chargers sit next to the batteries on the planes and operate as a system. Leon's hands were the last hands on the prototype chargers before they went out the door. He claimed that Securaplane, under extraordinary pressure to meet Boeing contract deadlines, took shortcuts and compromised human safety.

As part of his work years before, Leon discovered that the internal monitor in a prototype Dreamliner battery wasn't working properly. But Securaplane officials assured him it was safe. Two weeks later, he was in the company lab when the same battery exploded. It wasn't even hooked up to the charger.

"It was like an F-16 afterburner," Leon said. One cell after another exploded and spewed out toxic black smoke as thick as oil. It burned down Securaplane's three-story building. Leon suffered permanent injuries, including heart problems from the chemical smoke, but continued to work. Boeing claimed the battery caught fire due to an "improper test setup," but investigators were never able to determine the cause.

Now, seven years later, experts wondered whether whatever made the battery catch fire then might be a clue to the Dreamliner's current problems. But Boeing and Securaplane say it's unrelated.

Leon had also raised objections to what he felt were "dangerous" chargers. Once, during development, when he refused to sign off on the chargers for safety reasons, he learned that a colleague shipped them out anyway. (Boeing and Securaplane say the battery charger from the early testing is different than the final product so it shouldn't be a safety concern.)

Feeling as though his safety complaints were disregarded, and believing that management was targeting him, Leon filed a complaint with the Federal Aviation Administration (FAA) in 2007. Securaplane fired him. He sued for wrongful termination, but lost. The labor judge said that Leon wasn't fired for whistleblowing, but for his hostility and repeated misconduct. Leon argued that the hostility and supposed misconduct were a result of his managers marginalizing him when he raised safety concerns.

Interestingly, the labor judge did agree that "someone with Leon's level of expertise could reasonably believe Securaplane might be in violation of FAA regulations" and "Leon's concerns were objectively reasonable. They were the type of air safety concerns Congress intended to protect whistleblowers for raising."

The FAA—often rumored to favor industry—investigated Leon's complaint in 2007 and 2008 but took no action. The agency said that Leon complained about prototypes that are not installed in the Dreamliners that eventually went into service, so there was no concern.

As part of our research, Kim and I consulted numerous experts who said that the FAA's response in 2008 missed the point. Errors in prototypes can be perpetuated in the final product. Additionally, the company's practices were also at serious issue and so, theoretically, could affect any of its final products, not just certain prototypes.

So, we studied Leon's court testimony and documentation from 2006. We consulted with battery and air safety experts in the field to check out his claims. One of them went so far as to tell us he thought Leon's material qualified as a "smoking gun" in the current Dreamliner investigation.

Former National Transportation Safety Board chairman Jim Hall was on record as having said the 2006 battery fire which Leon claimed was caused by a faulty battery and/or poor company practices "is a significant event that the NTSB will want to look closely at." Former NTSB member John Goglia told us on camera that Leon's complaints took on new significance in light of the Dreamliner's grounding and "go right to the core of the battery and the battery charging system and they're really right on what we're looking for today."

Indeed, the NTSB investigation had narrowed to three areas, and Leon had touched upon each of them in his original complaints years before: the battery charger, battery construction and design, and defects introduced during manufacturing. The NTSB had recently interviewed Leon and so did a Democratic congressional staffer preparing for possible hearings. Leon's story and the facts revealed were interesting and important context in this developing story.

Best of all from a story standpoint, we had a compelling on-camera interview from Leon himself. A burly Vietnam vet who's part Native American, he came off as quirky, knowledgeable, sincere, and credible.

By late February 2013, we had nailed everything down. Kim, another *Evening New* producer, and I put the finishing touches on what we felt was an extremely strong script. It was approved by our senior producer and the CBS lawyers.

But what broadcast to offer the story to?

Evening News wouldn't want an original story like this. After all, the story took on Boeing and the FAA. But if we gave it to another broadcast and it got lots of attention and pickup, as it undoubtedly would, *Evening News* would be upset. Everybody would be asking why *they* didn't have the story. It had happened before. They didn't necessarily want a particular story, but they also didn't want to be called out for not running it if another broadcast did.

A CBS New York executive advised me to first offer the story to *Evening News,* as a formality, and then take it to *CBS This Morning* when *Evening News* declined.

Evening News executive producer Shevlin reviewed the script and either didn't get it or didn't want to. She wanted to gut it. Among other changes, she wanted to cut out the entire section about the 2006 fire, and the video of it.

"It doesn't have anything to do with what's going on today," she concluded, mistaken and uninformed. In one fell swoop she had disregarded our weeks of research and the opinions of seasoned experts. Shevlin sometimes had a difficult time grasping complex stories. Maybe I hadn't written it clearly enough. I offered to rewrite the section to better explain the fire's relevance. I was determined not to let her tear out the heart of the report. But she was intractable.

The confounding conversation dragged on—Shevlin in New York with three of us listening on telephone extensions in the Washington newsroom: me, one of my producers, and my senior producer. Each of us patiently took a stab at trying to help explain to Shevlin why her interpretations were so off base. She grew louder and more agitated as she dug in. The three of us in Washington made eye contact and shook our heads. Eventually, I made a knife-across-the-throat gesture signaling to my colleagues that there was no point continuing the discussion. We hung up and agreed that she just didn't like the story and wasn't going to air it. There was no sense continuing the charade.

I went straight to the *CBS Saturday Morning* broadcast, where I knew the executive producer was still receptive to great original stories and would give this one the time it needed to be well told. He viewed the script and the finished product, said it was terrific, and scheduled it to air the following weekend. I would fly to New York to introduce it on the set.

All was well until the Thursday before the air date. I got a strange call from Laura,* our ethics czar. That was never a good sign. Over the years, disgruntled CBS insiders sometimes went to Laura to complain about my reporting, especially if it stepped on their toes or was contrary to their personal beliefs. Managers had also employed Laura's services to try to soften or block my reporting on topics that riled corporate interests.

In this case, it seems somebody inside CBS had raised objections to our Dreamliner story, though it was yet to air. From what Laura said, this person falsely claimed that I had used Leon as an anonymous source for a previous Dreamliner story that was wrong.

Nothing like that had occurred: it was a complete fabrication on somebody's part. Leon hadn't been a source for me on *any* other story.

After we chatted, Laura was satisfied that the complainant had been mistaken and gave my script her seal of approval, commenting that it was "great."

I wondered which of my colleagues made up a disparaging story about me and my whistleblower, and why?

The next day, I was producing an unrelated story for the *Evening News* and preparing to fly to New York after the broadcast for the Saturday morning Dreamliner live shot.

A flurry of strange activity erupted.

First, the Saturday morning executive producer contacted me and said there had been some sort of meeting in New York, and he needed me to talk to Laura about my story again. Meanwhile, my senior producer in Washington told me he'd listened to that meeting via telephone. He said that among those in attendance were Shevlin,

---

* Not her real name.

CBS This Morning executive Chris Licht, and CBS president Rhodes. Apparently, they came up with endless reasons not to run my story—without seeking any input from me or my producers.

"It was a bloodbath," my senior producer told me.

"Did you defend the story?" I asked. After all, he knew it better than they did. He had approved the script and said it was a great story.

"There was no point," he answered. "Their minds were made up."

He was right. By the time I talked to Laura later that day, it was clear she'd been convinced or directed to find a way to pull the story.

Is this a feature story about a whistleblower or an investigative story about the Dreamliner? Laura asked me when we spoke on the phone.

Both, I explained. As with any good investigation, you like to have a strong human subject at the center of the story, as you expose important facts and information. It was an odd question for a seasoned producer like Laura to ask. She knows how we work.

Well, if it's a feature about a whistleblower, I'm not sure he's that compelling, Laura continued. *And if it's an investigation, why don't we just wait and see what the government finds and* then *do the story?*

I took a breath. I could tell the story was dead. This was all pro forma.

I didn't give up easily. I explained my philosophy about the type of reporting I try to do. I don't wait until a story is over, then join the pack and report what everyone else reports, I told Laura. And if we wait on the government to do the right thing before we report a story, we could be waiting forever. Afflicted by conflicts of interest, federal officials more often than not seem to bring up the rear in these types of investigations.

My explanations fell on deaf ears.

I hung up the phone and informed my senior producer the story was dead. He told me that if it was any consolation, *Evening News* probably wouldn't have aired it anyway once they saw what the quirky whistleblower looked like. It was like twisting the knife in my heart. TV likes pretty people who say predictable things and speak in homilies. I like real people who tell the truth.

Both of my producers and I lodged verbal and written objections. I told David Rhodes that my two terrific producers and I had worked at a combined four networks and three investigative units. To exclude our input and kill the story was dreadfully wrong.

The incident added a new sense of urgency to the discomfort I already had over the Benghazi affair. The day the Dreamliner story died, I told my senior producer, "I'm not going to walk out today or tomorrow. But I'm letting you know, I don't see how I can finish out my contract under these circumstances."

When Isham returned from vacation, he said he was sorry he hadn't been here to help intervene on my behalf. I told him I didn't foresee finishing my contract. It was late February 2013.

Deep down, Kim and I suspected what was going on. Boeing was in PR crisis mode. Experts and consultants felt threatened not to talk to the press about the Dreamliner. Many of these consultants depend on the airlines and airplane manufacturers for business. They couldn't afford to go up against Boeing.

I also knew that Boeing had been lobbying Congress to not convene hearings on the Dreamliner. And, in fact, hearings that were once reported to be imminent never materialized.

I could only assume that powerful interests had gotten to CBS, too. I had no way to know for sure. Nobody was going to tell me. Fueling my suspicions: it seemed like other media quit covering the Dreamliner's problems about the same time. The NTSB even halted its regular schedule of issuing updates. We all went from near-daily interest in the developing Dreamliner story, to more or less letting the topic fall off the planet.

Six months later, on August 1, 2013, a CBS colleague who knew about the fiasco over the Dreamliner story alerted me that United Airlines CEO Jeff Smisek was about to be interviewed live on *CBS This Morning*. United was the only U.S. airline flying Boeing Dreamliners.

I turned the TV to Channel 9, our local CBS Washington affiliate, and watched Smisek get several minutes of uninterrupted airtime on our news broadcast to promote his corporation and an upcoming merger that required government approval. A PR coup for United.

Midway through, the Dreamliner came up.

"Do you still believe in the 787 Dreamliner?" asked an anchor.

"Absolutely!" answered Smisek, adding, "It's a great airplane!"

The other anchor chimed in. "So you're here to say"—he points in time with the words for emphasis, as if a probing question is ahead—"the safety issues are behind you with respect to the Dreamliner?"

"I think the Dreamliner is absolutely a safe airplane . . ." agrees Smisek.

Much later, in June 2014, the National Transportation Safety Board would issue findings that Boeing's processes to certify its lithium-ion batteries in 2006 were "inadequate." The board also, in essence, criticized the FAA—the agency that had cast aside Leon's original complaint—and said that in the future, it should draw on the expertise of independent specialists outside the aviation industry so "that both the FAA and the aircraft manufacturer have access to the most current research and information related to the developing technology."

| AWARDS REBUFFED

It's against the backdrop of the Dreamliner disaster, the Benghazi bungling, and the green energy drubbing that the 2013 television news award season rolls around. The broadcasts enter their best work in various categories from the prior year, in hopes to gain professional recognition for their efforts and the public service provided.

But this year, nobody contacts me to see which of my stories I might recommend for the prestigious Emmys.

Kim and I talk about it. It had been a struggle, but we had managed to find homes for some excellent stories on various broadcasts that season. There was the one green energy story that aired on *CBS This Morning* before the Big Chill descended. And there were more that we managed to get on the *CBS Weekend News*.

There was an impressive spate of exclusive Benghazi stories that aired on *Evening News* prior to the curtain falling on that story.

And there was a mix of congressional oversight reporting we had done for various broadcasts, including an exposé on lobbying for *CBS Sunday Morning* and an undercover investigation into the fund-raising practices of congressional Republican freshmen.

We are proud of the work. So, we decide to enter the Emmys on our own. Who knows? The judges might find one of our entries worthy of a nomination, even if CBS didn't.

A couple of months later, I'm on vacation in Austria when I click on an email from a colleague.

"Congratulations on the Emmy nomination!" it reads.

The nominations have just been announced online. I click on the link for the full list and am pleased to see that our green energy stories had received a nomination. I scan to see what other stories made the list.

To my surprise, I find my name on another nomination. This one for our Benghazi stories.

As I keep reading, I see a third nomination: for the congressional stories. All three of our entries had received nominations. My strongest year ever in terms of this sort of commendation.

That recognition makes it more difficult for partisans and propagandists to credibly portray my work as shoddy, partisan, and agenda driven. It also makes the CBS insiders who tried to disparage the stories furious, because it appears to prove their judgment wrong.

| THE FINAL DAYS AT CBS

It's mid-February 2014. There are new discussions between my agent, Richard Leibner, and CBS over my possible departure. I'm at Reagan National Airport preparing to fly from Washington to New York.

I see my Isham browsing the magazine rack at the Delta Shuttle gate. The same one from which I'm departing.

I approach him.

"Hello, sir!" I say.

Isham looks up from the magazines. I ask if he's going to New York. He is. He asks if I'm going. I am. We ask each other what flight. We're both on the 2 p.m. Coincidence.

We're silent for a moment. Looking at each other. He looks stern. He's always tried to be an advocate for me and for investigative reporting. He was still trying at the end. He's an investigative guy to the core. But I know I'm a headache he doesn't need.

Suddenly, he breaks out into a smile and chuckles.

"Never a dull moment when you're around," he says.

I shrug and smile back. I don't think I'm the one creating the drama. But I guess there's a difference of opinion on that.

A couple of weeks later, it was finished. I ended the CBS stage of my career after twenty mostly happy, mostly successful, mostly satisfying years—and a couple that were really, really tough.

| MORELL POSTSCRIPT

I couldn't have been happier to be gone from CBS than when the Benghazi story again reared its head in earnest, in April 2014. It centered on former CIA deputy director and now CBS News consultant Morell.

First, on April 4, Morell was called to testify to Congress about newly released documents that show he heavily edited the Benghazi talking points. This wholly contradicted the original stories Morell told.

Free from CBS, I was able to write an unvarnished, factual account of his testimony and contradictions and publish it on my own website. Few others in the media seemed to assign any particular significance to Morell's highly evolved story and contradictions. (Yawn.)

But on April 29, it became difficult for the press at large to ignore incriminating new documents—even though they were obtained by a conservative watchdog group that many in the news media love to hate: Judicial Watch. Judicial Watch had obtained emails by suing the State Department over a denied Freedom of Information Act request.

These emails showed direct White House involvement in steering the Benghazi narrative toward the "spontaneous protest." The very thing that the administration had denied repeatedly, implicitly and explicitly.

One of the operative Judicial Watch documents, which the government had withheld from Congress and reporters for a year and a half, was an email circulated two day after the attacks by President Obama's assistant and deputy national security advisor Ben Rhodes. The September 14, 2012, email told White House press advisors that a goal of an upcoming call to prepare Ambassador Rice for her Sunday talk show appearances was "[t]o underscore that these protests are rooted in an Internet video, and not a broader failure of policy."

While many in the media would have liked to continue turning a blind eye to the Benghazi story, that changed when *USA Today* published an article on this revelation. I imagined it set off a flurry of meetings and frantic editorial discussions at major news outlets.

USA Today *covered it. Should we cover it, too?*

Will we look bad if we don't?

Jonathan Karl of ABC reported a full package on his network's evening newscast while NBC had a brief thirty-second "voice-over." CBS alone decided there was no news at all here. *Nothing to see. Move along.*

The media blog Mediabistro later noted, *"CBS Evening News with Scott Pelley* was the only evening newscast last night to not cover newly uncovered emails from White House adviser Ben Rhodes. . . ." In response, a CBS News spokesperson stated that there was "a thorough editorial discussion about it at *CBS Evening News* and David Rhodes [Ben's brother] was not involved [in the discussion]."

On May 1, 2014, I received a document that showed the State Department almost immediately concluded that the Islamic militia terrorist group Ansar al-Sharia was to blame for the Benghazi attacks. The State Department's Beth Jones said so in a private communication to the Libyan government, according to an internal email at 9:45 a.m. on September 12, 2012.

"When [the Libyan ambassador] said his government suspected that former Qaddafi regime elements carried out the attacks, I told him the group that conducted the attacks—Ansar al-Sharia—is affiliated with Islamic extremists," Jones reports in the email.

The private account between Jones and the Libyan government was entirely at odds with the messaging that President Obama, Clinton, Rice, and White House press secretary Carney delivered to the American public.

The Obama administration's entire Benghazi narrative had now fallen to pieces and was still crumbling. Imagine if the public had known prior to the 2012 election all that's been revealed since.

Were I still at CBS, there's little doubt I would be viewed by some as the network villain, offering stories on these important developments, pushing for them to air while the whisper campaign thundered on. Now dearly departed from my alma mater, I was free to commit unencumbered journalism without pressure.

Substitution Game: Is there anyone who really believes that if President Bush had claimed al-Qaeda was on the run, only to have the misfortune of a terrorist attack in Benghazi in 2012 and the event of ferocious jihadists taking over Iraqi cities in 2014, the press wouldn't have led the news highlighting the contradiction between his optimistic proclamations and the sordid reality? Bush, like all presidents, had plenty of imperfections. The difference is, they were usually, enthusiastically, and thoroughly probed by a persistent media.

| AFTER CBS

In April 2014, just a few weeks after leaving CBS, I attended an invitation-only investigative reporting conference at the University of California, Berkeley, called the Logan Symposium. The theme was apt: "Under Attack: Reporters and Their Sources." I was invited to moderate a panel called "The Third Rail: Stories We're Not Supposed to Tell." CBS had withheld the invitation from me when it first arrived before Christmas of 2013 and, I learned, intended to decline on my behalf without telling me. But the Logan organizers eventually reached out to me directly and I accepted.

At the symposium, I was greeted with a surprisingly warm reception from peers who were familiar with some of my travails. Many of them shared their own stories of undue political and corporate pressure and censorship. There was general agreement among the speakers that the Obama administration has advanced press restrictions beyond anything previously experienced, at least by us.

"The Obama administration is trying to narrow the playing field for reporters," said Pulitzer Prize–winning *New York Times* reporter James Risen, who faced the threat of jail time for refusing to turn over information about a confidential source.

"A Rip Van Winkle today would be shocked with what we accept in society and what we think of as normal," Risen told the audience of several hundred investigative journalists and Berkeley journalism graduate students. He warned that there's been a "fundamental change in society" since the September 11, 2001, terrorist attacks, and that Americans have given up civil liberties and press freedoms "slowly and incrementally."

"We've been too accepting of rules and mores of, first, the Bush administration and, now, the Obama administration. We have to stand up and begin to fight back. . . . [W]e need to think about how to challenge the government in the way we're supposed to challenge the government.

"[The Obama administration] want[s] to create an interstate highway for reporting in which there are police all along telling you to stay on that highway. As long as we accept this interstate highway of reporting, we are enabling and complicit in what's happening to society and the press," said Risen.

Lowell Bergman, director of the Investigative Reporting Program at UC Berkeley's Graduate School of Journalism, echoed the warnings, calling these "sad times" and telling the audience that reporters "have to take some more direct action, public action," to "raise the profile of what the government is doing or attempting to do."

Attendees sidled up to me to commiserate. Some said they've worked for bosses who shape or censor reporting in response to Obama administration threats to withhold "exclusive" interviews with administration officials. We marveled over the dynamic under which this administration and previous ones have convinced news organizations that serving as a government propaganda tool is actually a desirable thing. The White House and its agencies dole out officials for television news appearances in a rotation and lord over the schedule. We dutifully oblige, and promote the interviews as if they're special exclusives. In fact, they serve as little more than positive PR for the government and its officials.

We're next in line to get an interview with Michelle Obama, producers declare excitedly, after being told of the arrangement by the administration.

(That is, we're next as long as we stay on that interstate highway of reporting. *We'd better not run that pesky story looking into Michelle Obama's travels!*)

On April 10, 2013, the *New York Times'* Jill Abramson joined the growing chorus of journalists criticizing the Obama administration's press restrictions.

"The Obama years are a benchmark for a new level of secrecy and control," said Abramson in an interview. "It's created quite a challenging atmosphere for the *New York Times*, and for some of the best reporters in my newsroom who cover national security issues in Washington."

But one of the most personally telling anecdotes comes to me from a colleague named David Kirby, a self-described left-winger who authored the investigative award-winning book *Evidence of Harm: Mercury in Vaccines and the Autism Epidemic: A Medical Controversy.*

"I couldn't wait," says Kirby, speaking of Obama being elected president in 2008.

A "new era" was being ushered in. At last the GOP was out, and a new era of transparency was about to begin. He was the real deal, a Constitutional scholar who understood the fundamental importance of basic freedoms—the right to information and accountability, for example—to our democracy and its vaunted promise of "life, liberty and the pursuit of happiness."

Then I tried to get information out of the new gang.

The first six months of 2009 was a daily lesson in rejection, frustration and anger. I could not get any information out of *anyone*—not the USDA, not the EPA, and certainly not the White House. FOIA requests, the few that were actually fulfilled, came back with up to 90% of the text "redacted," blacked out like an angry child had taken an extra-wide Sharpie to the pages.

That summer I ran into an old friend from my early days in politics, a die-hard progressive, who would probably vote for the Communist Party if he could. Of course the subject of the new administration came up. "So how do you think he's doing so far?" my friend asked.

"Well, I gotta say," I replied, shuffling my feet, "At least when it comes to getting information out of the Obama people, I hate to say it, but it's worse than Bush. *Much* worse."

My comrade turned the color of farmed salmon, clashing with the red trumpet-vine blossoms behind the fence. He glared, he stammered, he yelled. I don't think he has spoken to me since.

Today I am deeply unsettled, yet sadly unsurprised, by the fumbling explanations from Democratic Party apparatchiks clumsily trying to play down recent scandals rocking the White House and the nation: NSA domestic spying; monitoring the Associated Press and Fox News like North Korean "minders."

Kirby is so moved by what's happened, he's writing his own book on the subject.

All of this makes me think back to that letter addressed to White House spokesman Carney, signed by many news organizations on November 21, 2013, referring to an arbitrary restraint and unwarranted interference on legiti-mate newsgathering activities . . . constitutional concerns . . . [a] troubling precedent with a direct and adverse impact on the public's ability to independently monitor and see what its government is doing . . .

From what I can see, our letter didn't spark any big changes. It'll take more than a letter.

Since CBS, I've heard from conservatives urging me to continue reporting on untouchable subjects. I've also heard from a great num-ber of people who claim to be either liberal or down the middle or politically disassociated altogether, and want me to know that they support journalism that follows a story no matter where it leads. There's not enough of it, they say. They're thirsty for it.

| **JUNE 20, 2014**

On this date, a new Gallup poll finds confidence in the news media is at an all-time low and confidence in TV news ranks even below the Internet. Liberals, conservatives, moderates: they all agree on this.

Can something good be born from something bad? With so much recognition that much is seriously broken, will the press fight to get back its mojo? Is it recoverable? Or too far gone?

Today, I feel as though I've taken a step forward. My heart is light. I breathe unrestricted, fresh air for the first time in several years. It smells different to me. It smells like freedom.

Do your own research. Consult those you trust. Make up your own mind.

Think for yourself.

INDEX